JAMES PATTERSON

WITCH & WIZARD

BATTLE FOR SHADOWLAND

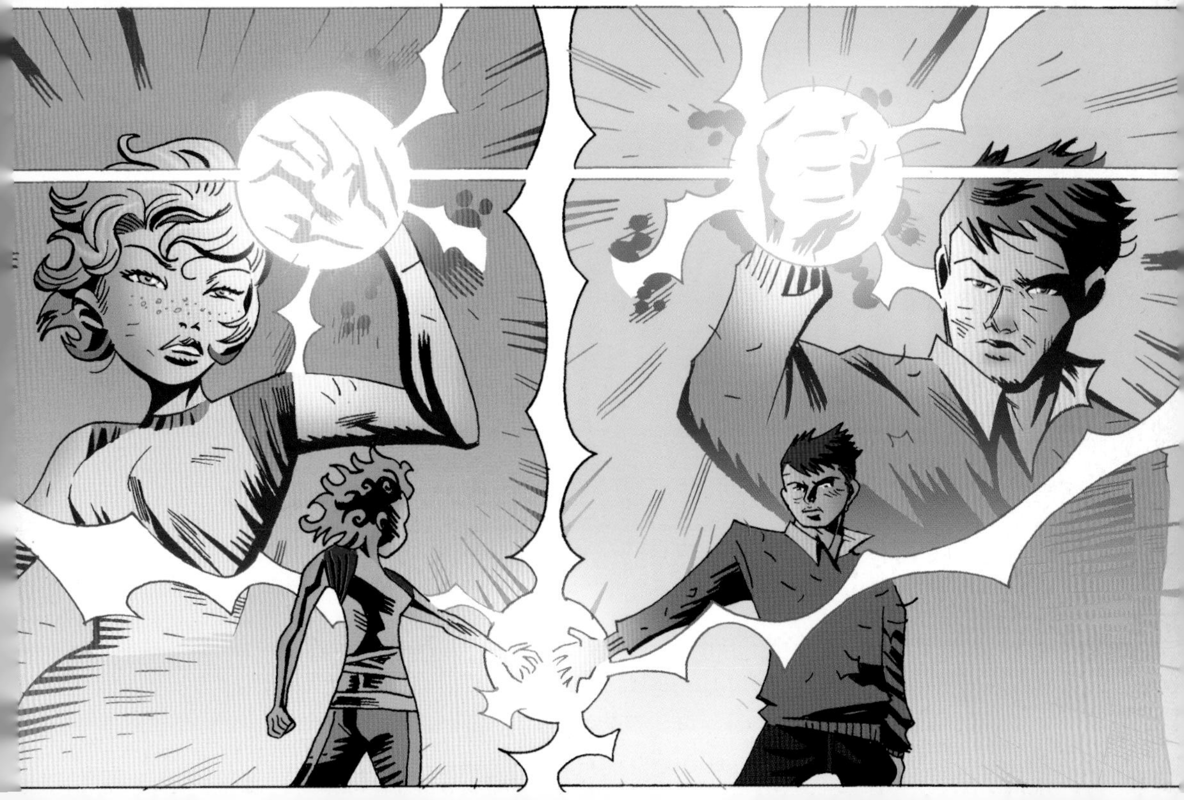

JAMES PATTERSON
WITCH & WIZARD
BATTLE FOR SHADOWLAND

Special thanks to Leopoldo Gout, Steve Bowen, Gabrielle Charbonnet, and James Patterson.

www.IDWPUBLISHING.com   ISBN: 978-1-60010-759-7   13 12 11 10   1 2 3 4

IDW™ IDW Publishing is: Operations: Ted Adams, CEO & Publisher • Greg Goldstein, Chief Operating Officer • Matthew Ruzicka, CPA, Chief Financial Officer • Alan Payne, VP of Sales • Lorelei Bunjes, Director of Digital Services • Jeff Webber, Director of ePublishing • AnnaMaria White, Dir., Marketing and Public Relations • Dirk Wood, Dir., Retail Marketing • Marci Hubbard, Executive Assistant • Alonzo Simon, Shipping Manager • Angela Loggins, Staff Accountant • Cherrie Go, Assistant Web Designer • Editorial: Chris Ryall, Chief Creative Officer, Editor-In-Chief • Scott Dunbier, Senior Editor, Special Projects • Andy Schmidt, Senior Editor • Bob Schreck, Senior Editor • Justin Eisinger, Senior Editor, Books • Kris Oprisko, Editor/Foreign Lic. • Denton J. Tipton, Editor • Tom Waltz, Editor • Mariah Huehner, Editor • Carlos Guzman, Assistant Editor • Bobby Curnow, Assistant Editor • Design: Robbie Robbins, EVP/Sr. Graphic Artist • Neil Uyetake, Senior Art Director • Chris Mowry, Senior Graphic Artist • Amauri Osorio, Graphic Artist • Gilberto Lazcano, Production Assistant • Shawn Lee, Graphic Artist

Originally published as JAMES PATTERSON'S WITCH & WIZARD: BATTLE FOR SHADOWLAND Issues #1–4.

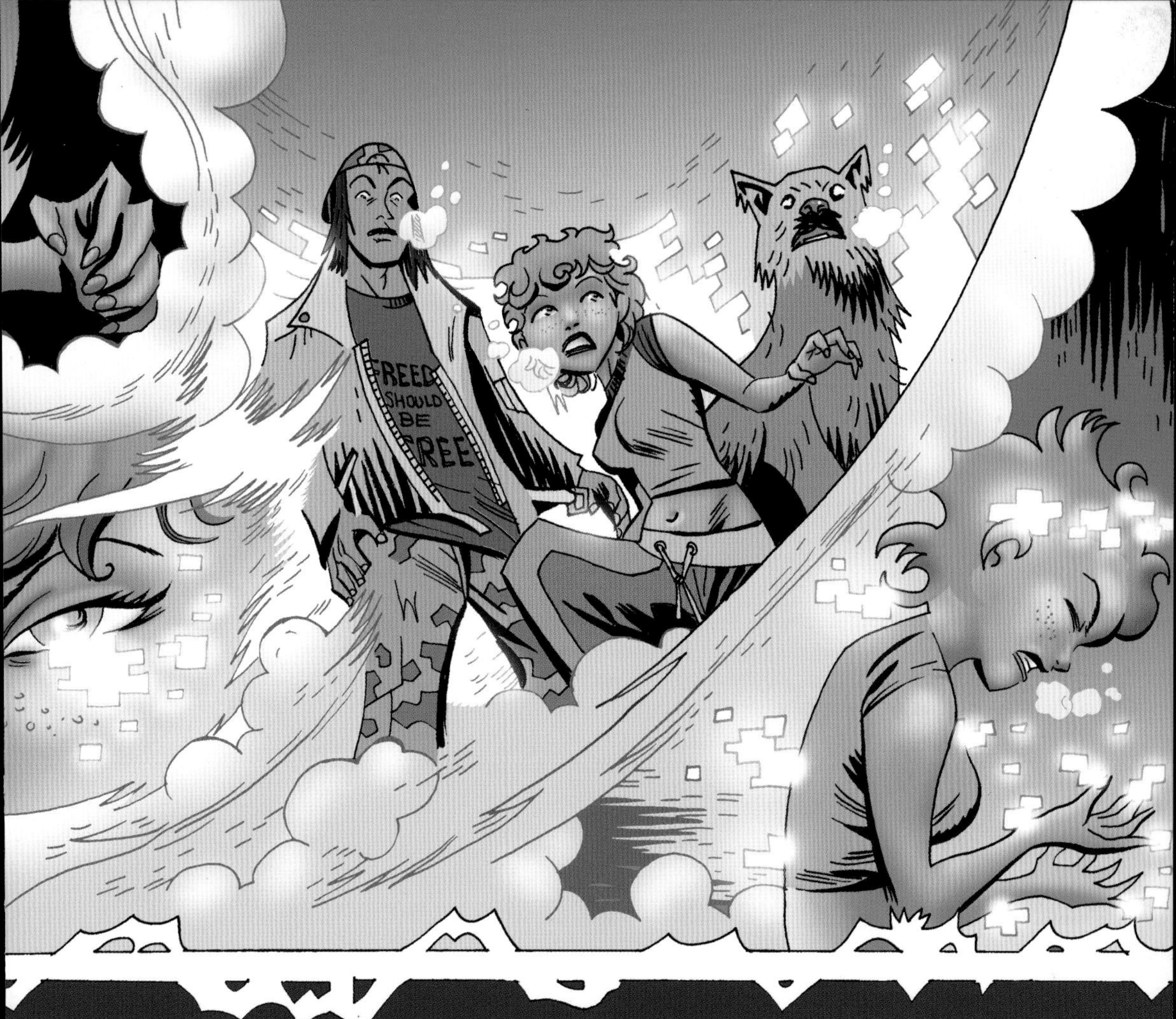

WRITERS
JAMES PATTERSON AND DARA NARAGHI

ARTIST
VICTOR SANTOS

COLORIST
JAMIE GRANT

LETTERERS
CHRIS MOWRY & NEIL UYETAKE

SERIES EDITOR
BOB SCHRECK

COLLECTION EDITOR
JUSTIN EISINGER

COLLECTION DESIGNER
NEIL UYETAKE

WITCH & WIZARD CREATED BY JAMES PATTERSON

Excerpts from "The Supreme Ascendancy of the New Order: A Brief History", pp. 58-72, by The One Who Records History, © 0001 A.O., New Order Press.

For the exclusive use of New Order Reformatory guests.

i.e. prisoners!

In retrospect, it is a simple task to identify the driving force behind the rise in popularity of the New Order political party. The people of this failed country, disillusioned by their so-called democracy and freedoms, embraced the values and principles of the New Order. This was a populist movement, a higher discipline led by smart, visionary leaders with a plan for a bright new future for every man, woman, and child.

What a joke! It was a total con job by a power-hungry evil sociopath

And so it was that on the first day of the first year of the New Order's Supreme Ascendancy, The Council Of Ones was established. Led by The One Who Is The One – our benevolent and capable leader – The Council took the necessary steps to elevate this nation to its rightful moral, cultural, and technological supremacy. This was achieved through a series of decrees designed to eliminate the corrupting influences of the old world. Superfluous and undesirable distractions such as art, music, and books were outlawed for the greater good of society.* Above all, the practice of the Foul Arts was strictly forbidden to all.

The aforementioned power-hungry evil sociopath

Yeah, as long as you obey their orders like a good little robot

i.e. totalitarian state!

i.e. everything worth living for, including freedom.

While these laws are supported unanimously by the citizenry, they are occasionally violated by deviants and criminals. Such offenders are treated sternly, yet with compassion, and are cured of their antisocial behaviors, returning to the populace as a capable and contributing member of society.

We're just kids!

Meaning magic, although its funny how The One uses magic himself

*See also: The One Who Writes New Laws, The One Who Judges, The One Who Imprisons, et al.

There's no "returning" from an execution

Suggested further reading: "Benjamin, Eliza, Whitford, and Wisteria: The Allgood Family of Deviants", by The One Who Hunts Fugitives.

i.e. kangaroo court, show trial, etc.

Stay strong, mom and dad! We love you

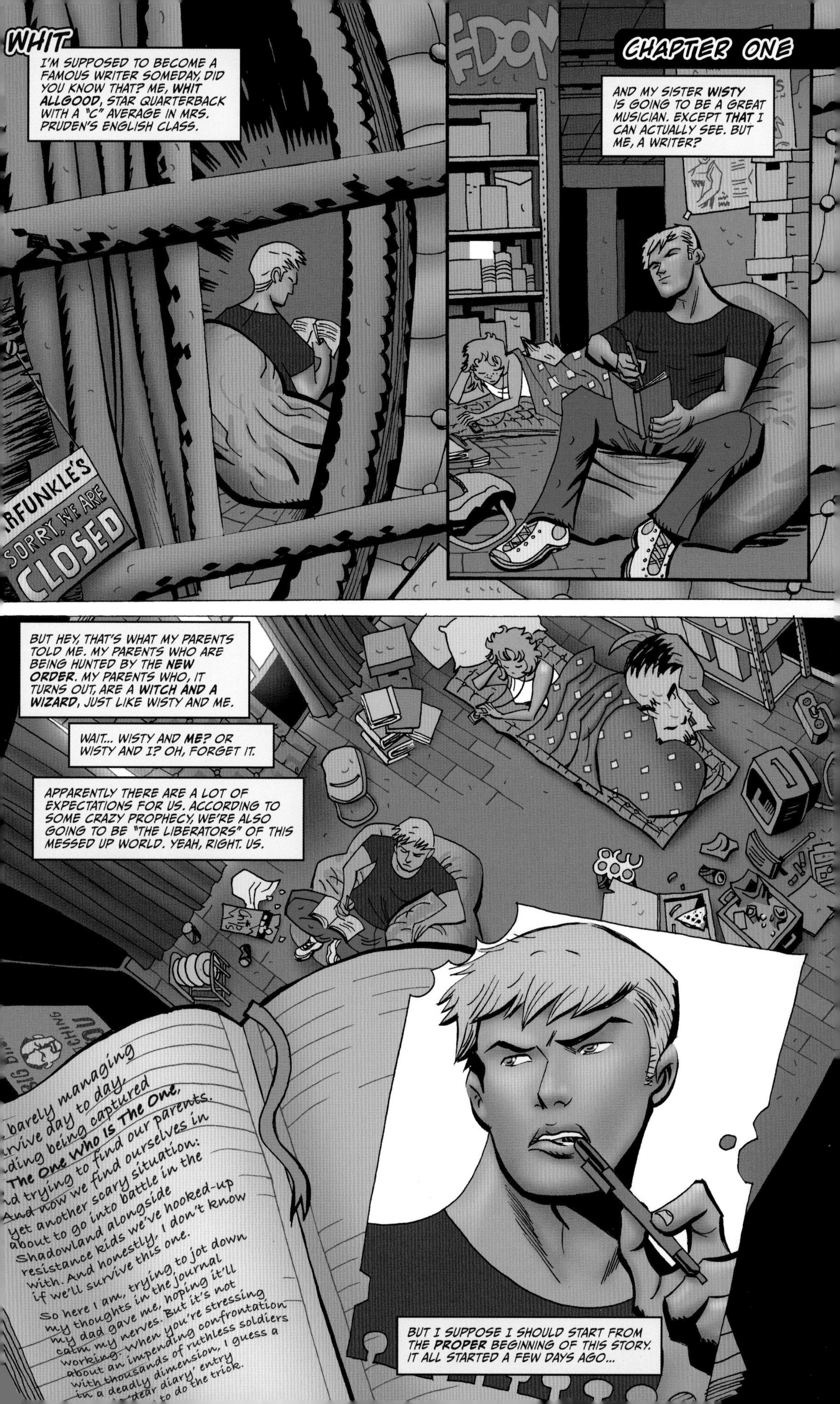
WHIT
I'M SUPPOSED TO BECOME A FAMOUS WRITER SOMEDAY, DID YOU KNOW THAT? ME, WHIT ALLGOOD, STAR QUARTERBACK WITH A "C" AVERAGE IN MRS. PRUDEN'S ENGLISH CLASS.
CHAPTER ONE
AND MY SISTER WISTY IS GOING TO BE A GREAT MUSICIAN. EXCEPT THAT I CAN ACTUALLY SEE. BUT ME, A WRITER?
RFUNKLE'S
SORRY, WE ARE
CLOSED
BUT HEY, THAT'S WHAT MY PARENTS TOLD ME. MY PARENTS WHO ARE BEING HUNTED BY THE NEW ORDER. MY PARENTS WHO, IT TURNS OUT, ARE A WITCH AND A WIZARD, JUST LIKE WISTY AND ME.
WAIT... WISTY AND ME? OR WISTY AND I? OH, FORGET IT.
APPARENTLY THERE ARE A LOT OF EXPECTATIONS FOR US. ACCORDING TO SOME CRAZY PROPHECY, WE'RE ALSO GOING TO BE "THE LIBERATORS" OF THIS MESSED UP WORLD. YEAH, RIGHT. US.
barely managing
rvive day to day,
ding being captured
The One Who Is The One,
d trying to find our parents.
And now we find ourselves in
yet another scary situation:
about to go into battle in the
Shadowland alongside
resistance kids we've hooked-up
with. And honestly, I don't know
if we'll survive this one.
So here I am, trying to jot down
my thoughts in the journal
my dad gave me, hoping it'll
calm my nerves. But it's not
working. When you're stressing
about an impending confrontation
with thousands of ruthless soldiers
in a deadly dimension, I guess a
'dear diary' entry
to do the trick.
BUT I SUPPOSE I SHOULD START FROM THE PROPER BEGINNING OF THIS STORY. IT ALL STARTED A FEW DAYS AGO...

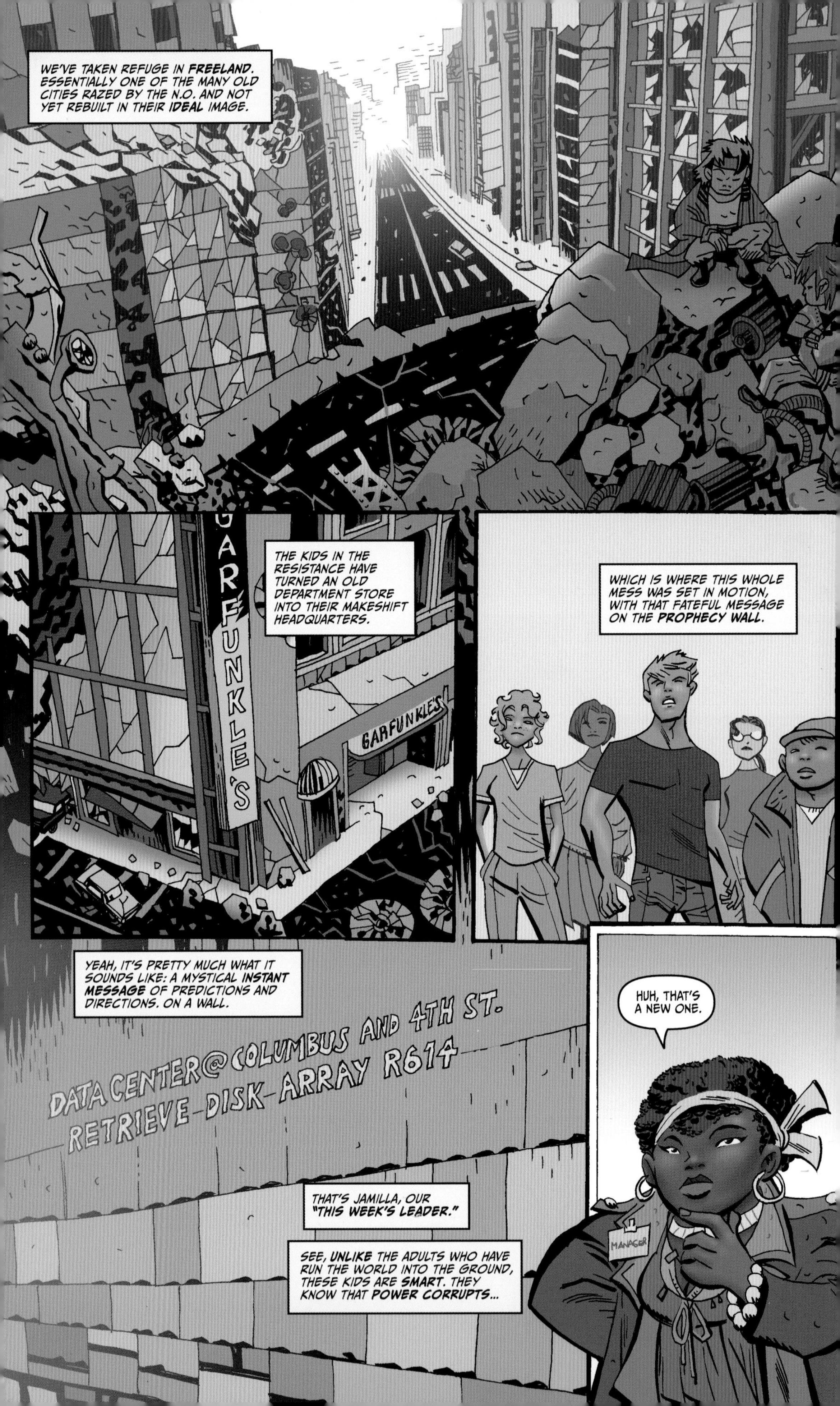
WE'VE TAKEN REFUGE IN FREELAND. ESSENTIALLY ONE OF THE MANY OLD CITIES RAZED BY THE N.O. AND NOT YET REBUILT IN THEIR IDEAL IMAGE.
GARFUNKLE'S
THE KIDS IN THE RESISTANCE HAVE TURNED AN OLD DEPARTMENT STORE INTO THEIR MAKESHIFT HEADQUARTERS.
GARFUNKLE'S
GARFUNKLE'S
WHICH IS WHERE THIS WHOLE MESS WAS SET IN MOTION, WITH THAT FATEFUL MESSAGE ON THE PROPHECY WALL.
YEAH, IT'S PRETTY MUCH WHAT IT SOUNDS LIKE: A MYSTICAL INSTANT MESSAGE OF PREDICTIONS AND DIRECTIONS. ON A WALL.
DATA CENTER@COLUMBUS AND 4TH ST.
RETRIEVE-DISK-ARRAY R614
HUH, THAT'S A NEW ONE.
THAT'S JAMILLA, OUR "THIS WEEK'S LEADER."
SEE, UNLIKE THE ADULTS WHO HAVE RUN THE WORLD INTO THE GROUND, THESE KIDS ARE SMART. THEY KNOW THAT POWER CORRUPTS...
MANAGER

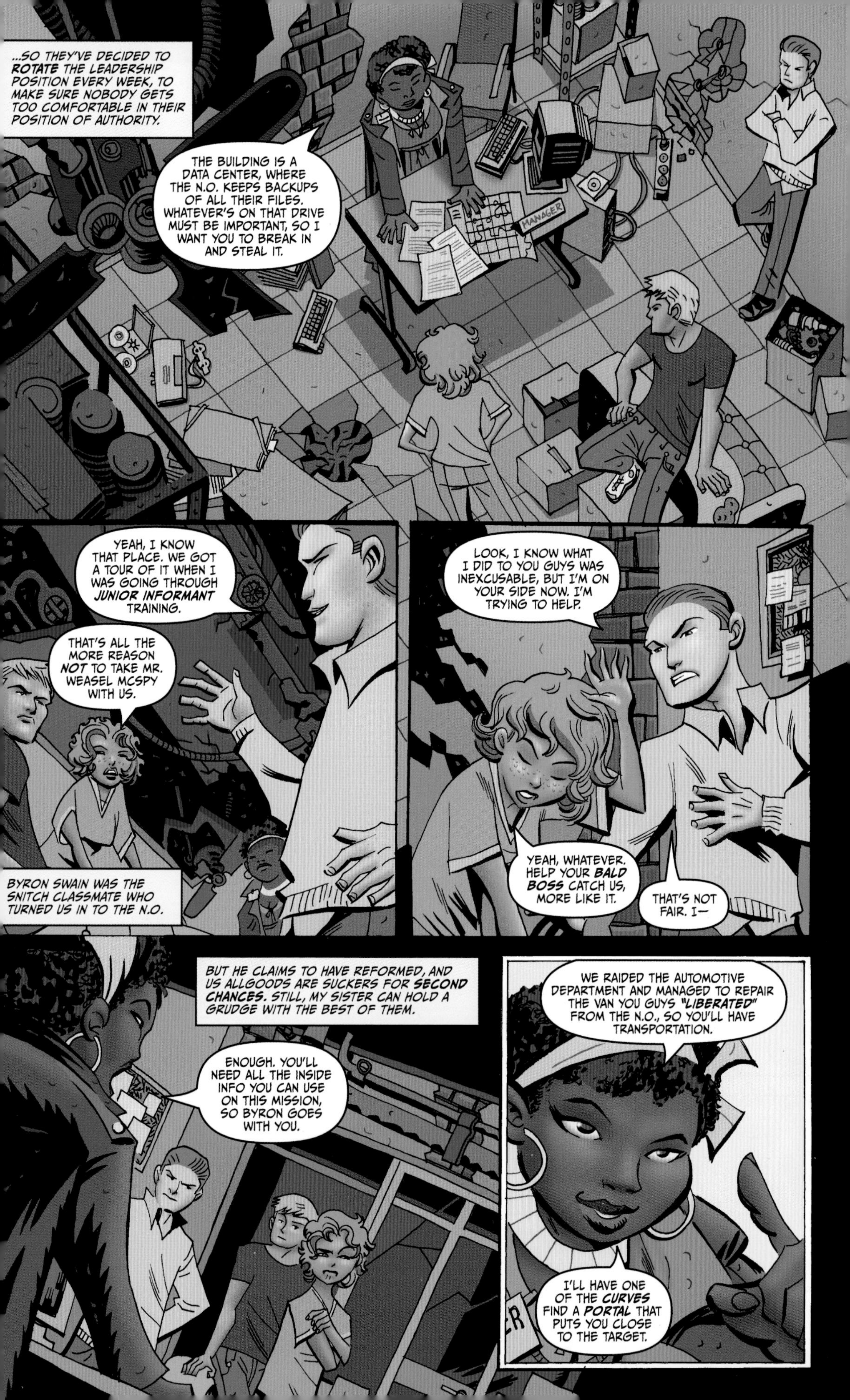
...SO THEY'VE DECIDED TO ROTATE THE LEADERSHIP POSITION EVERY WEEK, TO MAKE SURE NOBODY GETS TOO COMFORTABLE IN THEIR POSITION OF AUTHORITY.
THE BUILDING IS A DATA CENTER, WHERE THE N.O. KEEPS BACKUPS OF ALL THEIR FILES. WHATEVER'S ON THAT DRIVE MUST BE IMPORTANT, SO I WANT YOU TO BREAK IN AND STEAL IT.
MANAGER
YEAH, I KNOW THAT PLACE. WE GOT A TOUR OF IT WHEN I WAS GOING THROUGH JUNIOR INFORMANT TRAINING.
THAT'S ALL THE MORE REASON NOT TO TAKE MR. WEASEL MCSPY WITH US.
BYRON SWAIN WAS THE SNITCH CLASSMATE WHO TURNED US IN TO THE N.O.
LOOK, I KNOW WHAT I DID TO YOU GUYS WAS INEXCUSABLE, BUT I'M ON YOUR SIDE NOW. I'M TRYING TO HELP.
YEAH, WHATEVER. HELP YOUR BALD BOSS CATCH US, MORE LIKE IT.
THAT'S NOT FAIR. I—
BUT HE CLAIMS TO HAVE REFORMED, AND US ALLGOODS ARE SUCKERS FOR SECOND CHANCES. STILL, MY SISTER CAN HOLD A GRUDGE WITH THE BEST OF THEM.
ENOUGH. YOU'LL NEED ALL THE INSIDE INFO YOU CAN USE ON THIS MISSION, SO BYRON GOES WITH YOU.
WE RAIDED THE AUTOMOTIVE DEPARTMENT AND MANAGED TO REPAIR THE VAN YOU GUYS "LIBERATED" FROM THE N.O., SO YOU'LL HAVE TRANSPORTATION.
I'LL HAVE ONE OF THE CURVES FIND A PORTAL THAT PUTS YOU CLOSE TO THE TARGET.

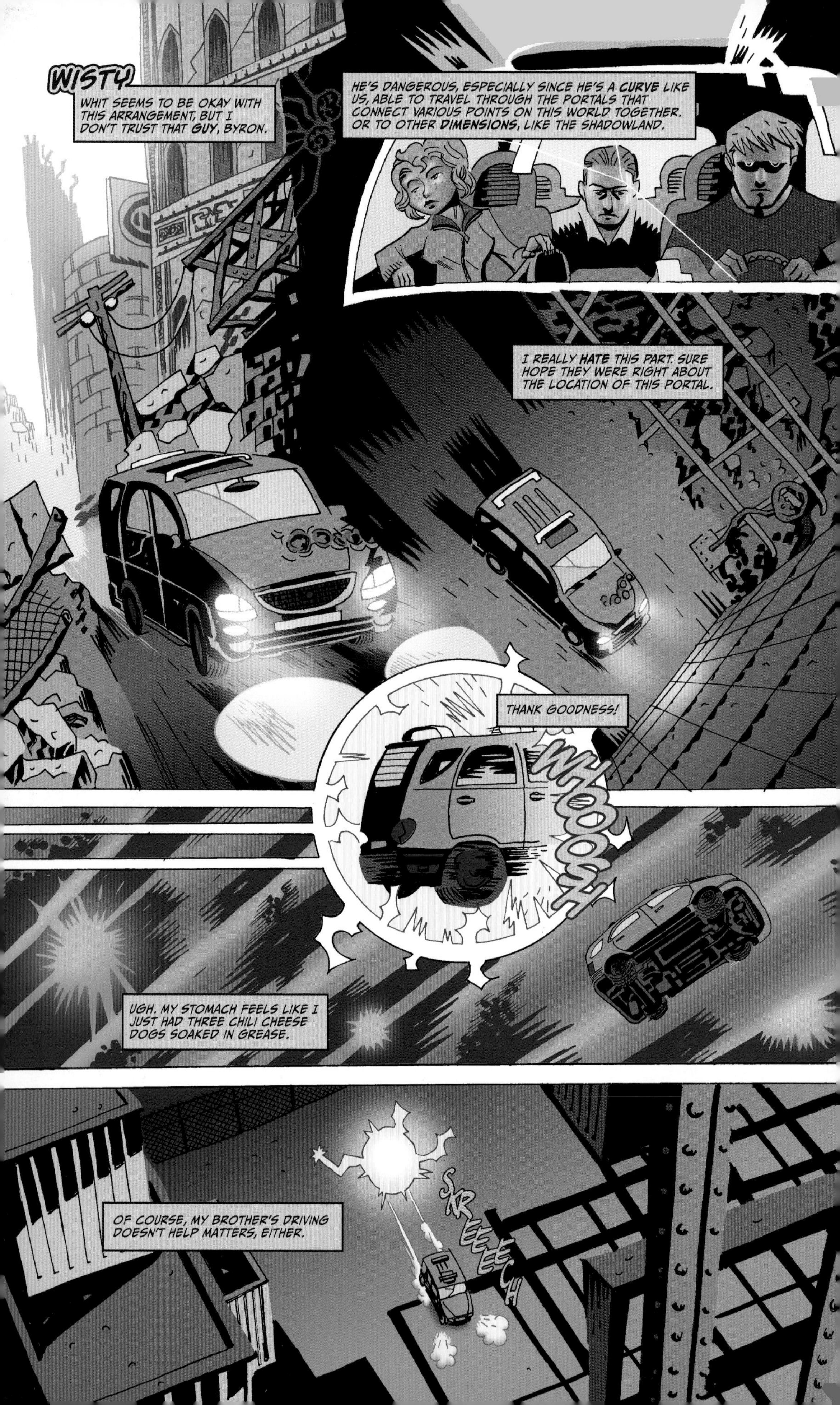
WISTY
WHIT SEEMS TO BE OKAY WITH THIS ARRANGEMENT, BUT I DON'T TRUST THAT GUY, BYRON.
HE'S DANGEROUS, ESPECIALLY SINCE HE'S A CURVE LIKE US, ABLE TO TRAVEL THROUGH THE PORTALS THAT CONNECT VARIOUS POINTS ON THIS WORLD TOGETHER. OR TO OTHER DIMENSIONS, LIKE THE SHADOWLAND.
I REALLY HATE THIS PART. SURE HOPE THEY WERE RIGHT ABOUT THE LOCATION OF THIS PORTAL.
THANK GOODNESS!
WHOOOM
UGH. MY STOMACH FEELS LIKE I JUST HAD THREE CHILI CHEESE DOGS SOAKED IN GREASE.
OF COURSE, MY BROTHER'S DRIVING DOESN'T HELP MATTERS, EITHER.
SKREEEECH

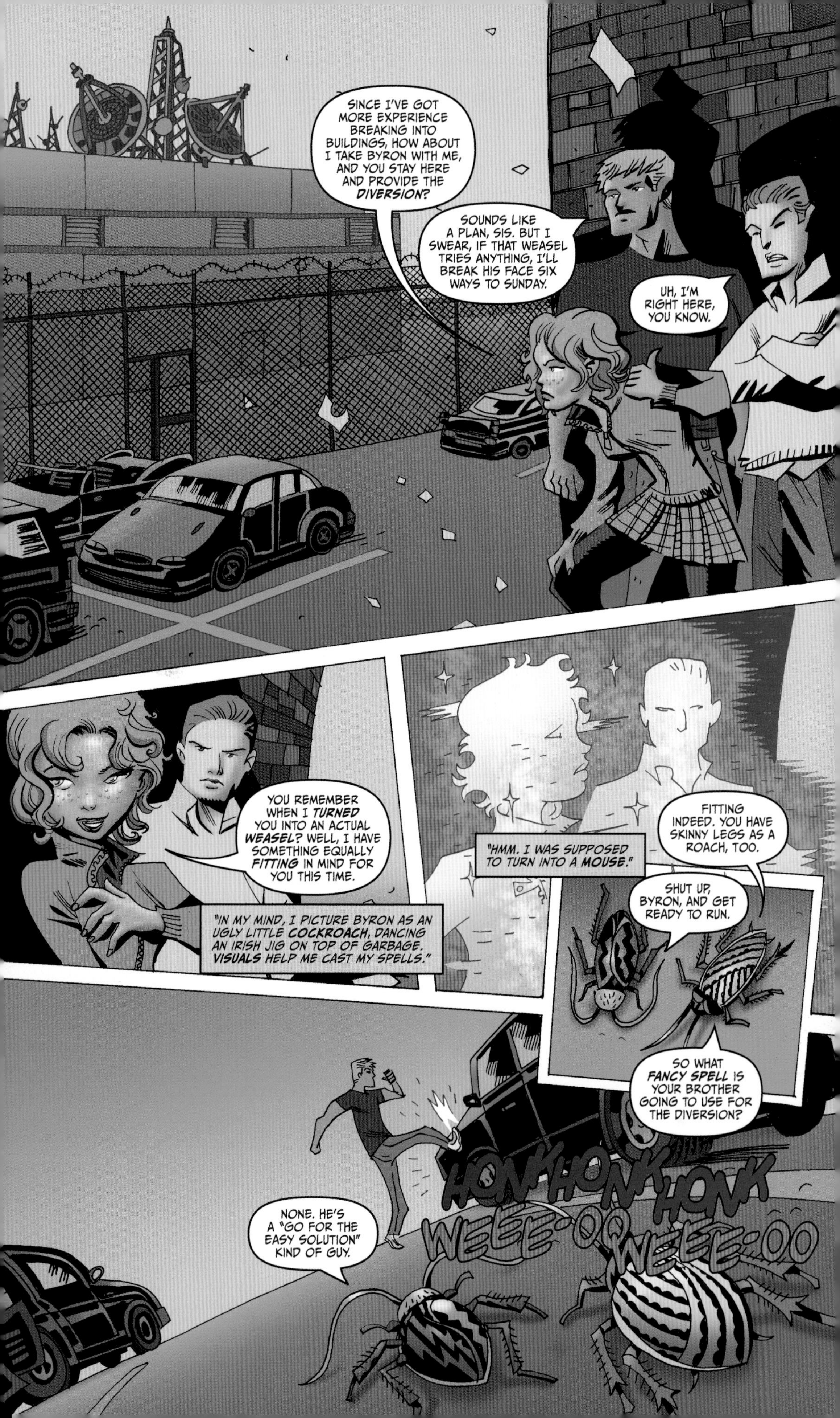
SINCE I'VE GOT MORE EXPERIENCE BREAKING INTO BUILDINGS, HOW ABOUT I TAKE BYRON WITH ME, AND YOU STAY HERE AND PROVIDE THE *DIVERSION*?
SOUNDS LIKE A PLAN, SIS. BUT I SWEAR, IF THAT WEASEL TRIES ANYTHING, I'LL BREAK HIS FACE SIX WAYS TO SUNDAY.
UH, I'M RIGHT HERE, YOU KNOW.
YOU REMEMBER WHEN I *TURNED* YOU INTO AN ACTUAL *WEASEL*? WELL, I HAVE SOMETHING EQUALLY *FITTING* IN MIND FOR YOU THIS TIME.
"IN MY MIND, I PICTURE BYRON AS AN UGLY LITTLE *COCKROACH*, DANCING AN IRISH JIG ON TOP OF GARBAGE. *VISUALS* HELP ME CAST MY SPELLS."
"HMM. I WAS SUPPOSED TO TURN INTO A *MOUSE*."
FITTING INDEED. YOU HAVE SKINNY LEGS AS A ROACH, TOO.
SHUT UP, BYRON, AND GET READY TO RUN.
SO WHAT *FANCY SPELL* IS YOUR BROTHER GOING TO USE FOR THE DIVERSION?
HONK HONK HONK
WEEE-OO WEEE-OO
NONE. HE'S A "GO FOR THE EASY SOLUTION" KIND OF GUY.

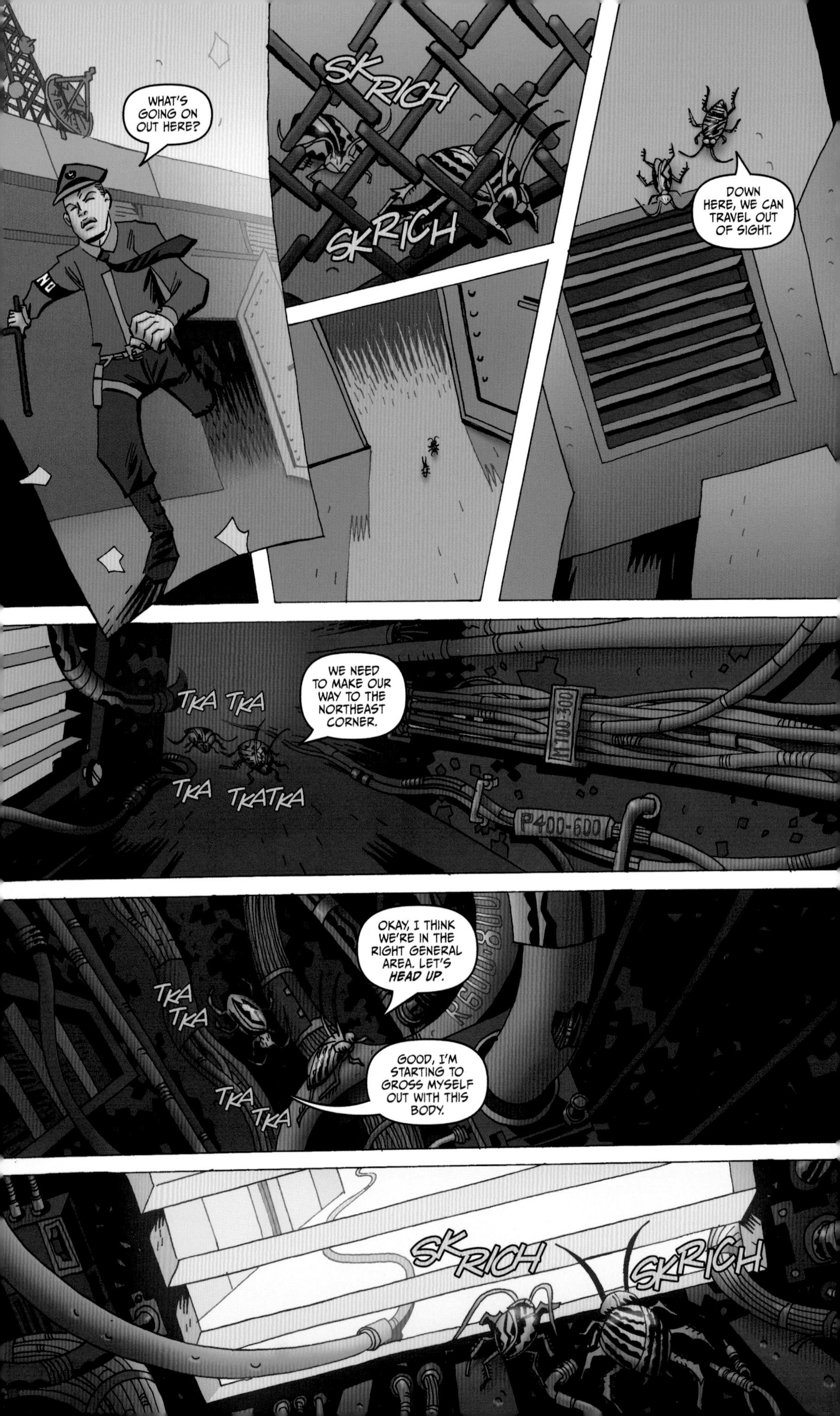
WHAT'S GOING ON OUT HERE?
SKRICH
SKRICH
DOWN HERE, WE CAN TRAVEL OUT OF SIGHT.
TKA TKA
WE NEED TO MAKE OUR WAY TO THE NORTHEAST CORNER.
TKA TKATKA
M100-300
P400-600
OKAY, I THINK WE'RE IN THE RIGHT GENERAL AREA. LET'S *HEAD UP*.
TKA TKA
GOOD, I'M STARTING TO GROSS MYSELF OUT WITH THIS BODY.
TKA TKA
SKRICH
SKRICH

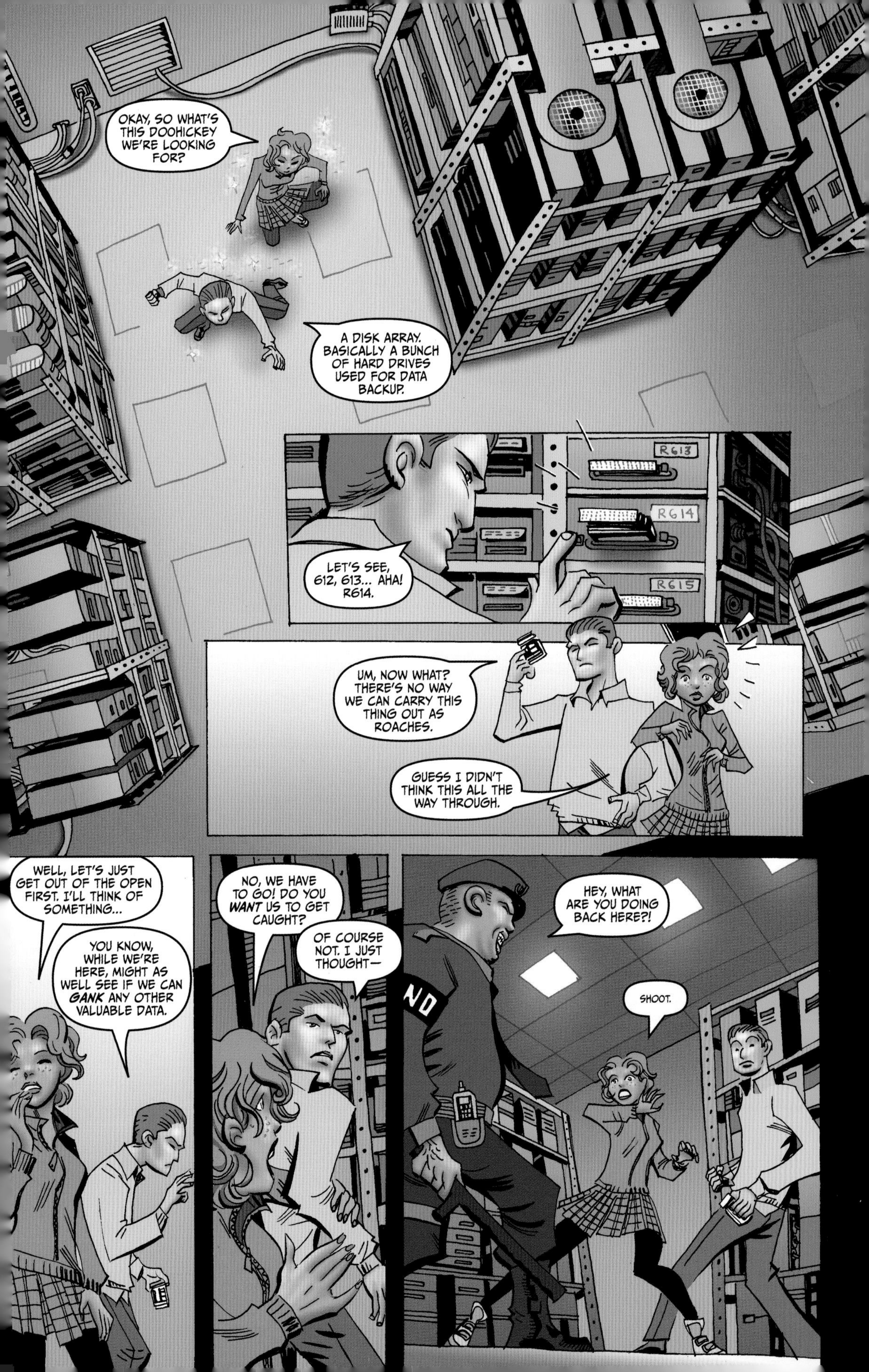
OKAY, SO WHAT'S THIS DOOHICKEY WE'RE LOOKING FOR?
A DISK ARRAY. BASICALLY A BUNCH OF HARD DRIVES USED FOR DATA BACKUP.
R613
R614
R615
LET'S SEE, 612, 613... AHA! R614.
UM, NOW WHAT? THERE'S NO WAY WE CAN CARRY THIS THING OUT AS ROACHES.
GUESS I DIDN'T THINK THIS ALL THE WAY THROUGH.
WELL, LET'S JUST GET OUT OF THE OPEN FIRST. I'LL THINK OF SOMETHING...
YOU KNOW, WHILE WE'RE HERE, MIGHT AS WELL SEE IF WE CAN *GANK* ANY OTHER VALUABLE DATA.
NO, WE HAVE TO GO! DO YOU *WANT* US TO GET CAUGHT?
OF COURSE NOT. I JUST THOUGHT—
HEY, WHAT ARE YOU DOING BACK HERE?!
SHOOT.

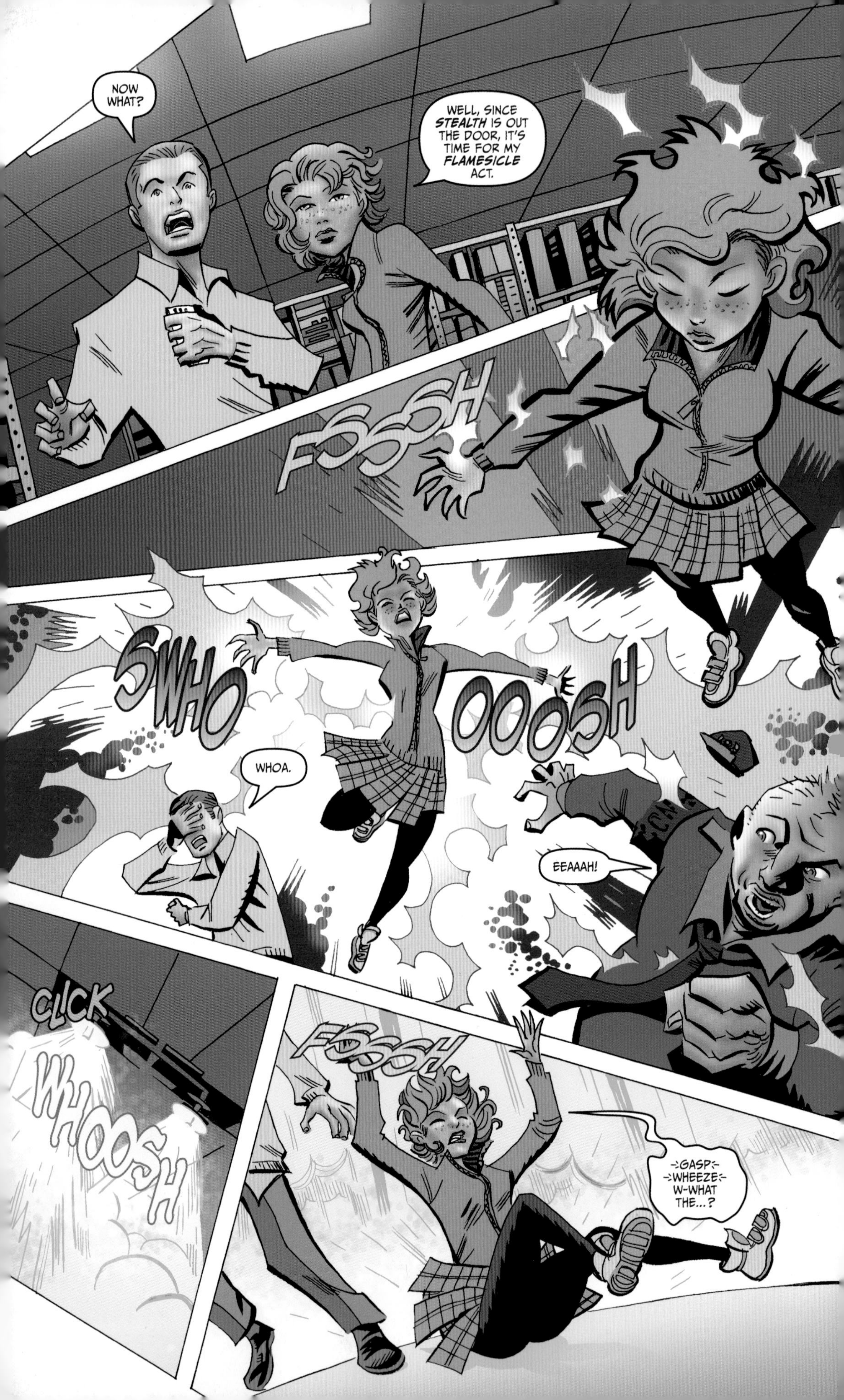
NOW WHAT?
WELL, SINCE STEALTH IS OUT THE DOOR, IT'S TIME FOR MY FLAMESICLE ACT.
FSSSH
SWHOOOOSH
WHOA.
EEAAAH!
CLICK
WHOOSH
FSSSH
-GASP- -WHEEZE- W-WHAT THE...?

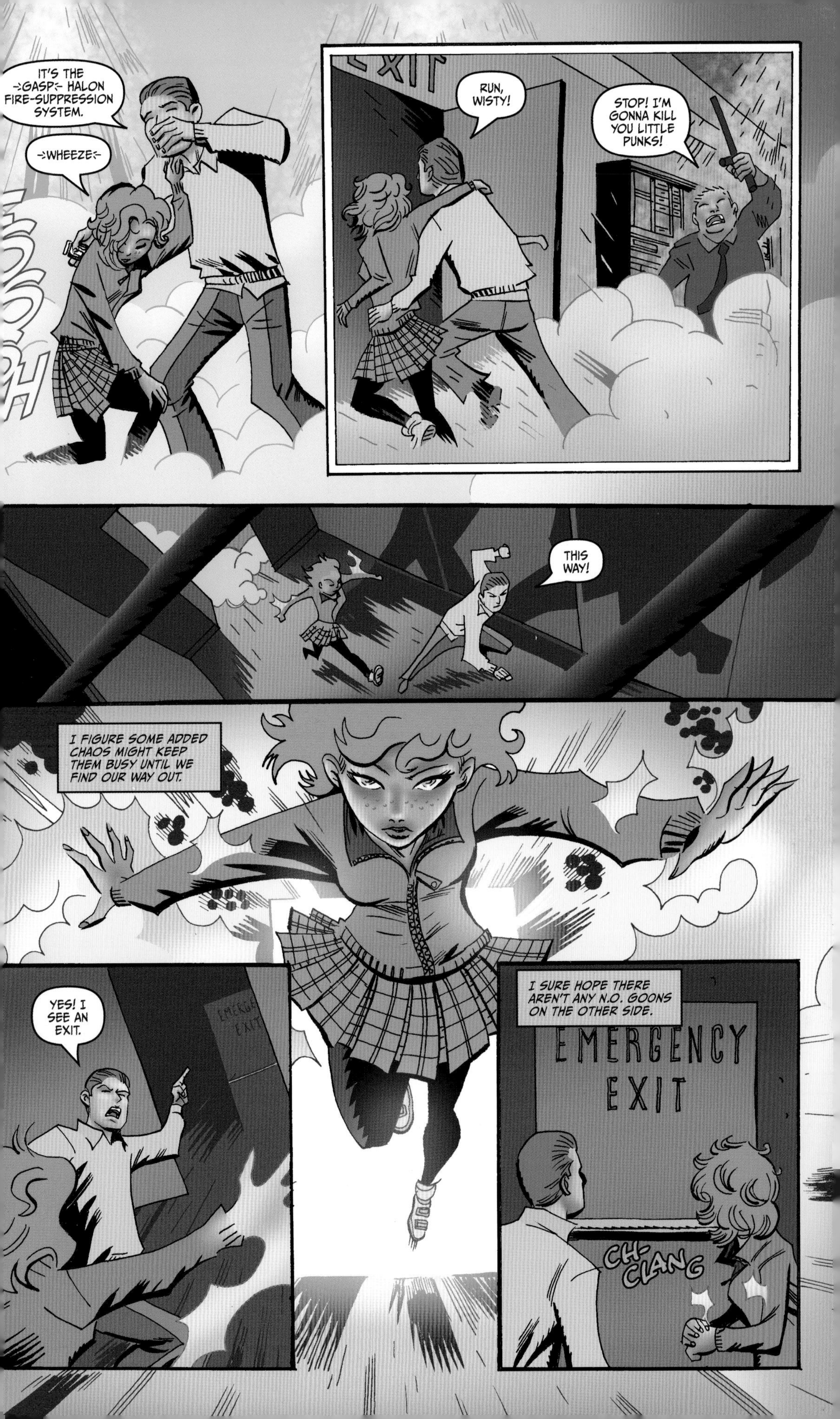

IT'S THE -GASP- HALON FIRE-SUPPRESSION SYSTEM.
-WHEEZE-
WHOOSH
RUN, WISTY!
STOP! I'M GONNA KILL YOU LITTLE PUNKS!
EXIT
THIS WAY!
I FIGURE SOME ADDED CHAOS MIGHT KEEP THEM BUSY UNTIL WE FIND OUR WAY OUT.
YES! I SEE AN EXIT.
I SURE HOPE THERE AREN'T ANY N.O. GOONS ON THE OTHER SIDE.
EMERGENCY EXIT
CH-CLANG

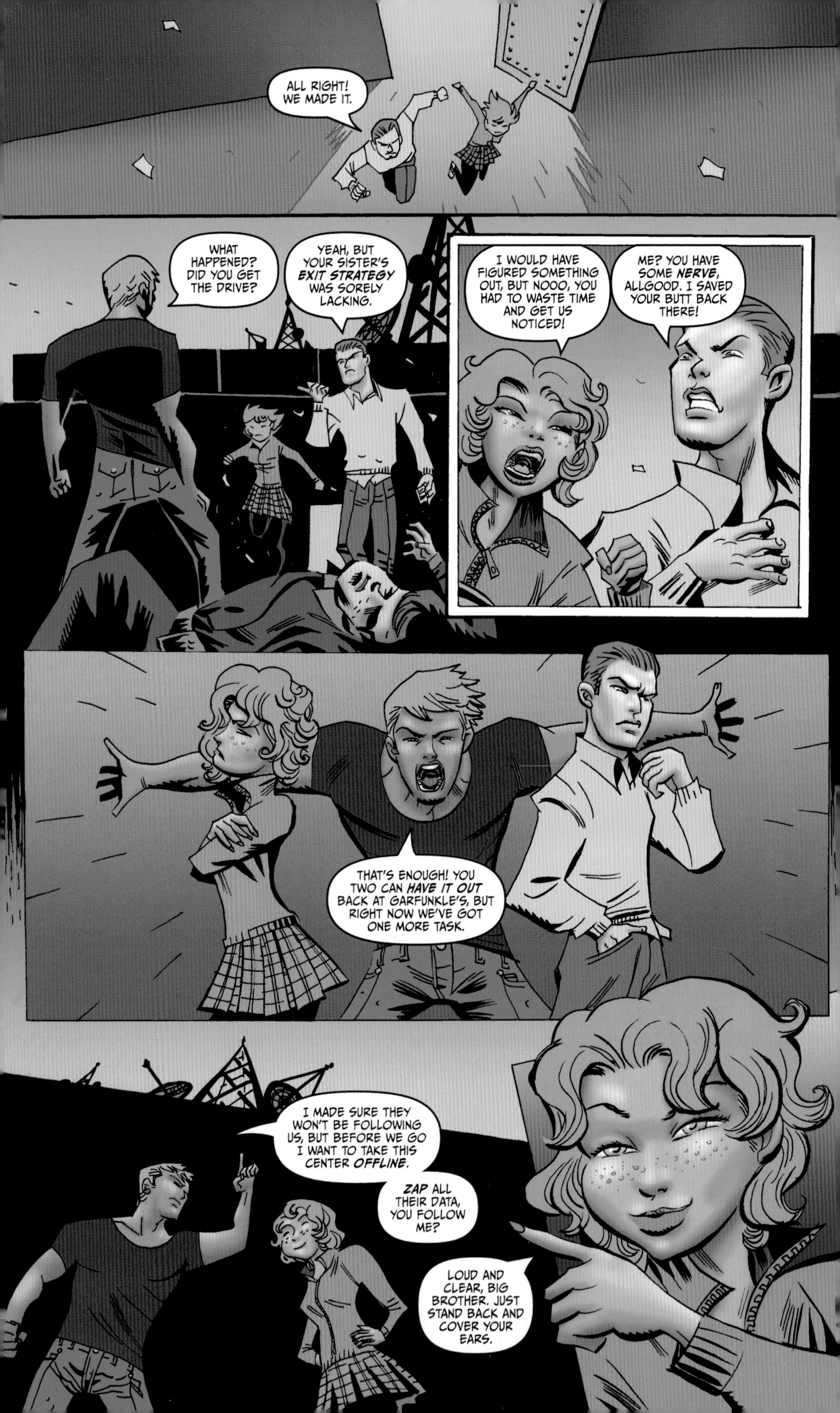
ALL RIGHT! WE MADE IT.
WHAT HAPPENED? DID YOU GET THE DRIVE?
YEAH, BUT YOUR SISTER'S EXIT STRATEGY WAS SORELY LACKING.
I WOULD HAVE FIGURED SOMETHING OUT, BUT NOOO, YOU HAD TO WASTE TIME AND GET US NOTICED!
ME? YOU HAVE SOME NERVE, ALLGOOD. I SAVED YOUR BUTT BACK THERE!
THAT'S ENOUGH! YOU TWO CAN HAVE IT OUT BACK AT GARFUNKLE'S, BUT RIGHT NOW WE'VE GOT ONE MORE TASK.
I MADE SURE THEY WON'T BE FOLLOWING US, BUT BEFORE WE GO I WANT TO TAKE THIS CENTER OFFLINE.
ZAP ALL THEIR DATA, YOU FOLLOW ME?
LOUD AND CLEAR, BIG BROTHER. JUST STAND BACK AND COVER YOUR EARS.

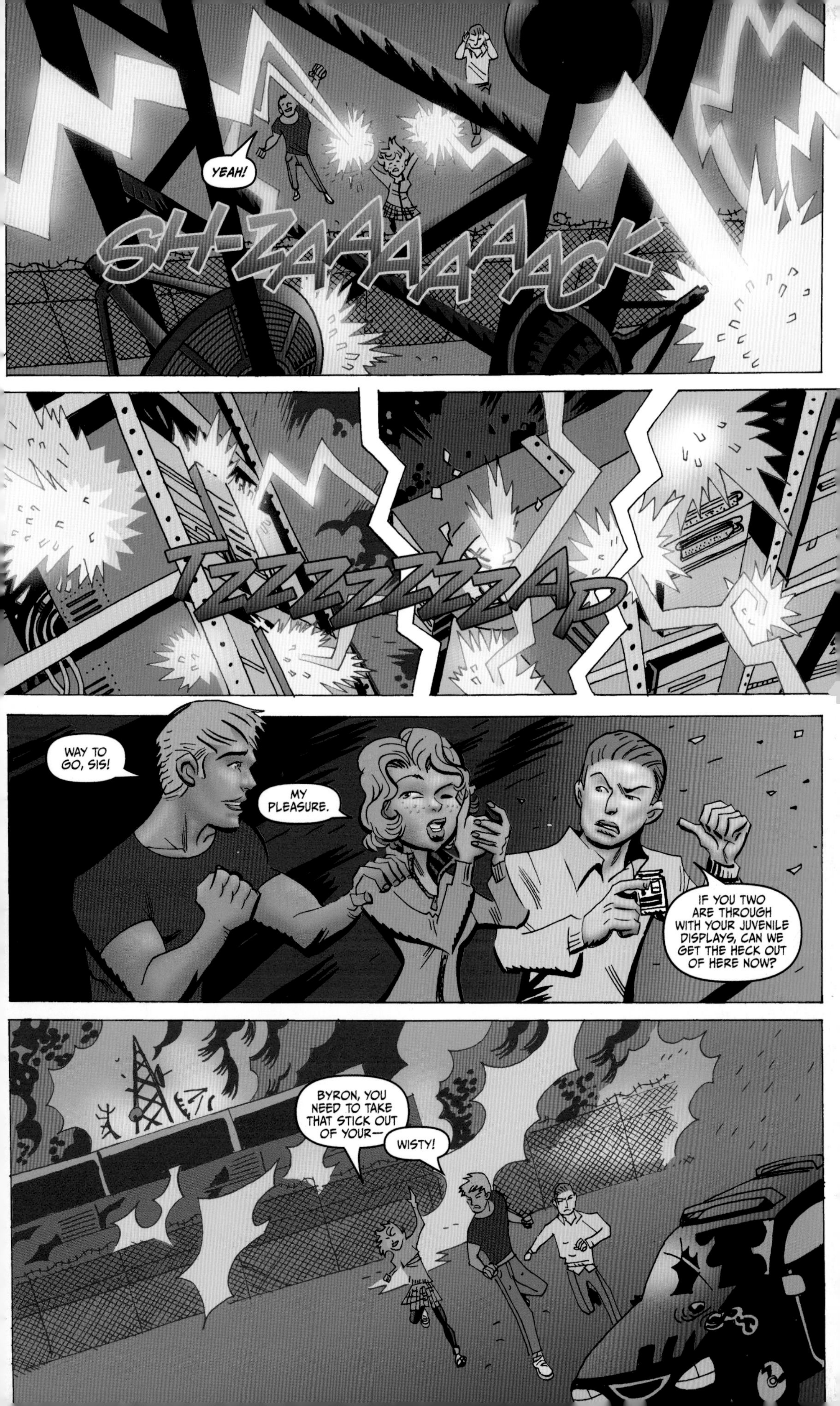
YEAH!
SH-ZAAAAAAACK
TZZZZZZZAP
WAY TO GO, SIS!
MY PLEASURE.
IF YOU TWO ARE THROUGH WITH YOUR JUVENILE DISPLAYS, CAN WE GET THE HECK OUT OF HERE NOW?
BYRON, YOU NEED TO TAKE THAT STICK OUT OF YOUR—
WISTY!

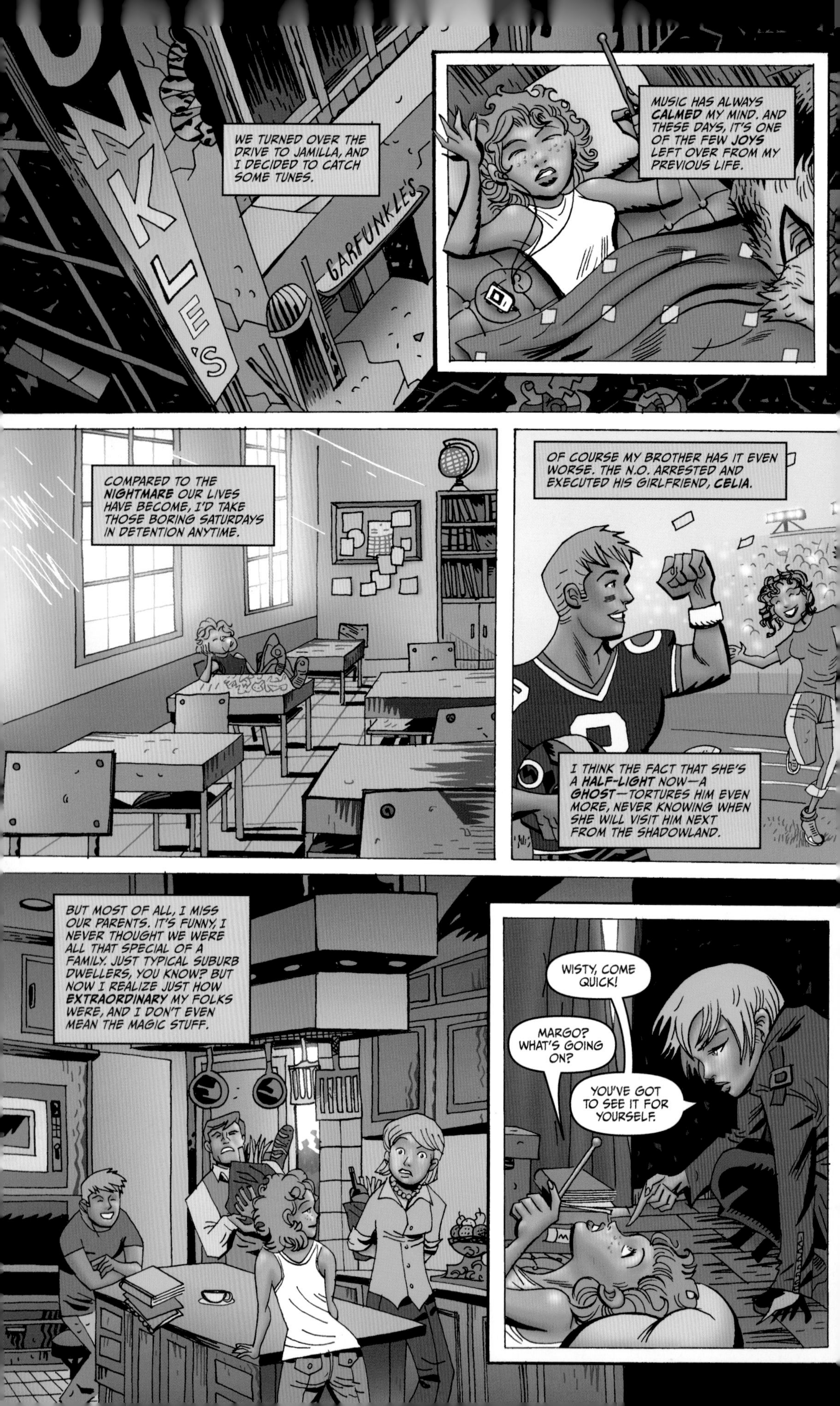

NKLE'S
GARFUNKLE'S
WE TURNED OVER THE DRIVE TO JAMILLA, AND I DECIDED TO CATCH SOME TUNES.
MUSIC HAS ALWAYS **CALMED** MY MIND. AND THESE DAYS, IT'S ONE OF THE FEW **JOYS** LEFT OVER FROM MY PREVIOUS LIFE.
COMPARED TO THE **NIGHTMARE** OUR LIVES HAVE BECOME, I'D TAKE THOSE BORING SATURDAYS IN DETENTION ANYTIME.
OF COURSE MY BROTHER HAS IT EVEN WORSE. THE N.O. ARRESTED AND EXECUTED HIS GIRLFRIEND, **CELIA**.
I THINK THE FACT THAT SHE'S A **HALF-LIGHT** NOW—A **GHOST**—TORTURES HIM EVEN MORE, NEVER KNOWING WHEN SHE WILL VISIT HIM NEXT FROM THE SHADOWLAND.
BUT MOST OF ALL, I MISS OUR PARENTS. IT'S FUNNY, I NEVER THOUGHT WE WERE ALL THAT SPECIAL OF A FAMILY. JUST TYPICAL SUBURB DWELLERS, YOU KNOW? BUT NOW I REALIZE JUST HOW **EXTRAORDINARY** MY FOLKS WERE, AND I DON'T EVEN MEAN THE MAGIC STUFF.
WISTY, COME QUICK!
MARGO? WHAT'S GOING ON?
YOU'VE GOT TO SEE IT FOR YOURSELF.

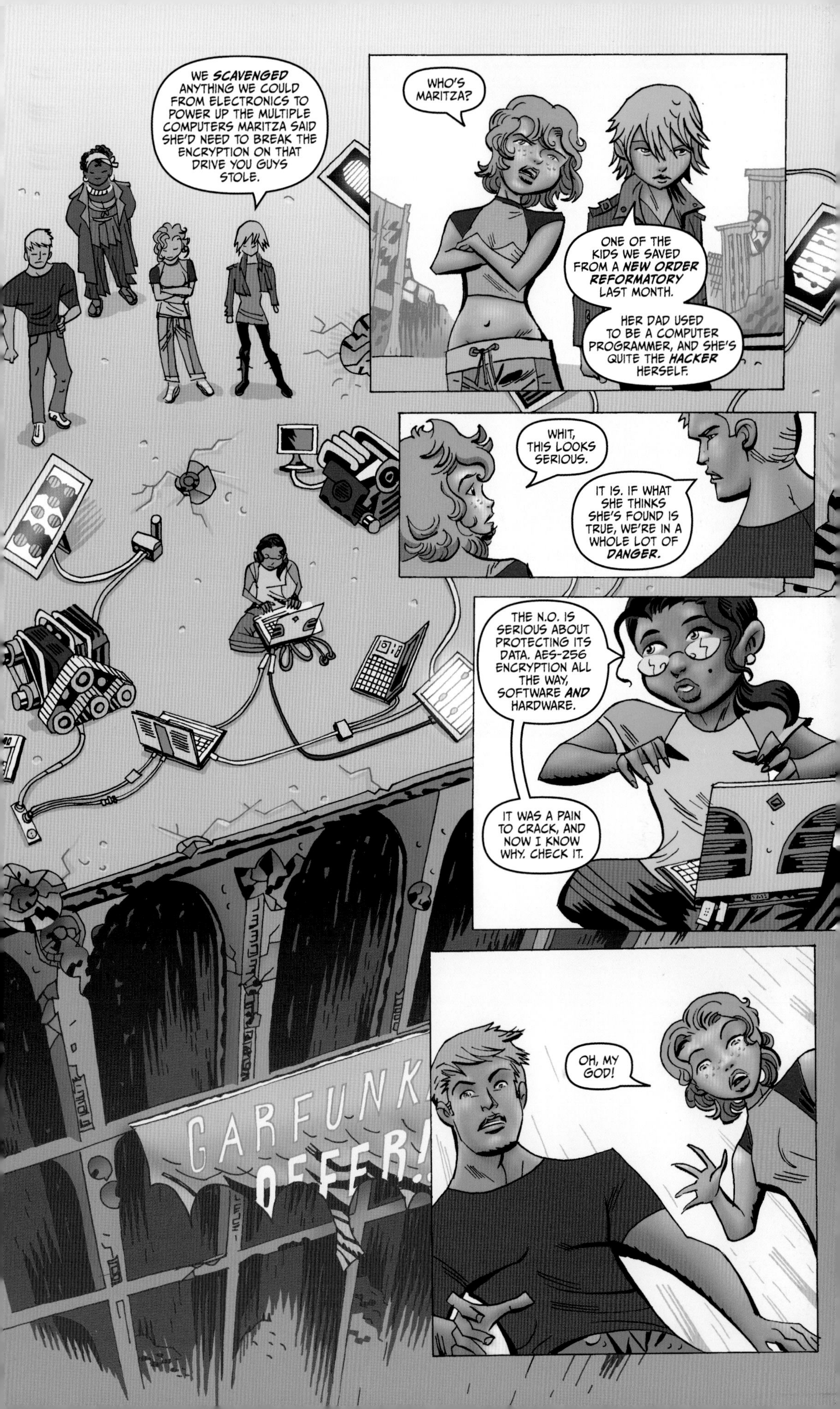

WE SCAVENGED ANYTHING WE COULD FROM ELECTRONICS TO POWER UP THE MULTIPLE COMPUTERS MARITZA SAID SHE'D NEED TO BREAK THE ENCRYPTION ON THAT DRIVE YOU GUYS STOLE.
WHO'S MARITZA?
ONE OF THE KIDS WE SAVED FROM A NEW ORDER REFORMATORY LAST MONTH.
HER DAD USED TO BE A COMPUTER PROGRAMMER, AND SHE'S QUITE THE HACKER HERSELF.
WHIT, THIS LOOKS SERIOUS.
IT IS. IF WHAT SHE THINKS SHE'S FOUND IS TRUE, WE'RE IN A WHOLE LOT OF DANGER.
THE N.O. IS SERIOUS ABOUT PROTECTING ITS DATA. AES-256 ENCRYPTION ALL THE WAY, SOFTWARE AND HARDWARE.
IT WAS A PAIN TO CRACK, AND NOW I KNOW WHY. CHECK IT.
GARFUNK
OFFER!
OH, MY GOD!

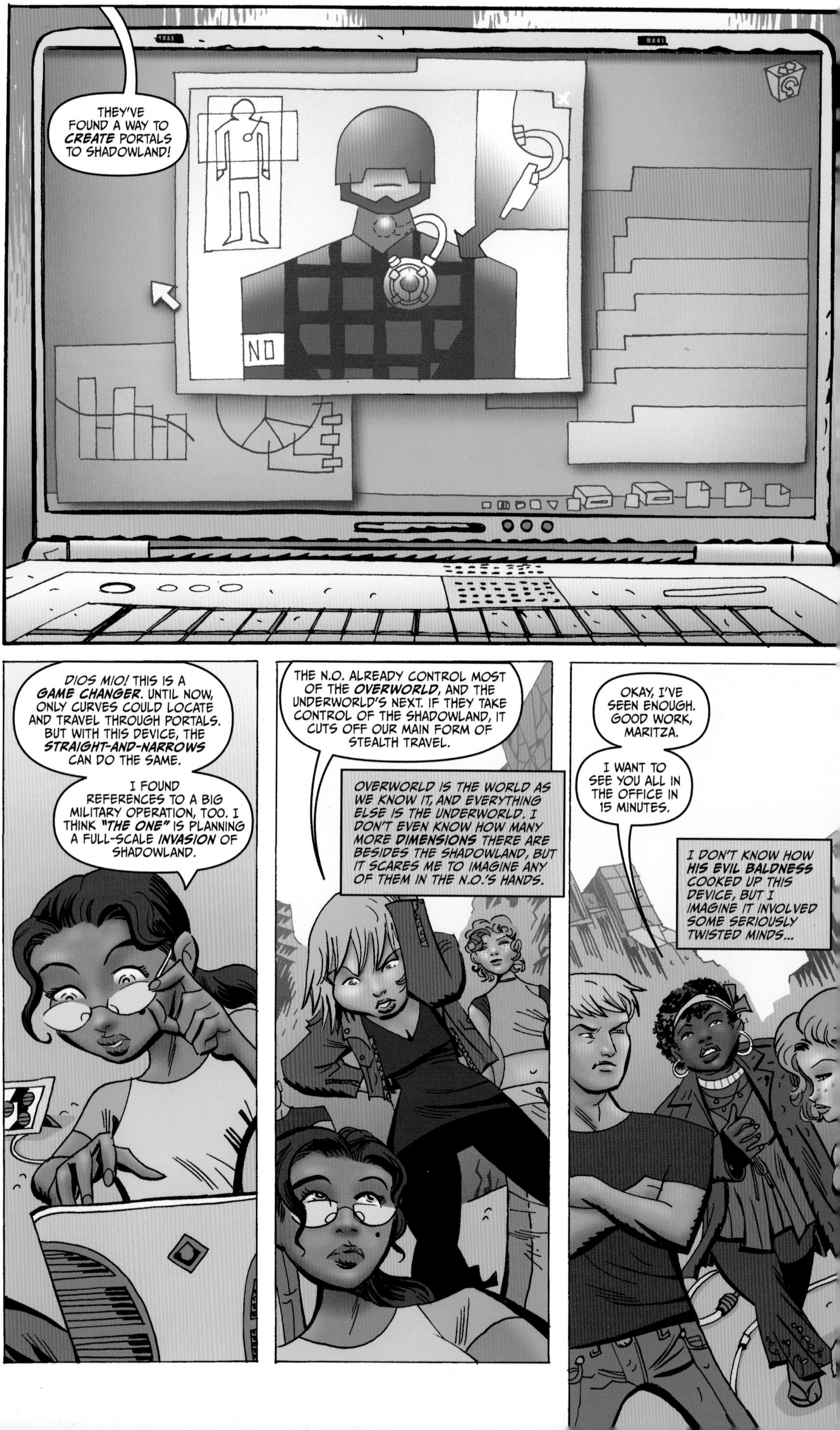
THEY'VE FOUND A WAY TO CREATE PORTALS TO SHADOWLAND!
NO
DIOS MIO! THIS IS A GAME CHANGER. UNTIL NOW, ONLY CURVES COULD LOCATE AND TRAVEL THROUGH PORTALS. BUT WITH THIS DEVICE, THE STRAIGHT-AND-NARROWS CAN DO THE SAME.
I FOUND REFERENCES TO A BIG MILITARY OPERATION, TOO. I THINK "THE ONE" IS PLANNING A FULL-SCALE INVASION OF SHADOWLAND.
THE N.O. ALREADY CONTROL MOST OF THE OVERWORLD, AND THE UNDERWORLD'S NEXT. IF THEY TAKE CONTROL OF THE SHADOWLAND, IT CUTS OFF OUR MAIN FORM OF STEALTH TRAVEL.
OVERWORLD IS THE WORLD AS WE KNOW IT, AND EVERYTHING ELSE IS THE UNDERWORLD. I DON'T EVEN KNOW HOW MANY MORE DIMENSIONS THERE ARE BESIDES THE SHADOWLAND, BUT IT SCARES ME TO IMAGINE ANY OF THEM IN THE N.O.'S HANDS.
OKAY, I'VE SEEN ENOUGH. GOOD WORK, MARITZA.
I WANT TO SEE YOU ALL IN THE OFFICE IN 15 MINUTES.
I DON'T KNOW HOW HIS EVIL BALDNESS COOKED UP THIS DEVICE, BUT I IMAGINE IT INVOLVED SOME SERIOUSLY TWISTED MINDS...

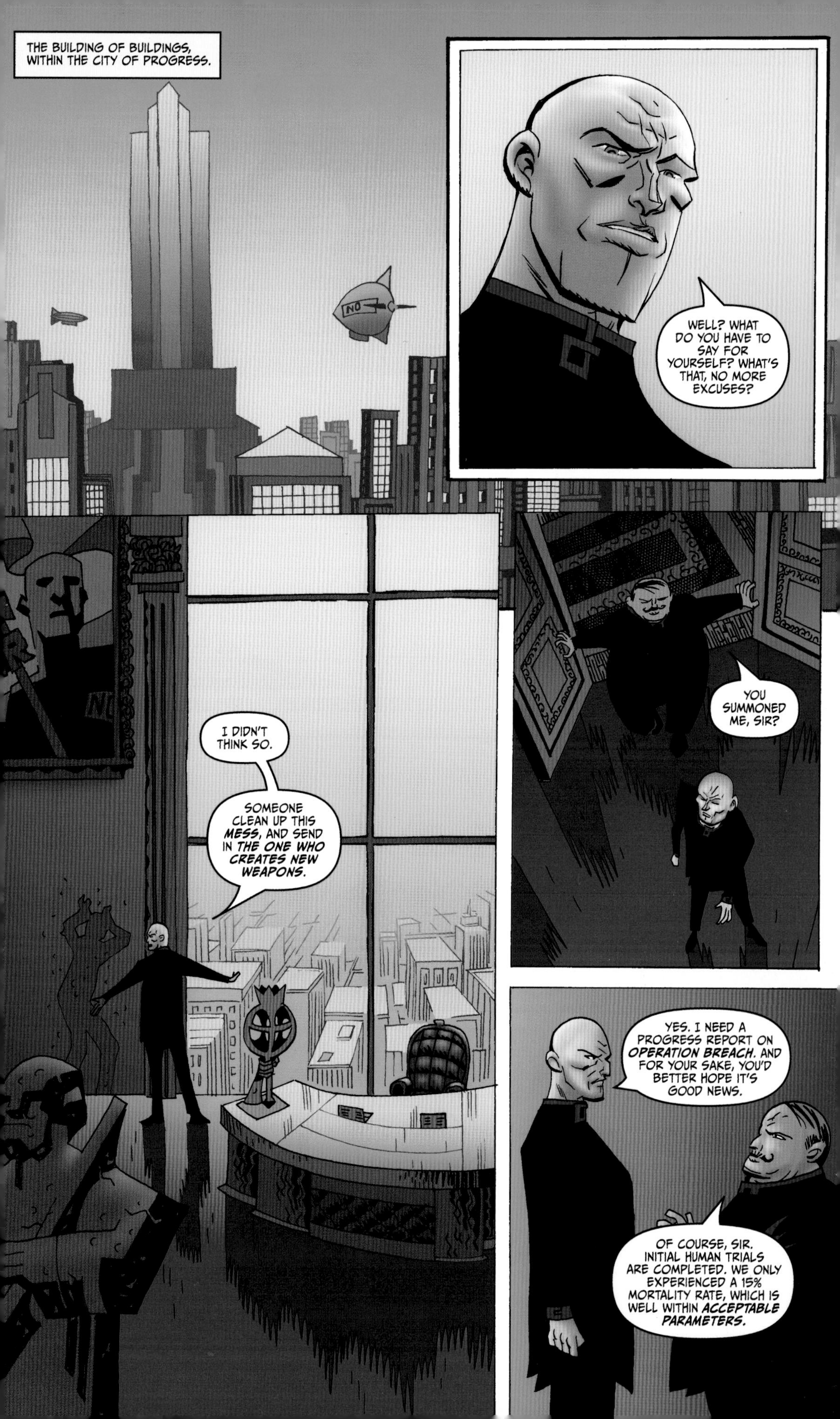
THE BUILDING OF BUILDINGS, WITHIN THE CITY OF PROGRESS.
NO
WELL? WHAT DO YOU HAVE TO SAY FOR YOURSELF? WHAT'S THAT, NO MORE EXCUSES?
I DIDN'T THINK SO.
SOMEONE CLEAN UP THIS *MESS*, AND SEND IN *THE ONE WHO CREATES NEW WEAPONS*.
YOU SUMMONED ME, SIR?
YES. I NEED A PROGRESS REPORT ON *OPERATION BREACH*. AND FOR YOUR SAKE, YOU'D BETTER HOPE IT'S GOOD NEWS.
OF COURSE, SIR. INITIAL HUMAN TRIALS ARE COMPLETED. WE ONLY EXPERIENCED A 15% MORTALITY RATE, WHICH IS WELL WITHIN *ACCEPTABLE PARAMETERS*.

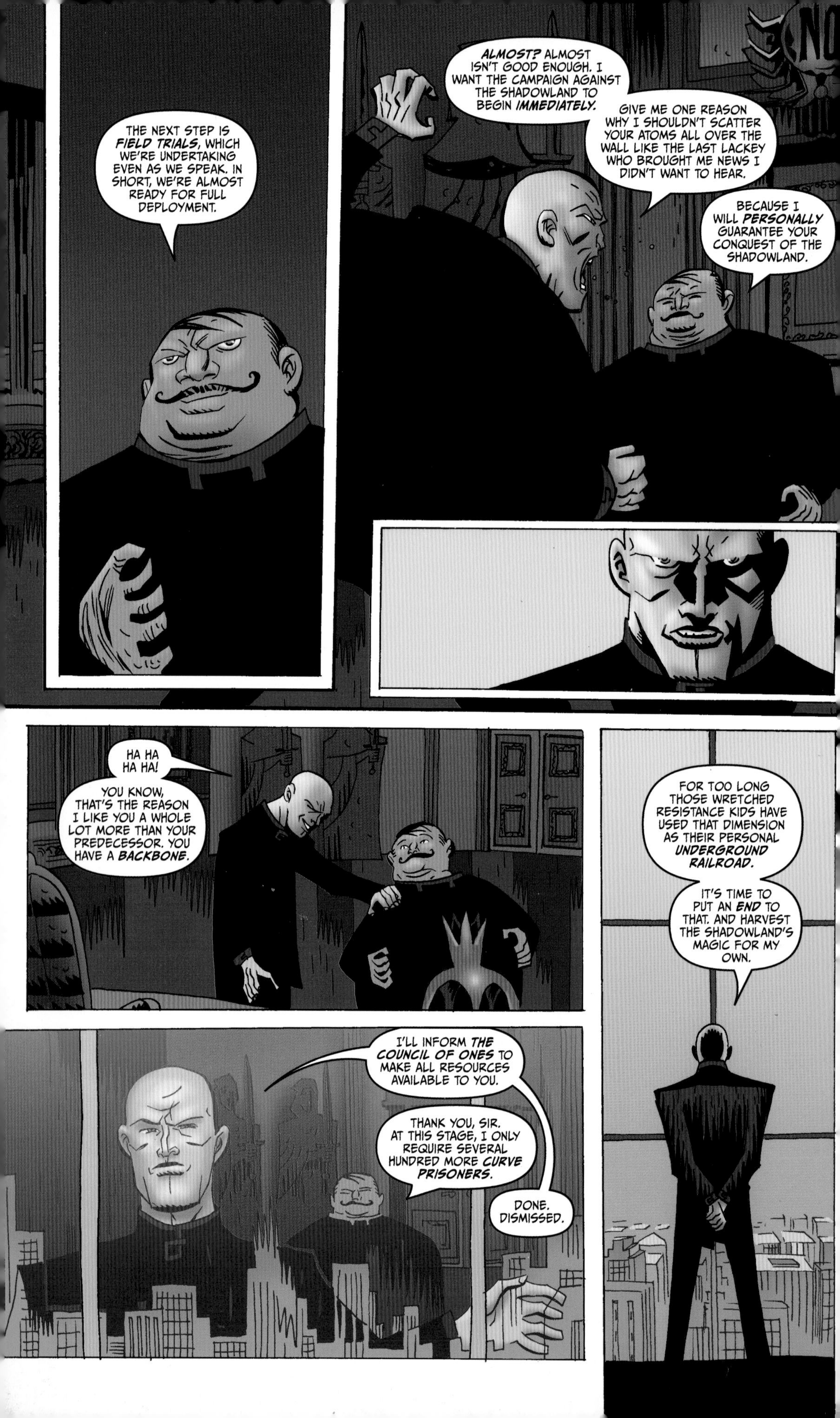
THE NEXT STEP IS FIELD TRIALS, WHICH WE'RE UNDERTAKING EVEN AS WE SPEAK. IN SHORT, WE'RE ALMOST READY FOR FULL DEPLOYMENT.
ALMOST? ALMOST ISN'T GOOD ENOUGH. I WANT THE CAMPAIGN AGAINST THE SHADOWLAND TO BEGIN IMMEDIATELY.
GIVE ME ONE REASON WHY I SHOULDN'T SCATTER YOUR ATOMS ALL OVER THE WALL LIKE THE LAST LACKEY WHO BROUGHT ME NEWS I DIDN'T WANT TO HEAR.
BECAUSE I WILL PERSONALLY GUARANTEE YOUR CONQUEST OF THE SHADOWLAND.
HA HA HA HA!
YOU KNOW, THAT'S THE REASON I LIKE YOU A WHOLE LOT MORE THAN YOUR PREDECESSOR. YOU HAVE A BACKBONE.
FOR TOO LONG THOSE WRETCHED RESISTANCE KIDS HAVE USED THAT DIMENSION AS THEIR PERSONAL UNDERGROUND RAILROAD.
IT'S TIME TO PUT AN END TO THAT. AND HARVEST THE SHADOWLAND'S MAGIC FOR MY OWN.
I'LL INFORM THE COUNCIL OF ONES TO MAKE ALL RESOURCES AVAILABLE TO YOU.
THANK YOU, SIR. AT THIS STAGE, I ONLY REQUIRE SEVERAL HUNDRED MORE CURVE PRISONERS.
DONE. DISMISSED.

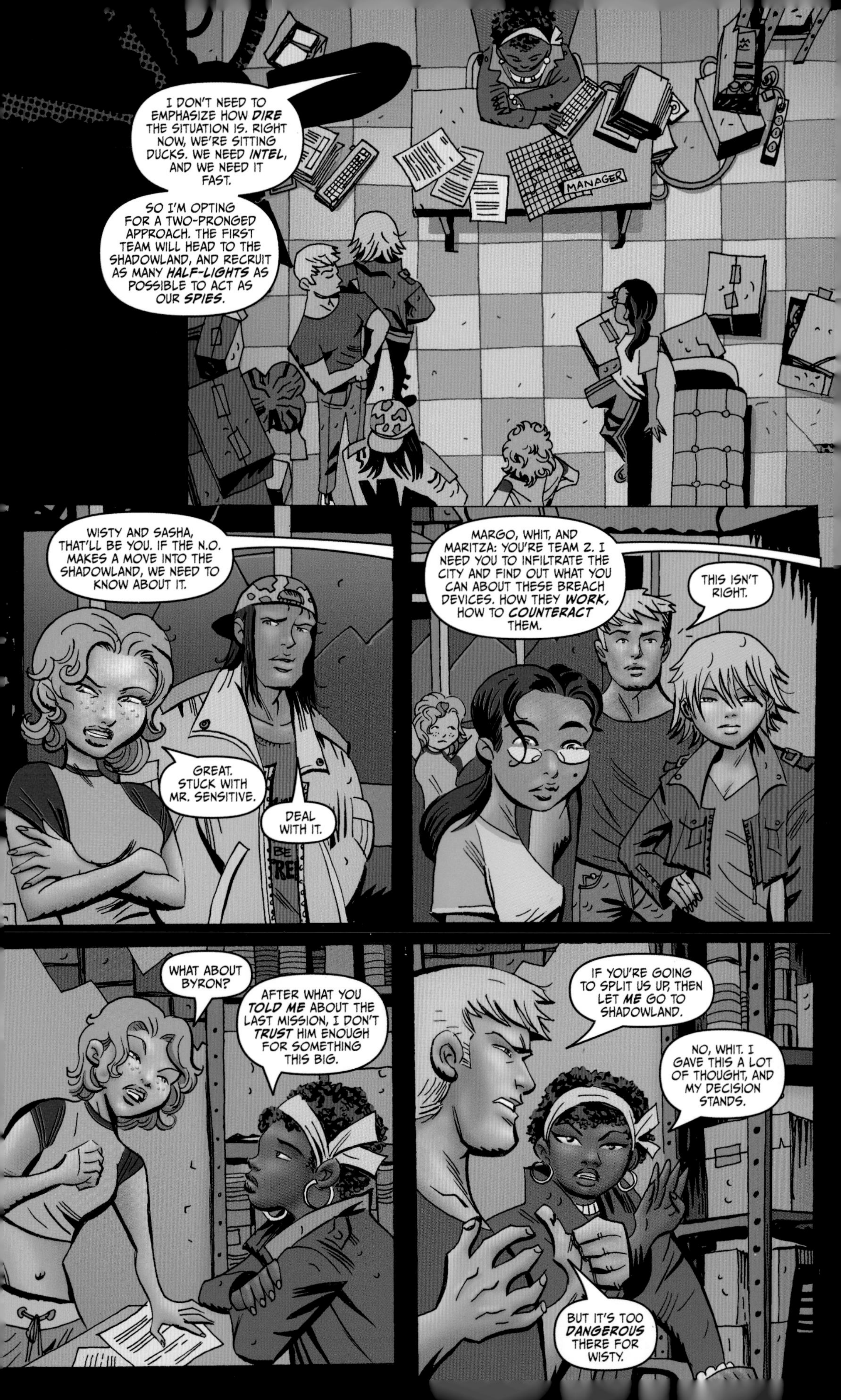
I DON'T NEED TO EMPHASIZE HOW DIRE THE SITUATION IS. RIGHT NOW, WE'RE SITTING DUCKS. WE NEED INTEL, AND WE NEED IT FAST.
SO I'M OPTING FOR A TWO-PRONGED APPROACH. THE FIRST TEAM WILL HEAD TO THE SHADOWLAND, AND RECRUIT AS MANY HALF-LIGHTS AS POSSIBLE TO ACT AS OUR SPIES.
MANAGER
WISTY AND SASHA, THAT'LL BE YOU. IF THE N.O. MAKES A MOVE INTO THE SHADOWLAND, WE NEED TO KNOW ABOUT IT.
GREAT. STUCK WITH MR. SENSITIVE.
DEAL WITH IT.
MARGO, WHIT, AND MARITZA: YOU'RE TEAM 2. I NEED YOU TO INFILTRATE THE CITY AND FIND OUT WHAT YOU CAN ABOUT THESE BREACH DEVICES. HOW THEY WORK, HOW TO COUNTERACT THEM.
THIS ISN'T RIGHT.
WHAT ABOUT BYRON?
AFTER WHAT YOU TOLD ME ABOUT THE LAST MISSION, I DON'T TRUST HIM ENOUGH FOR SOMETHING THIS BIG.
IF YOU'RE GOING TO SPLIT US UP, THEN LET ME GO TO SHADOWLAND.
NO, WHIT. I GAVE THIS A LOT OF THOUGHT, AND MY DECISION STANDS.
BUT IT'S TOO DANGEROUS THERE FOR WISTY.

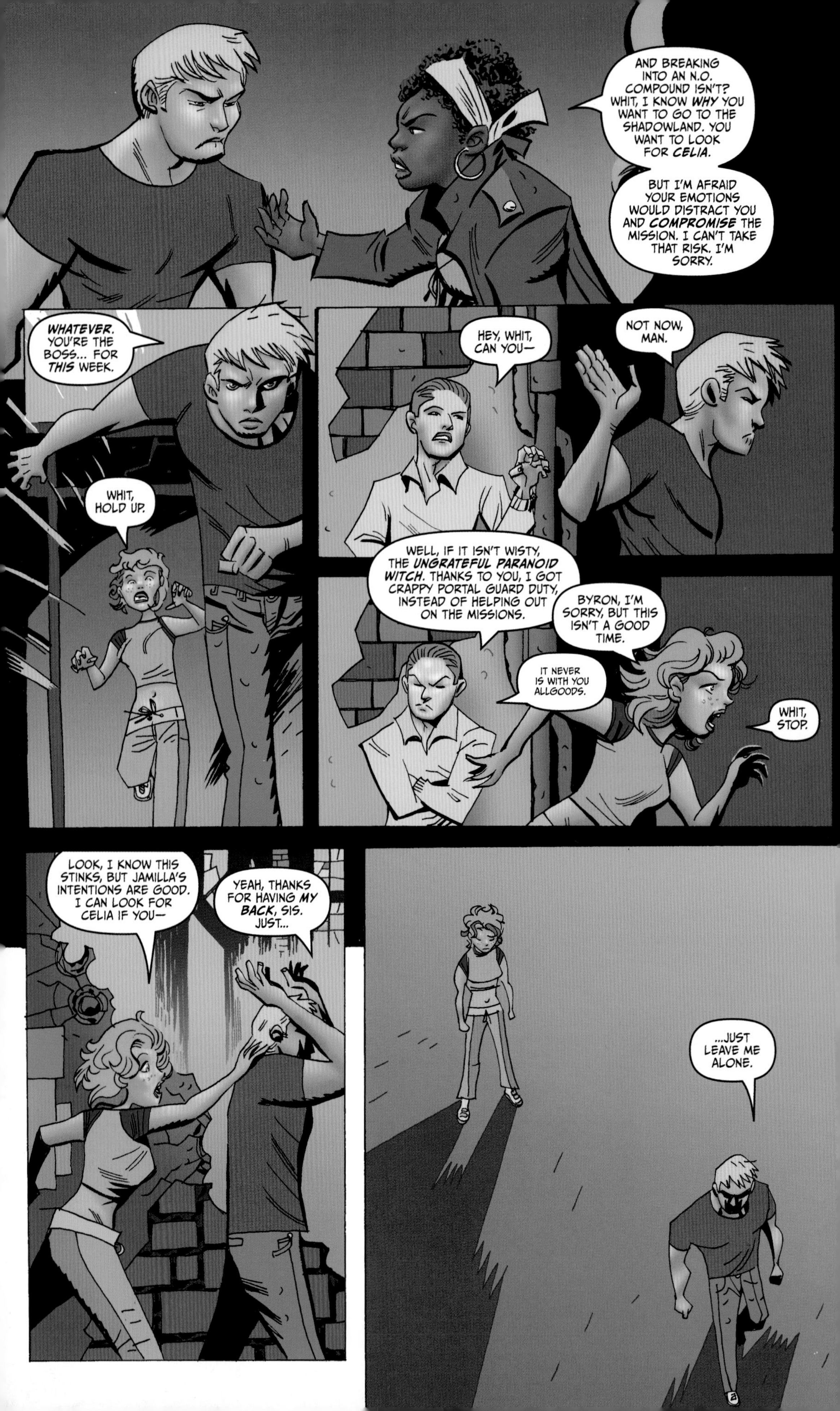
AND BREAKING INTO AN N.O. COMPOUND ISN'T? WHIT, I KNOW *WHY* YOU WANT TO GO TO THE SHADOWLAND. YOU WANT TO LOOK FOR *CELIA*.
BUT I'M AFRAID YOUR EMOTIONS WOULD DISTRACT YOU AND *COMPROMISE* THE MISSION. I CAN'T TAKE THAT RISK. I'M SORRY.
WHATEVER. YOU'RE THE BOSS... FOR *THIS* WEEK.
WHIT, HOLD UP.
HEY, WHIT, CAN YOU—
NOT NOW, MAN.
WELL, IF IT ISN'T WISTY, THE *UNGRATEFUL PARANOID WITCH*. THANKS TO YOU, I GOT CRAPPY PORTAL GUARD DUTY, INSTEAD OF HELPING OUT ON THE MISSIONS.
BYRON, I'M SORRY, BUT THIS ISN'T A GOOD TIME.
IT NEVER IS WITH YOU ALLGOODS.
WHIT, STOP.
LOOK, I KNOW THIS STINKS, BUT JAMILLA'S INTENTIONS ARE GOOD. I CAN LOOK FOR CELIA IF YOU—
YEAH, THANKS FOR HAVING *MY BACK*, SIS. JUST...
...JUST LEAVE ME ALONE.

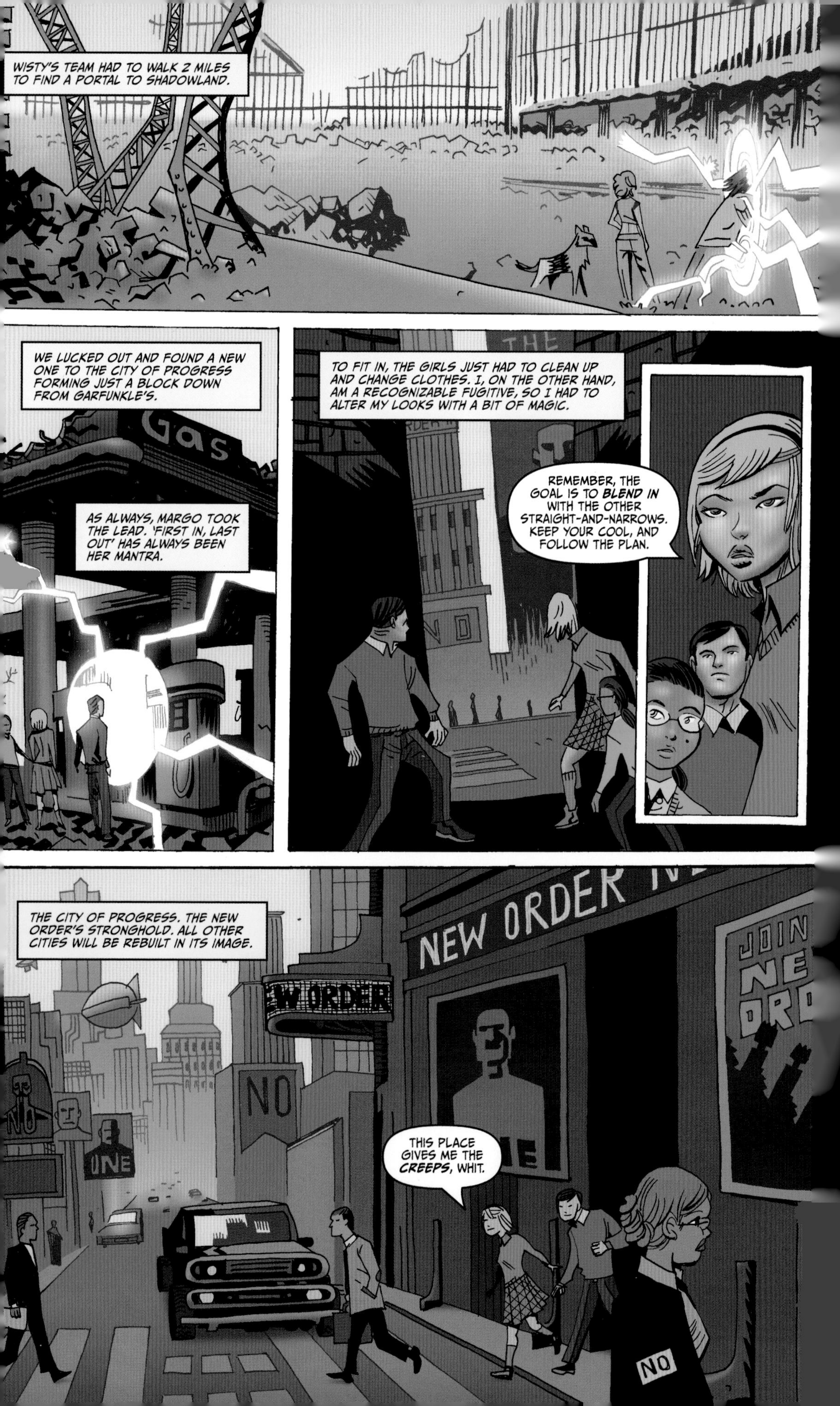
WISTY'S TEAM HAD TO WALK 2 MILES TO FIND A PORTAL TO SHADOWLAND.
WE LUCKED OUT AND FOUND A NEW ONE TO THE CITY OF PROGRESS FORMING JUST A BLOCK DOWN FROM GARFUNKLE'S.
GAS
AS ALWAYS, MARGO TOOK THE LEAD. 'FIRST IN, LAST OUT' HAS ALWAYS BEEN HER MANTRA.
TO FIT IN, THE GIRLS JUST HAD TO CLEAN UP AND CHANGE CLOTHES. I, ON THE OTHER HAND, AM A RECOGNIZABLE FUGITIVE, SO I HAD TO ALTER MY LOOKS WITH A BIT OF MAGIC.
REMEMBER, THE GOAL IS TO BLEND IN WITH THE OTHER STRAIGHT-AND-NARROWS. KEEP YOUR COOL, AND FOLLOW THE PLAN.
THE CITY OF PROGRESS. THE NEW ORDER'S STRONGHOLD. ALL OTHER CITIES WILL BE REBUILT IN ITS IMAGE.
NEW ORDER
W ORDER
NO
ONE
THIS PLACE GIVES ME THE CREEPS, WHIT.
NO

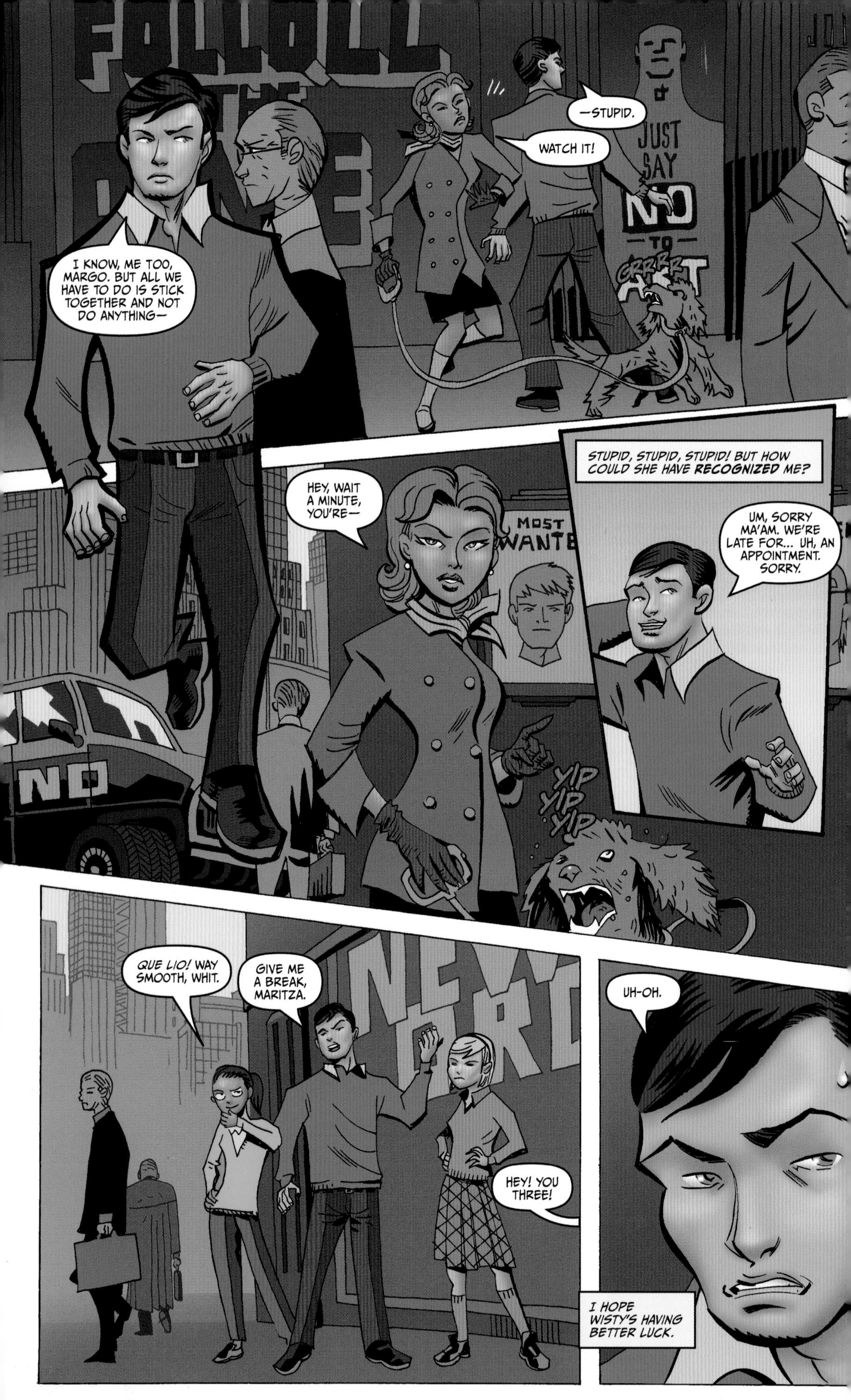
FOLLOW THE
JUST SAY NO TO ART
—STUPID.
WATCH IT!
I KNOW, ME TOO, MARGO. BUT ALL WE HAVE TO DO IS STICK TOGETHER AND NOT DO ANYTHING—
CRRRR
HEY, WAIT A MINUTE, YOU'RE—
MOST WANTE
NO
YIP YIP YIP
STUPID, STUPID, STUPID! BUT HOW COULD SHE HAVE RECOGNIZED ME?
UM, SORRY MA'AM. WE'RE LATE FOR... UH, AN APPOINTMENT. SORRY.
QUE LIO! WAY SMOOTH, WHIT.
GIVE ME A BREAK, MARITZA.
HEY! YOU THREE!
UH-OH.
I HOPE WISTY'S HAVING BETTER LUCK.

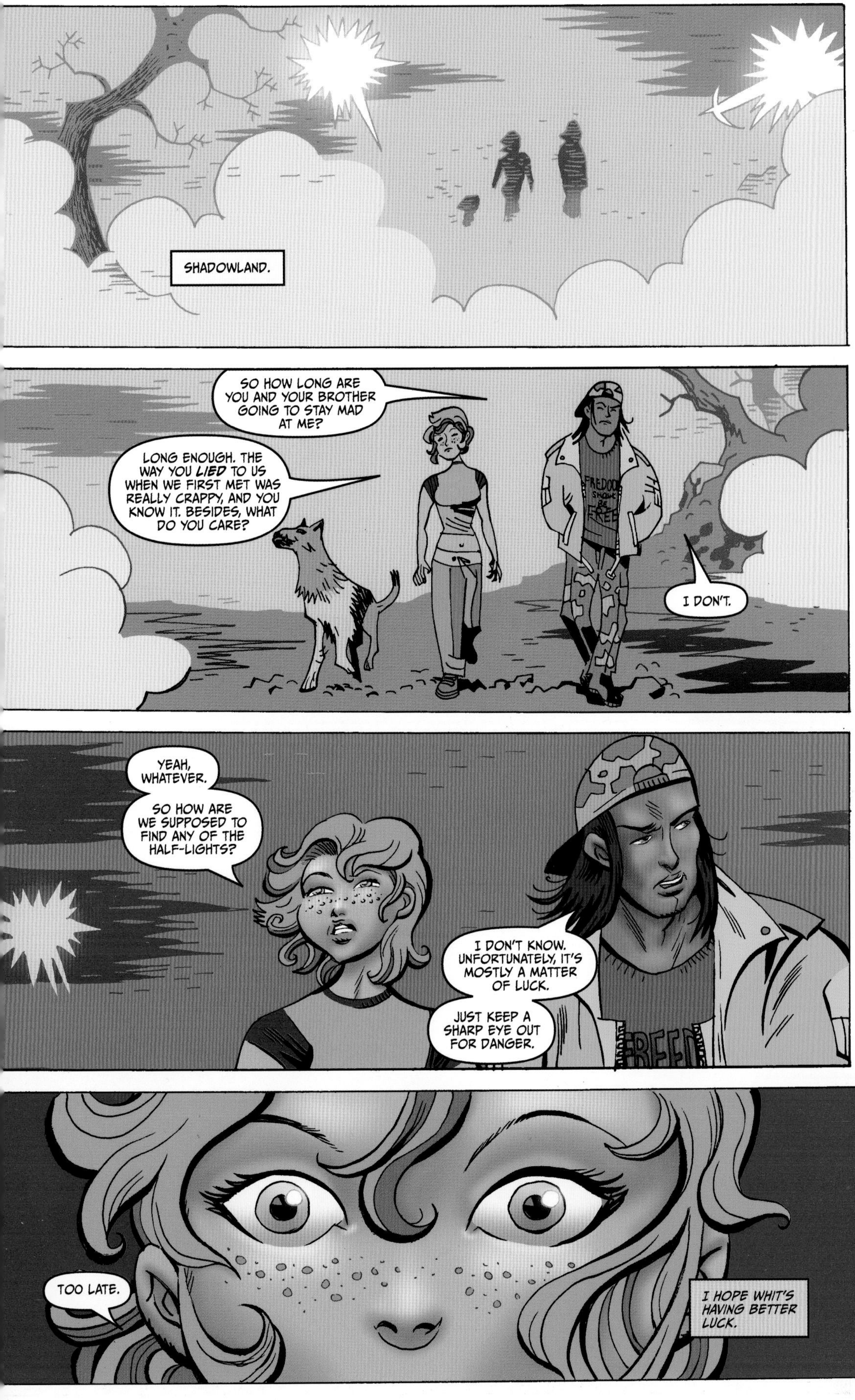
SHADOWLAND.
SO HOW LONG ARE YOU AND YOUR BROTHER GOING TO STAY MAD AT ME?
LONG ENOUGH. THE WAY YOU *LIED* TO US WHEN WE FIRST MET WAS REALLY CRAPPY, AND YOU KNOW IT. BESIDES, WHAT DO YOU CARE?
I DON'T.
YEAH, WHATEVER.
SO HOW ARE WE SUPPOSED TO FIND ANY OF THE HALF-LIGHTS?
I DON'T KNOW. UNFORTUNATELY, IT'S MOSTLY A MATTER OF LUCK.
JUST KEEP A SHARP EYE OUT FOR DANGER.
TOO LATE.
I HOPE WHIT'S HAVING BETTER LUCK.

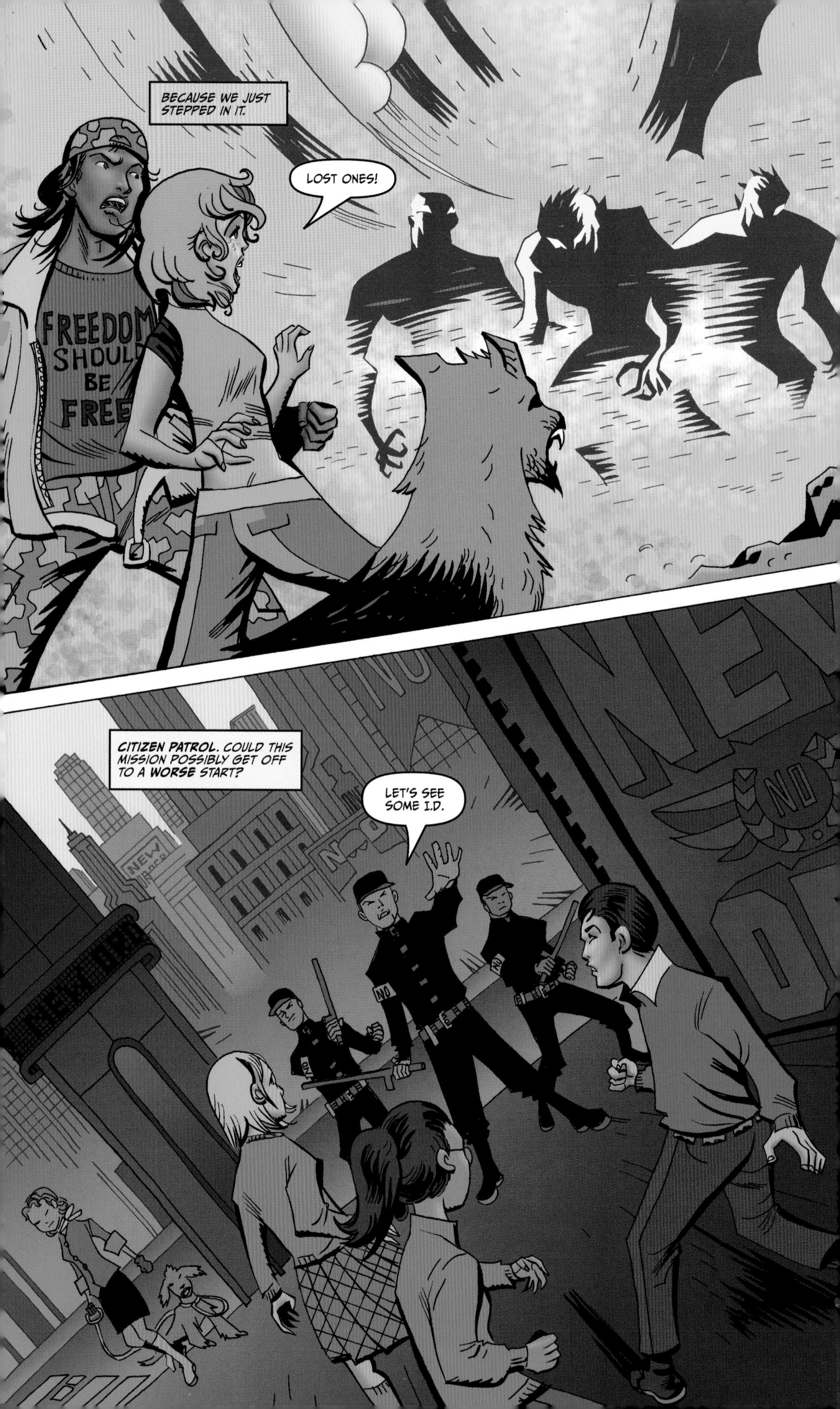
BECAUSE WE JUST STEPPED IN IT.
LOST ONES!
CITIZEN PATROL. COULD THIS MISSION POSSIBLY GET OFF TO A WORSE START?
LET'S SEE SOME I.D.

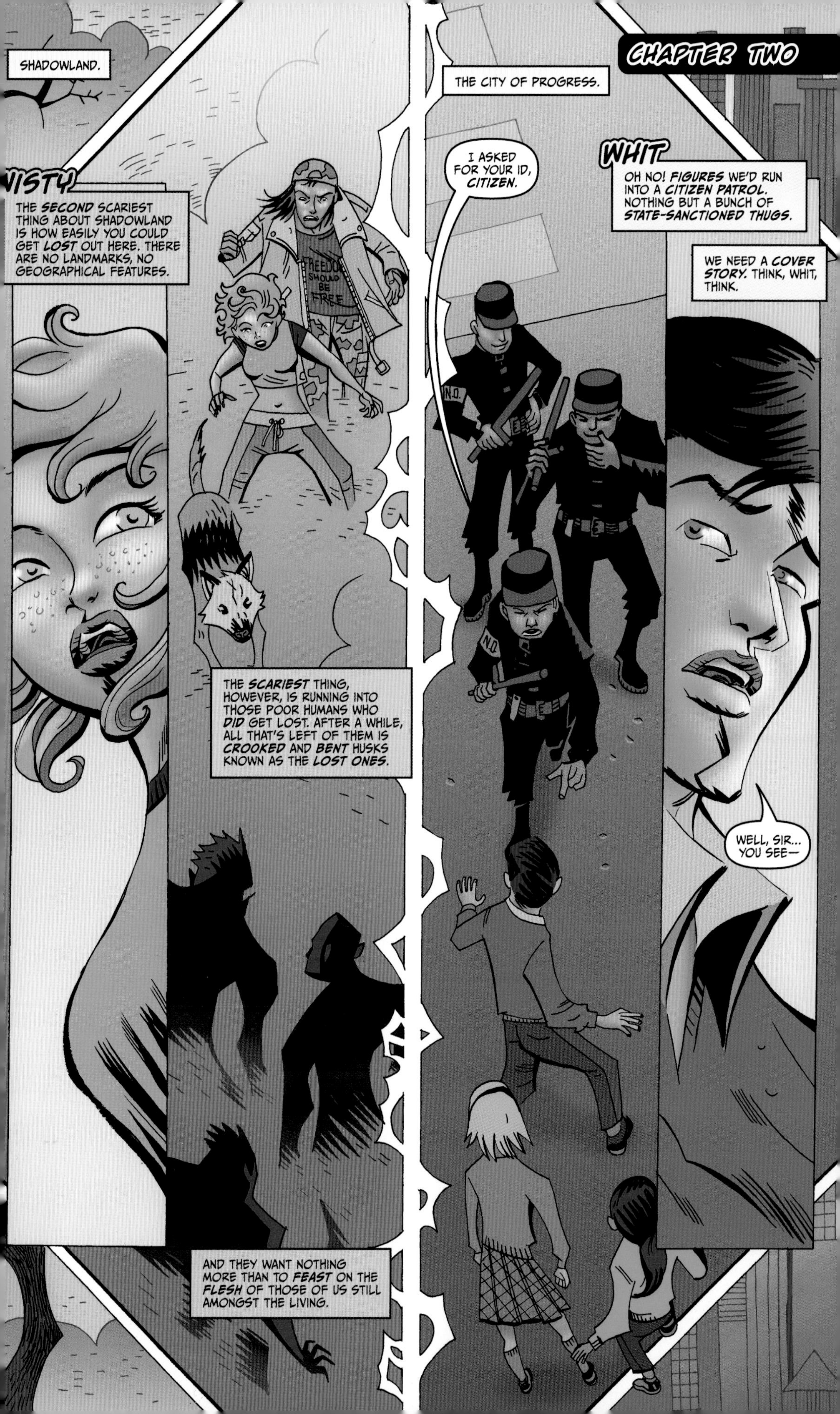
CHAPTER TWO
SHADOWLAND.
NISTY
THE SECOND SCARIEST THING ABOUT SHADOWLAND IS HOW EASILY YOU COULD GET LOST OUT HERE. THERE ARE NO LANDMARKS, NO GEOGRAPHICAL FEATURES.
FREEDOM SHOULD BE FREE
THE SCARIEST THING, HOWEVER, IS RUNNING INTO THOSE POOR HUMANS WHO DID GET LOST. AFTER A WHILE, ALL THAT'S LEFT OF THEM IS CROOKED AND BENT HUSKS KNOWN AS THE LOST ONES.
AND THEY WANT NOTHING MORE THAN TO FEAST ON THE FLESH OF THOSE OF US STILL AMONGST THE LIVING.
THE CITY OF PROGRESS.
I ASKED FOR YOUR ID, CITIZEN.
N.O.
WHIT
OH NO! FIGURES WE'D RUN INTO A CITIZEN PATROL. NOTHING BUT A BUNCH OF STATE-SANCTIONED THUGS.
WE NEED A COVER STORY. THINK, WHIT, THINK.
WELL, SIR... YOU SEE—

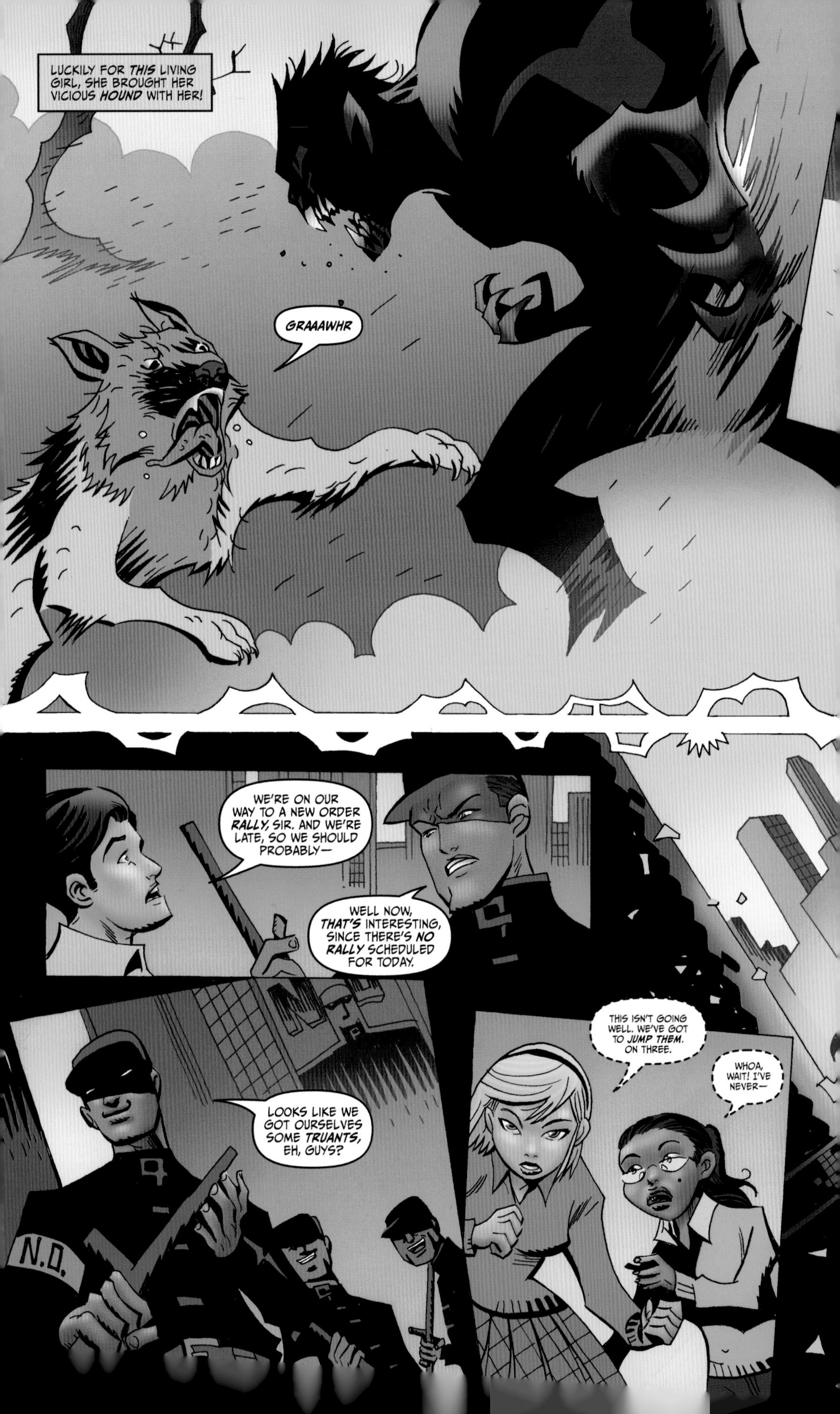
LUCKILY FOR THIS LIVING GIRL, SHE BROUGHT HER VICIOUS HOUND WITH HER!
GRAAAWHR
WE'RE ON OUR WAY TO A NEW ORDER RALLY, SIR. AND WE'RE LATE, SO WE SHOULD PROBABLY—
WELL NOW, THAT'S INTERESTING, SINCE THERE'S NO RALLY SCHEDULED FOR TODAY.
LOOKS LIKE WE GOT OURSELVES SOME TRUANTS, EH, GUYS?
N.D.
THIS ISN'T GOING WELL. WE'VE GOT TO JUMP THEM. ON THREE.
WHOA, WAIT! I'VE NEVER—

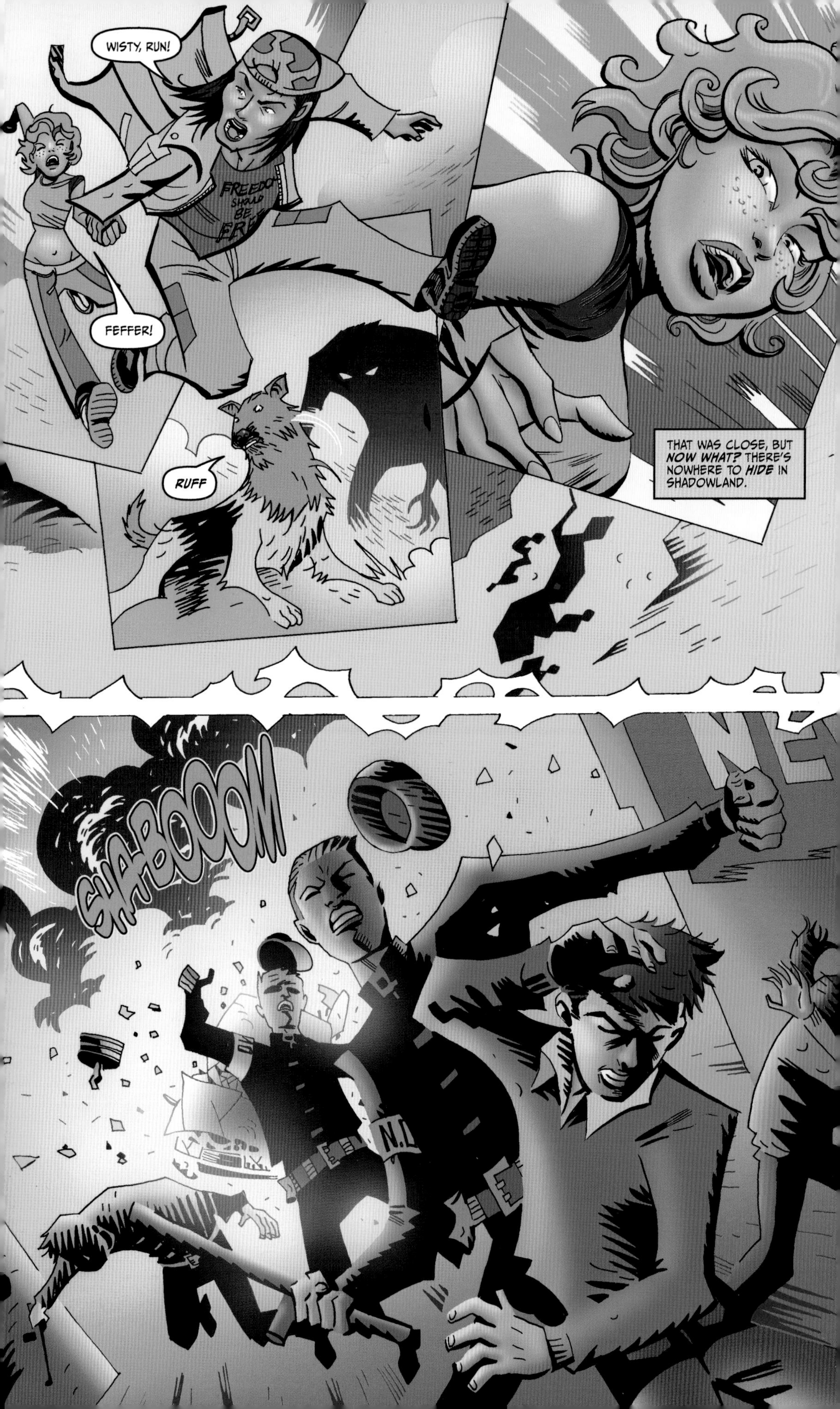
WISTY, RUN!
FREEDOM SHOULD BE FREE
FEFFER!
RUFF
THAT WAS CLOSE, BUT *NOW WHAT?* THERE'S NOWHERE TO *HIDE* IN SHADOWLAND.
SHABOOOM
N.O.

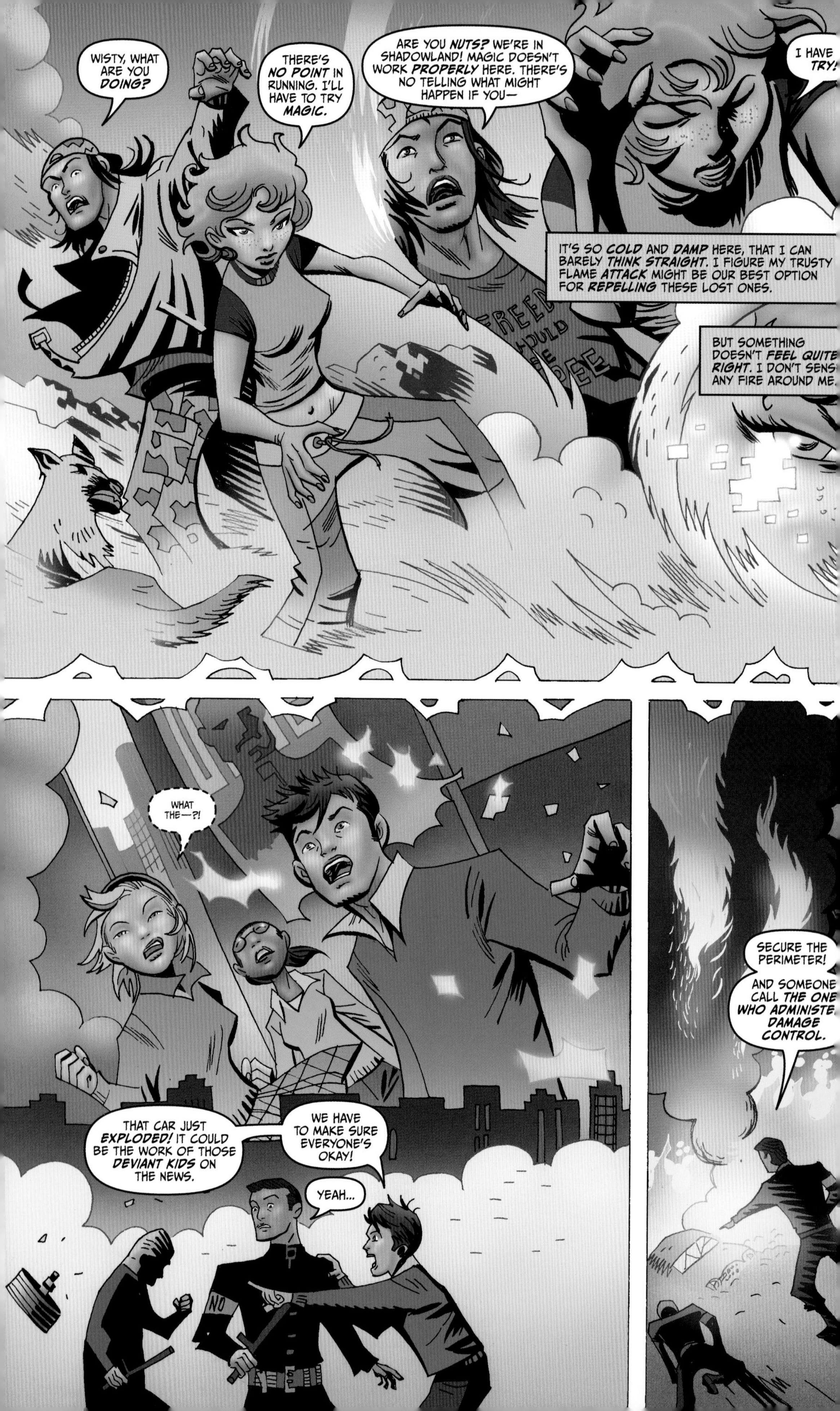
WISTY, WHAT ARE YOU DOING?
THERE'S NO POINT IN RUNNING. I'LL HAVE TO TRY MAGIC.
ARE YOU NUTS? WE'RE IN SHADOWLAND! MAGIC DOESN'T WORK PROPERLY HERE. THERE'S NO TELLING WHAT MIGHT HAPPEN IF YOU—
I HAVE TRY!
IT'S SO COLD AND DAMP HERE, THAT I CAN BARELY THINK STRAIGHT. I FIGURE MY TRUSTY FLAME ATTACK MIGHT BE OUR BEST OPTION FOR REPELLING THESE LOST ONES.
BUT SOMETHING DOESN'T FEEL QUITE RIGHT. I DON'T SENS ANY FIRE AROUND ME.
WHAT THE—?!
THAT CAR JUST EXPLODED! IT COULD BE THE WORK OF THOSE DEVIANT KIDS ON THE NEWS.
WE HAVE TO MAKE SURE EVERYONE'S OKAY!
YEAH...
SECURE THE PERIMETER!
AND SOMEONE CALL THE ONE WHO ADMINISTE DAMAGE CONTROL.

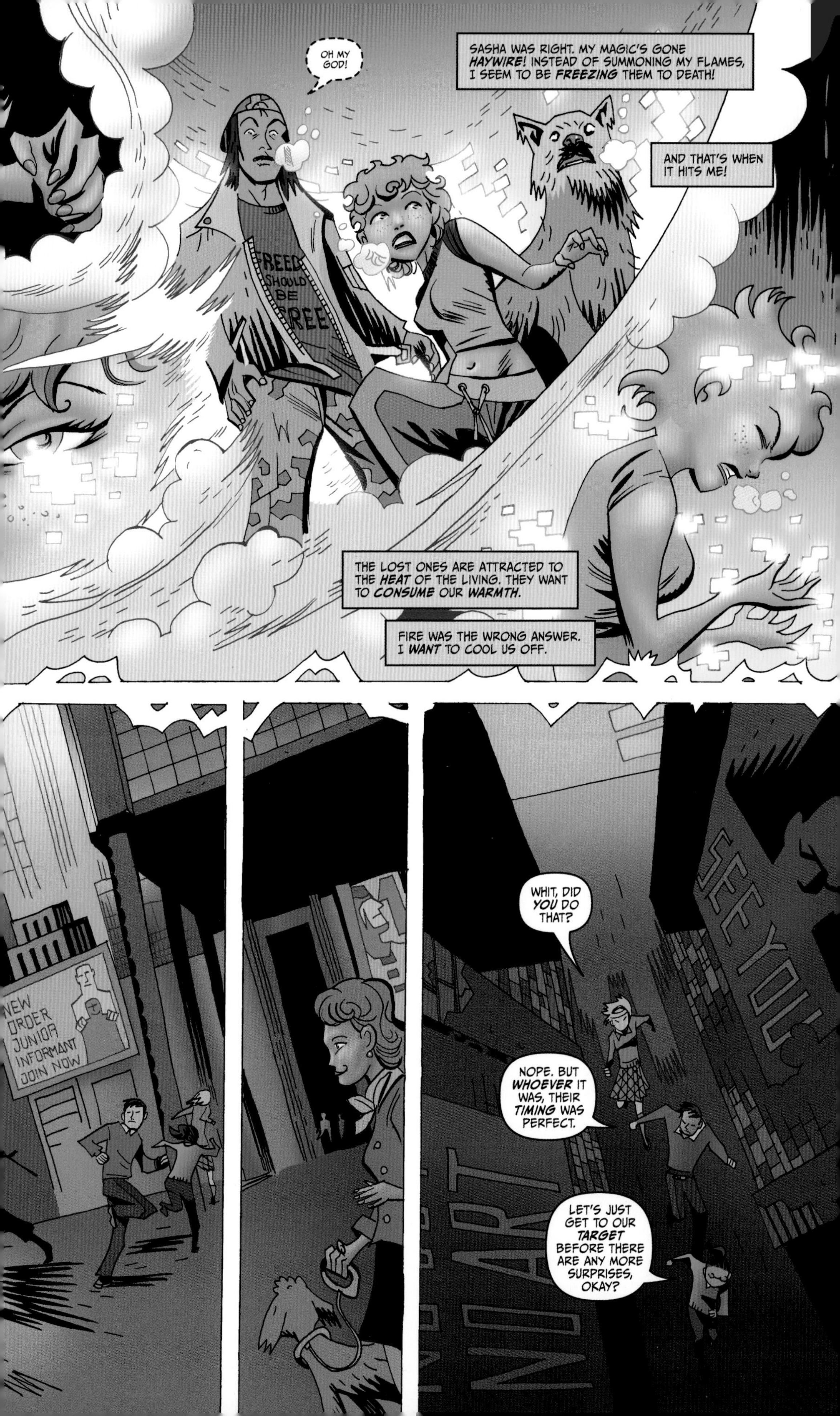
OH MY GOD!
SASHA WAS RIGHT. MY MAGIC'S GONE HAYWIRE! INSTEAD OF SUMMONING MY FLAMES, I SEEM TO BE FREEZING THEM TO DEATH!
AND THAT'S WHEN IT HITS ME!
FREED SHOULD BE FREE
THE LOST ONES ARE ATTRACTED TO THE HEAT OF THE LIVING. THEY WANT TO CONSUME OUR WARMTH.
FIRE WAS THE WRONG ANSWER. I WANT TO COOL US OFF.
NEW ORDER JUNIOR INFORMANT JOIN NOW
WHIT, DID YOU DO THAT?
NOPE. BUT WHOEVER IT WAS, THEIR TIMING WAS PERFECT.
LET'S JUST GET TO OUR TARGET BEFORE THERE ARE ANY MORE SURPRISES, OKAY?
SEE YOU

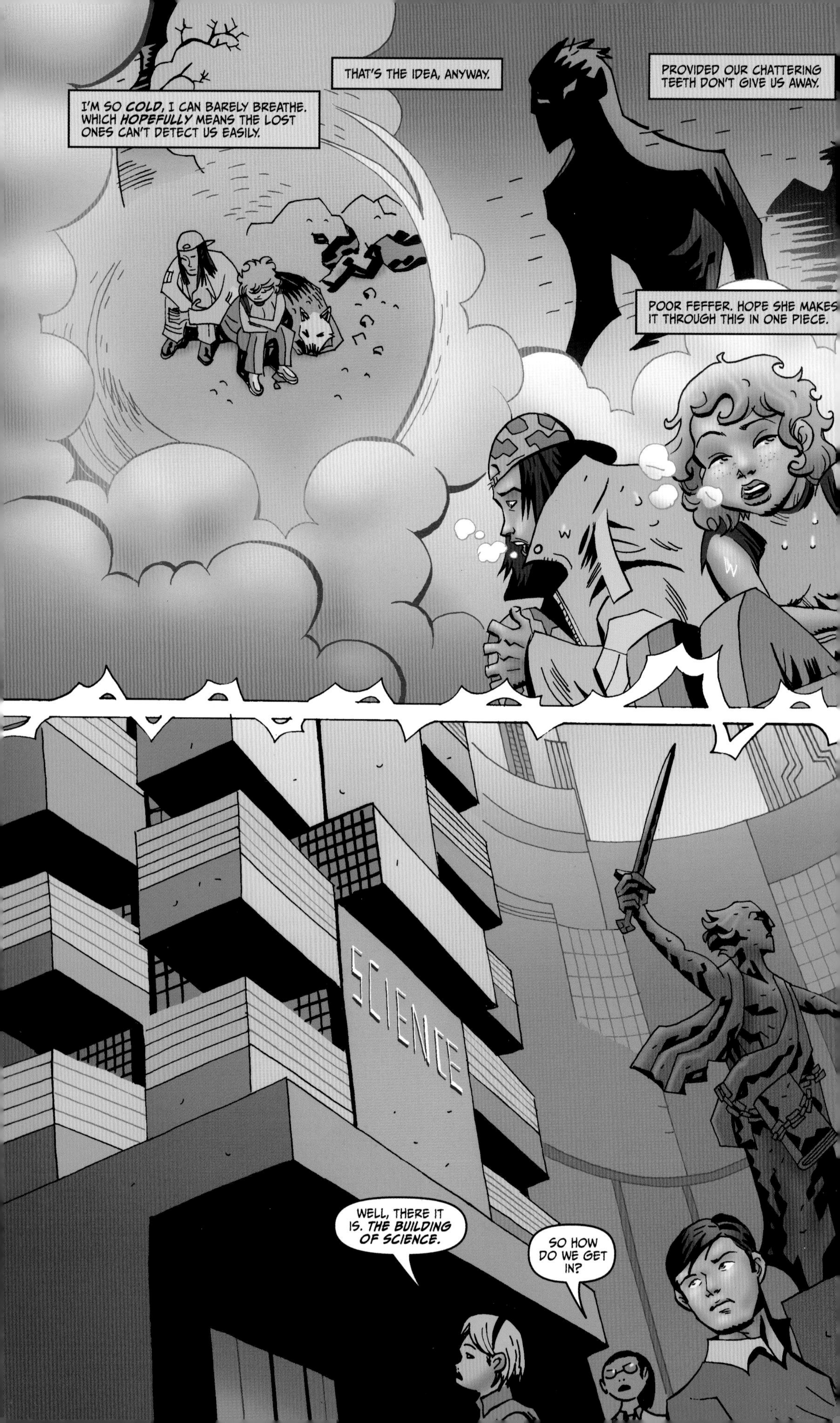

I'M SO *COLD*, I CAN BARELY BREATHE. WHICH *HOPEFULLY* MEANS THE LOST ONES CAN'T DETECT US EASILY.
THAT'S THE IDEA, ANYWAY.
PROVIDED OUR CHATTERING TEETH DON'T GIVE US AWAY.
POOR FEFFER. HOPE SHE MAKES IT THROUGH THIS IN ONE PIECE.
SCIENCE
WELL, THERE IT IS. *THE BUILDING OF SCIENCE.*
SO HOW DO WE GET IN?

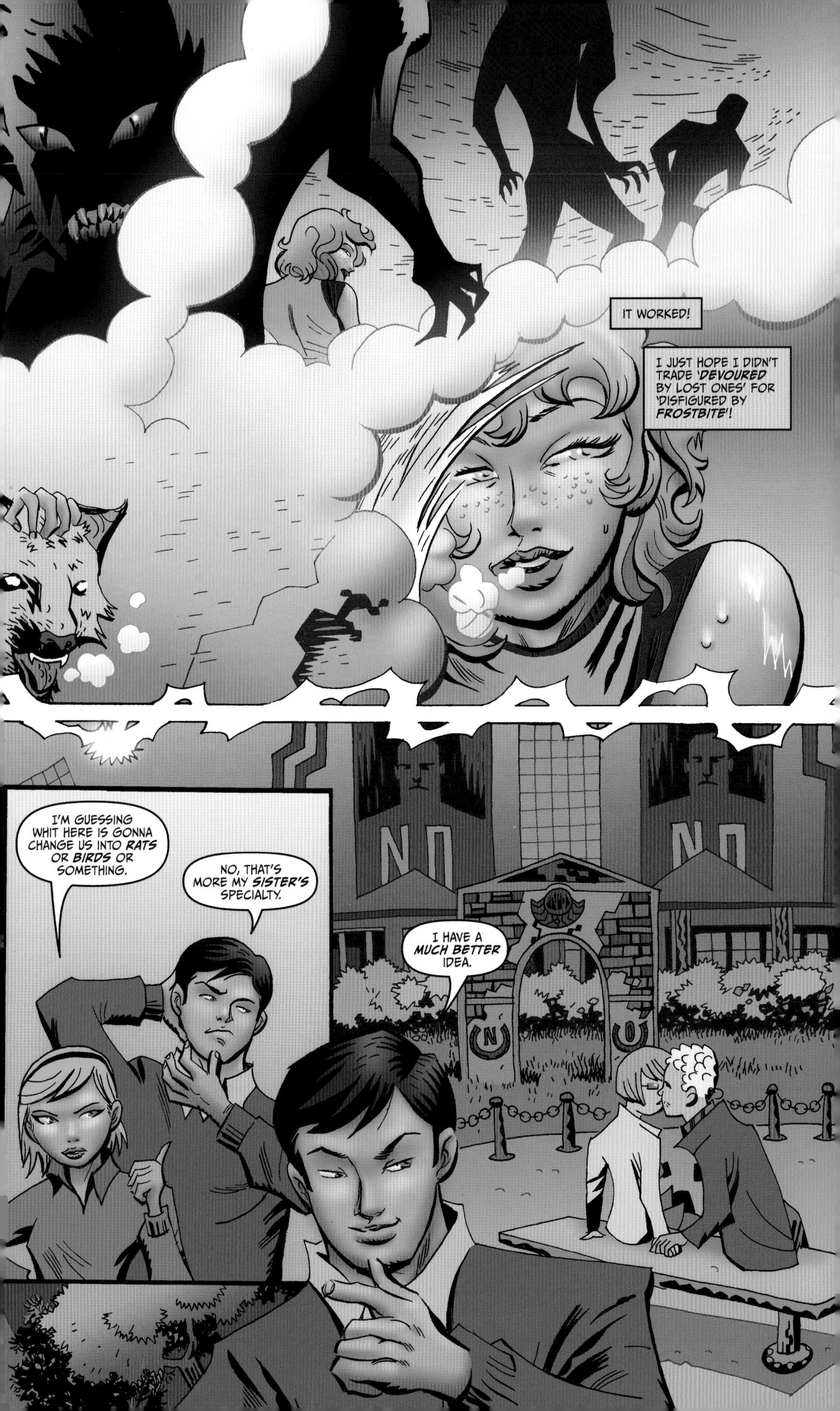

IT WORKED!
I JUST HOPE I DIDN'T TRADE 'DEVOURED BY LOST ONES' FOR 'DISFIGURED BY FROSTBITE'!
I'M GUESSING WHIT HERE IS GONNA CHANGE US INTO RATS OR BIRDS OR SOMETHING.
NO, THAT'S MORE MY SISTER'S SPECIALTY.
I HAVE A MUCH BETTER IDEA.

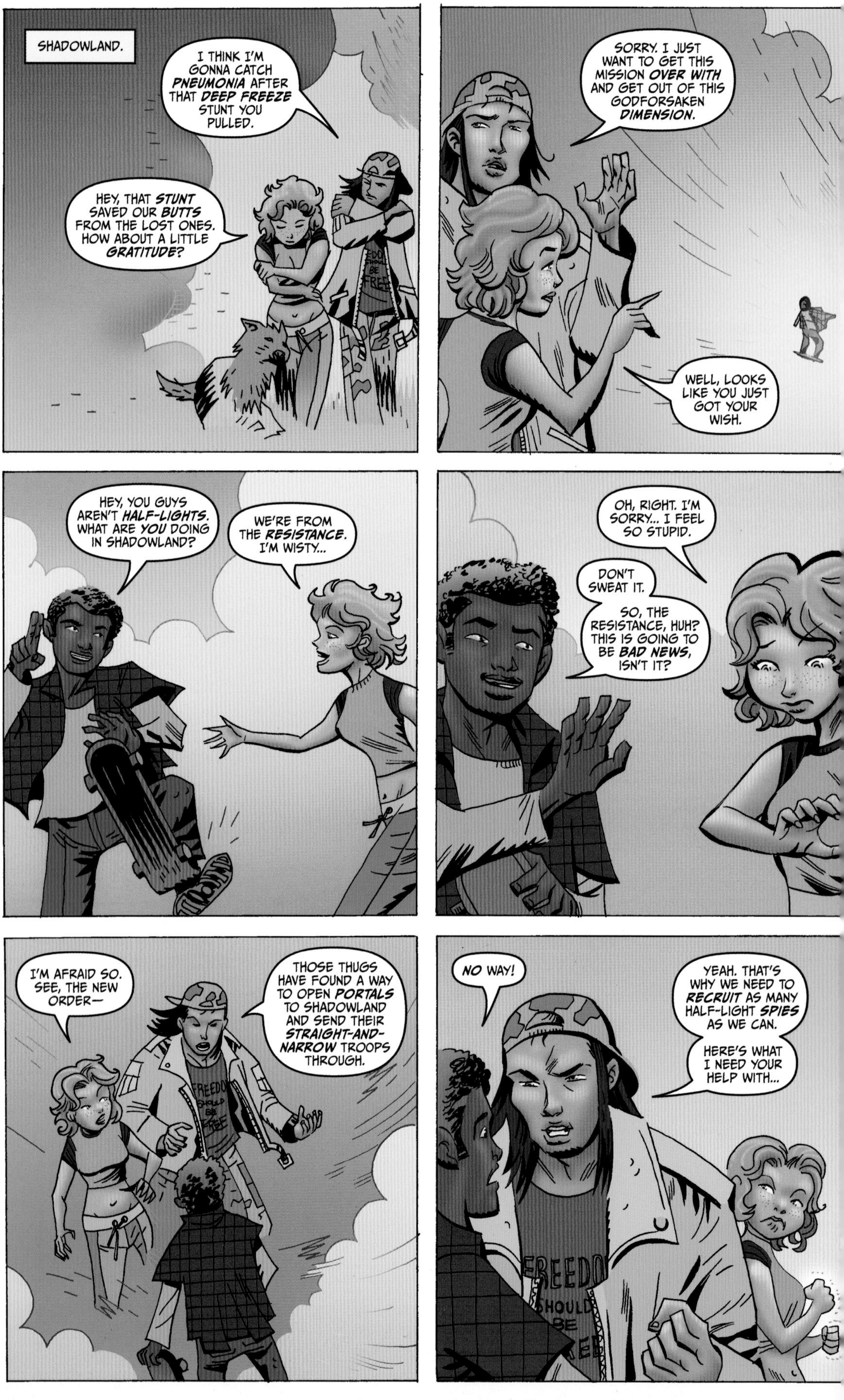

SHADOWLAND.
I THINK I'M GONNA CATCH PNEUMONIA AFTER THAT DEEP FREEZE STUNT YOU PULLED.
HEY, THAT STUNT SAVED OUR BUTTS FROM THE LOST ONES. HOW ABOUT A LITTLE GRATITUDE?
SORRY. I JUST WANT TO GET THIS MISSION OVER WITH AND GET OUT OF THIS GODFORSAKEN DIMENSION.
WELL, LOOKS LIKE YOU JUST GOT YOUR WISH.
HEY, YOU GUYS AREN'T HALF-LIGHTS. WHAT ARE YOU DOING IN SHADOWLAND?
WE'RE FROM THE RESISTANCE. I'M WISTY...
OH, RIGHT. I'M SORRY... I FEEL SO STUPID.
DON'T SWEAT IT.
SO, THE RESISTANCE, HUH? THIS IS GOING TO BE BAD NEWS, ISN'T IT?
I'M AFRAID SO. SEE, THE NEW ORDER—
THOSE THUGS HAVE FOUND A WAY TO OPEN PORTALS TO SHADOWLAND AND SEND THEIR STRAIGHT-AND-NARROW TROOPS THROUGH.
NO WAY!
YEAH. THAT'S WHY WE NEED TO RECRUIT AS MANY HALF-LIGHT SPIES AS WE CAN.
HERE'S WHAT I NEED YOUR HELP WITH...

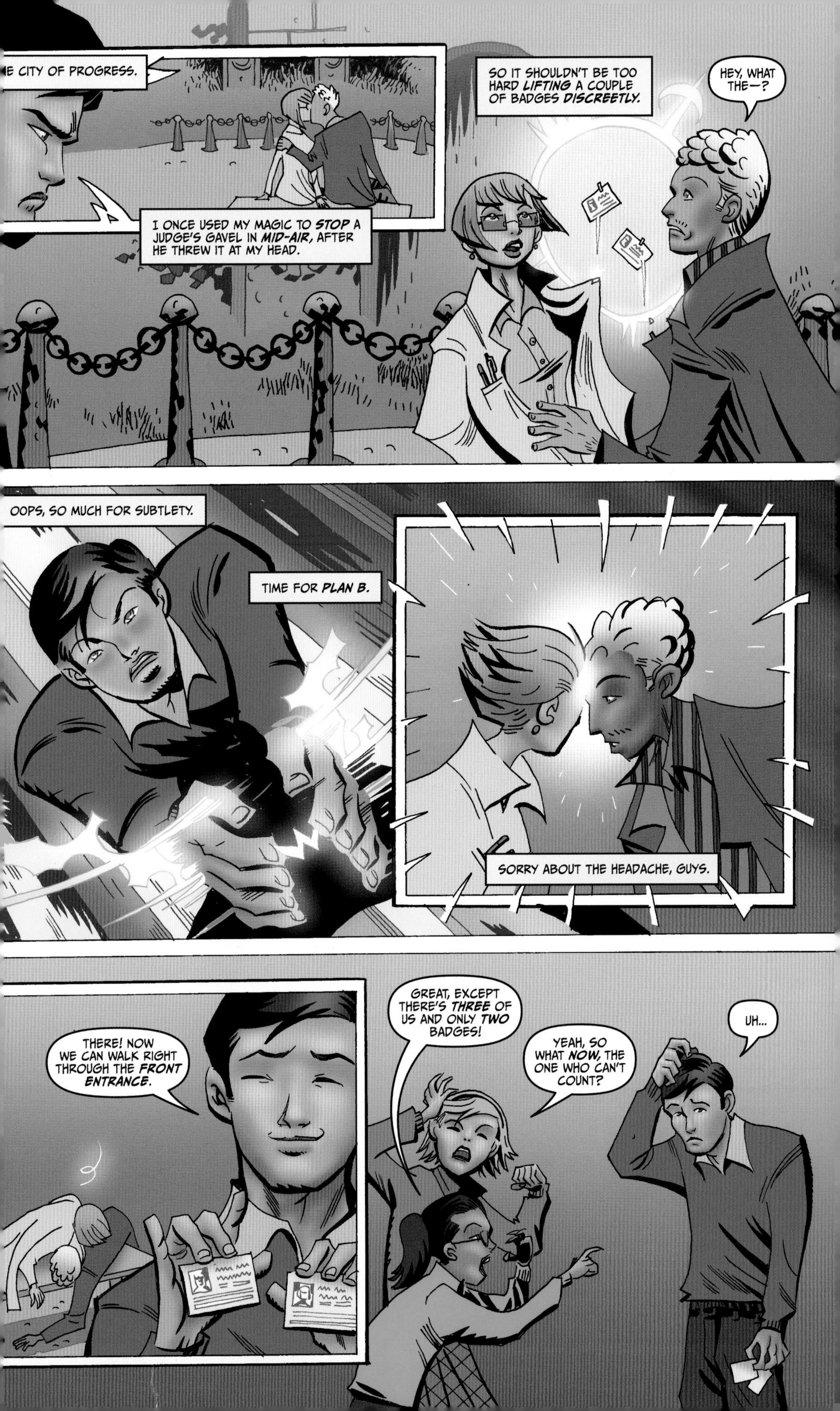
E CITY OF PROGRESS.
I ONCE USED MY MAGIC TO STOP A JUDGE'S GAVEL IN MID-AIR, AFTER HE THREW IT AT MY HEAD.
SO IT SHOULDN'T BE TOO HARD LIFTING A COUPLE OF BADGES DISCREETLY.
HEY, WHAT THE—?
OOPS, SO MUCH FOR SUBTLETY.
TIME FOR PLAN B.
SORRY ABOUT THE HEADACHE, GUYS.
THERE! NOW WE CAN WALK RIGHT THROUGH THE FRONT ENTRANCE.
GREAT, EXCEPT THERE'S THREE OF US AND ONLY TWO BADGES!
YEAH, SO WHAT NOW, THE ONE WHO CAN'T COUNT?
UH...

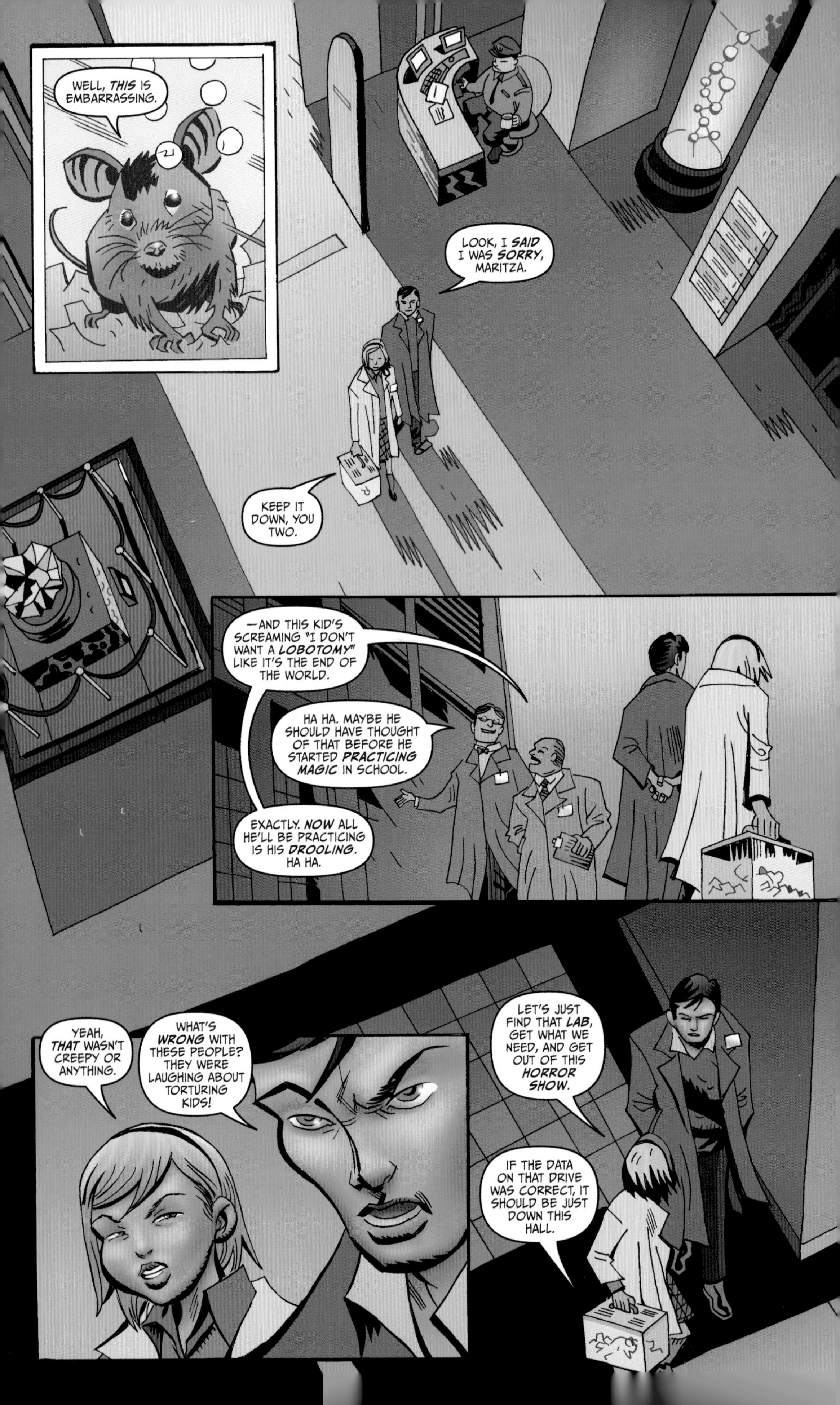
WELL, *THIS* IS EMBARRASSING.
LOOK, I *SAID* I WAS *SORRY*, MARITZA.
KEEP IT DOWN, YOU TWO.
—AND THIS KID'S SCREAMING "I DON'T WANT A *LOBOTOMY*" LIKE IT'S THE END OF THE WORLD.
HA HA. MAYBE HE SHOULD HAVE THOUGHT OF THAT BEFORE HE STARTED *PRACTICING MAGIC* IN SCHOOL.
EXACTLY. *NOW* ALL HE'LL BE PRACTICING IS HIS *DROOLING*. HA HA.
YEAH, *THAT* WASN'T CREEPY OR ANYTHING.
WHAT'S *WRONG* WITH THESE PEOPLE? THEY WERE LAUGHING ABOUT TORTURING KIDS!
LET'S JUST FIND THAT *LAB*, GET WHAT WE NEED, AND GET OUT OF THIS *HORROR SHOW*.
IF THE DATA ON THAT DRIVE WAS CORRECT, IT SHOULD BE JUST DOWN THIS HALL.

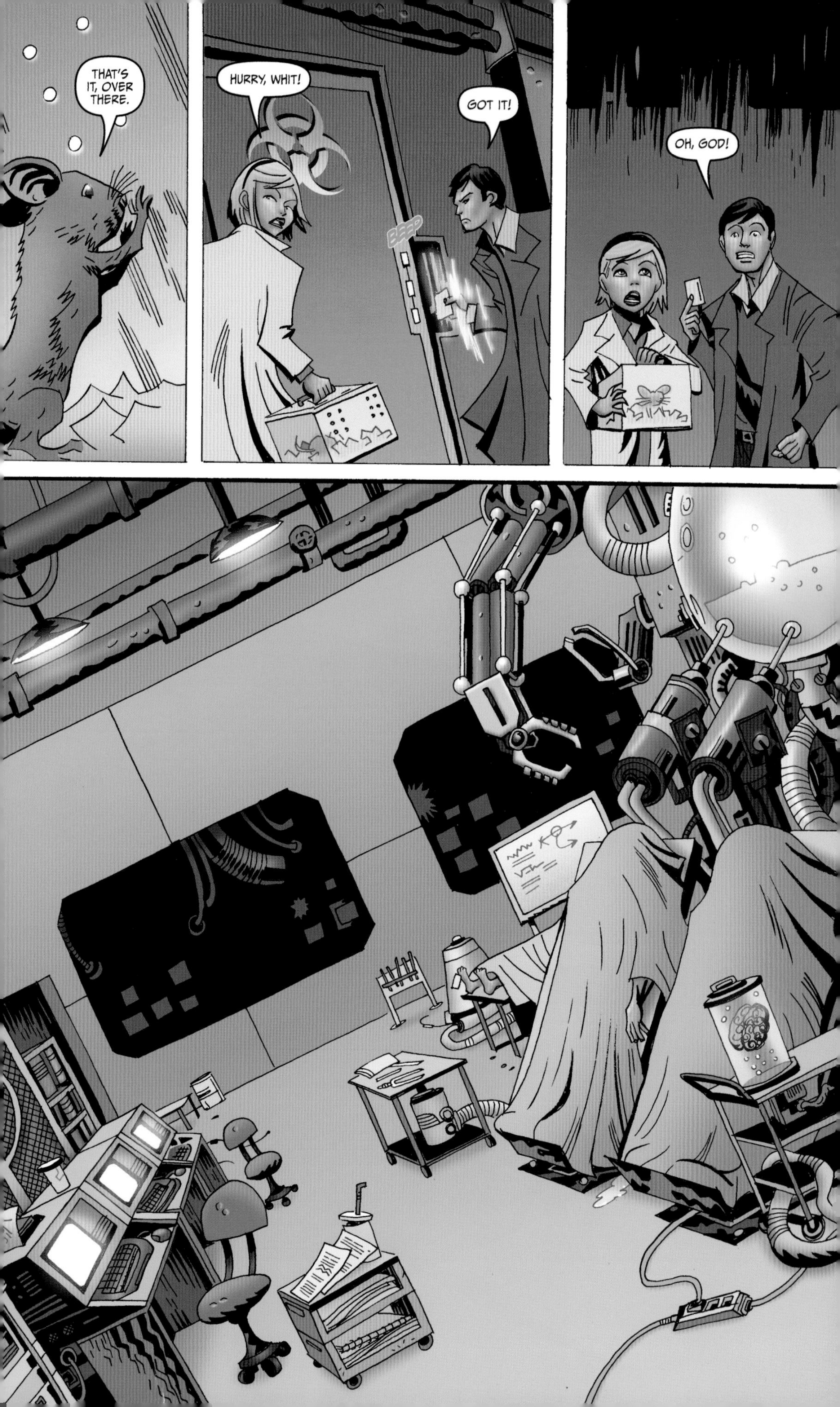
THAT'S IT, OVER THERE.
HURRY, WHIT!
BEEP
GOT IT!
OH, GOD!

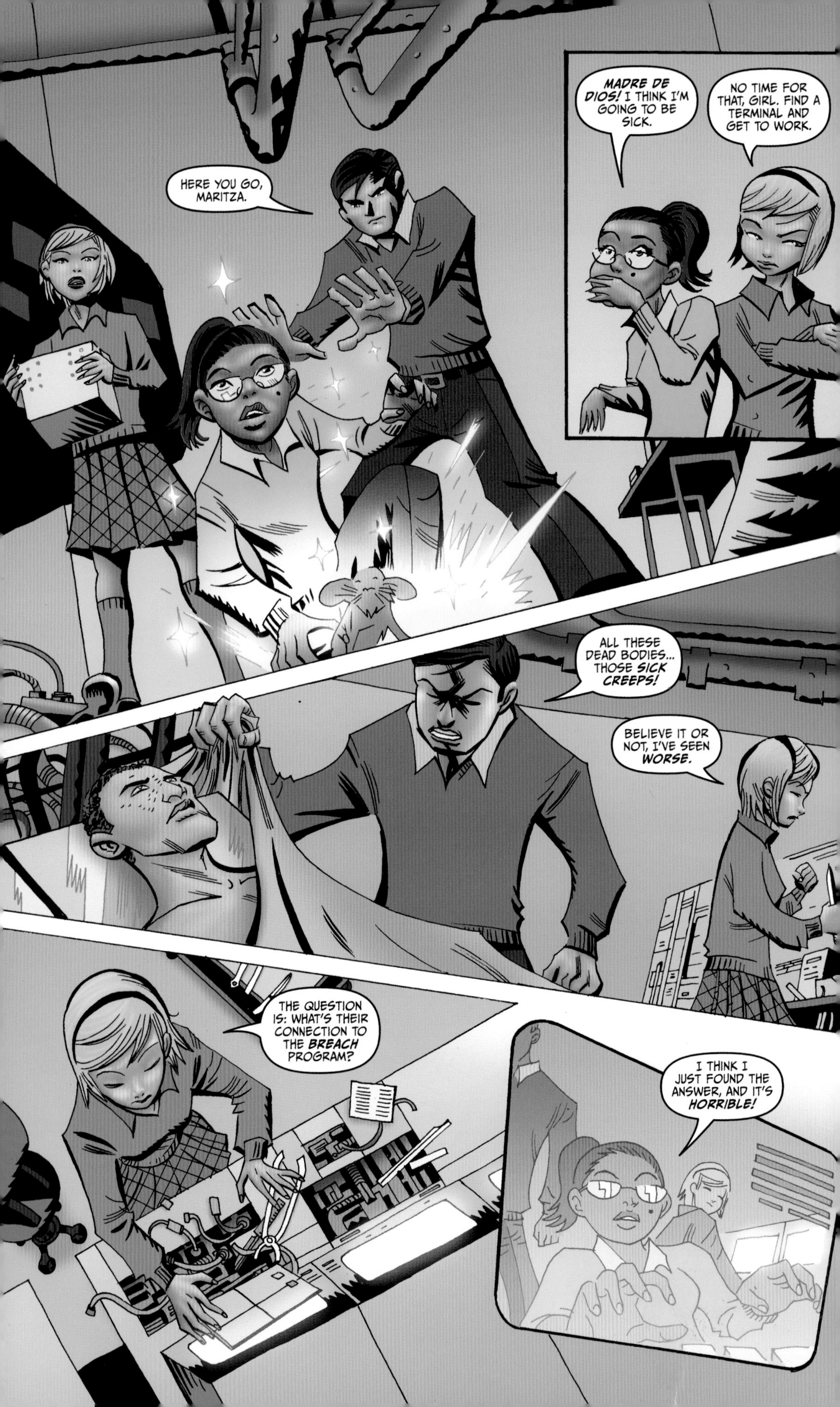
HERE YOU GO, MARITZA.
MADRE DE DIOS! I THINK I'M GOING TO BE SICK.
NO TIME FOR THAT, GIRL. FIND A TERMINAL AND GET TO WORK.
ALL THESE DEAD BODIES... THOSE SICK CREEPS!
BELIEVE IT OR NOT, I'VE SEEN WORSE.
THE QUESTION IS: WHAT'S THEIR CONNECTION TO THE BREACH PROGRAM?
I THINK I JUST FOUND THE ANSWER, AND IT'S HORRIBLE!

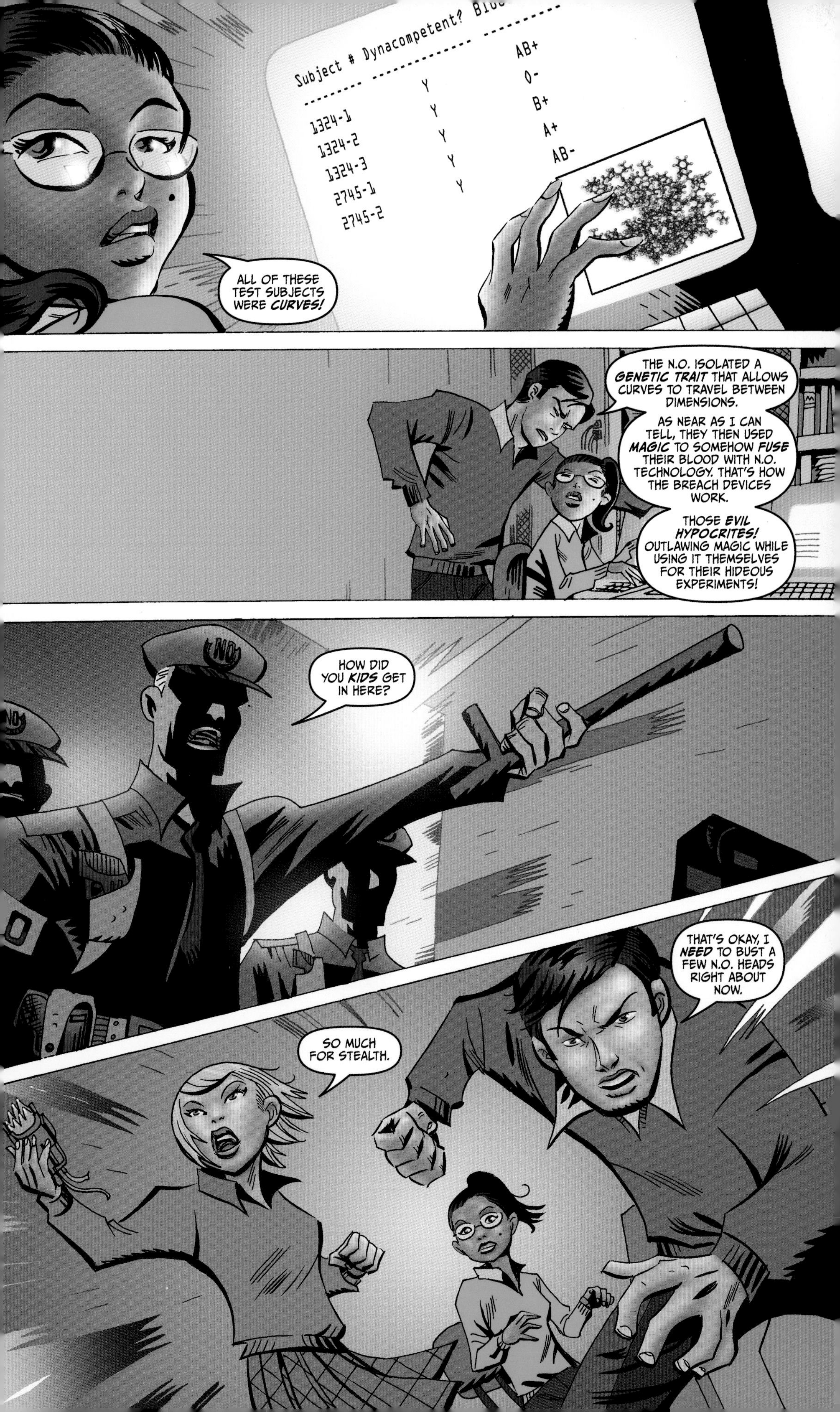

Subject # Dynacompetent?
1324-1 Y AB+
1324-2 Y O-
1324-3 Y B+
2745-1 Y A+
2745-2 Y AB-
ALL OF THESE TEST SUBJECTS WERE *CURVES!*
THE N.O. ISOLATED A ***GENETIC TRAIT*** THAT ALLOWS CURVES TO TRAVEL BETWEEN DIMENSIONS.
AS NEAR AS I CAN TELL, THEY THEN USED ***MAGIC*** TO SOMEHOW ***FUSE*** THEIR BLOOD WITH N.O. TECHNOLOGY. THAT'S HOW THE BREACH DEVICES WORK.
THOSE ***EVIL HYPOCRITES!*** OUTLAWING MAGIC WHILE USING IT THEMSELVES FOR THEIR HIDEOUS EXPERIMENTS!
HOW DID YOU ***KIDS*** GET IN HERE?
THAT'S OKAY, I ***NEED*** TO BUST A FEW N.O. HEADS RIGHT ABOUT NOW.
SO MUCH FOR STEALTH.

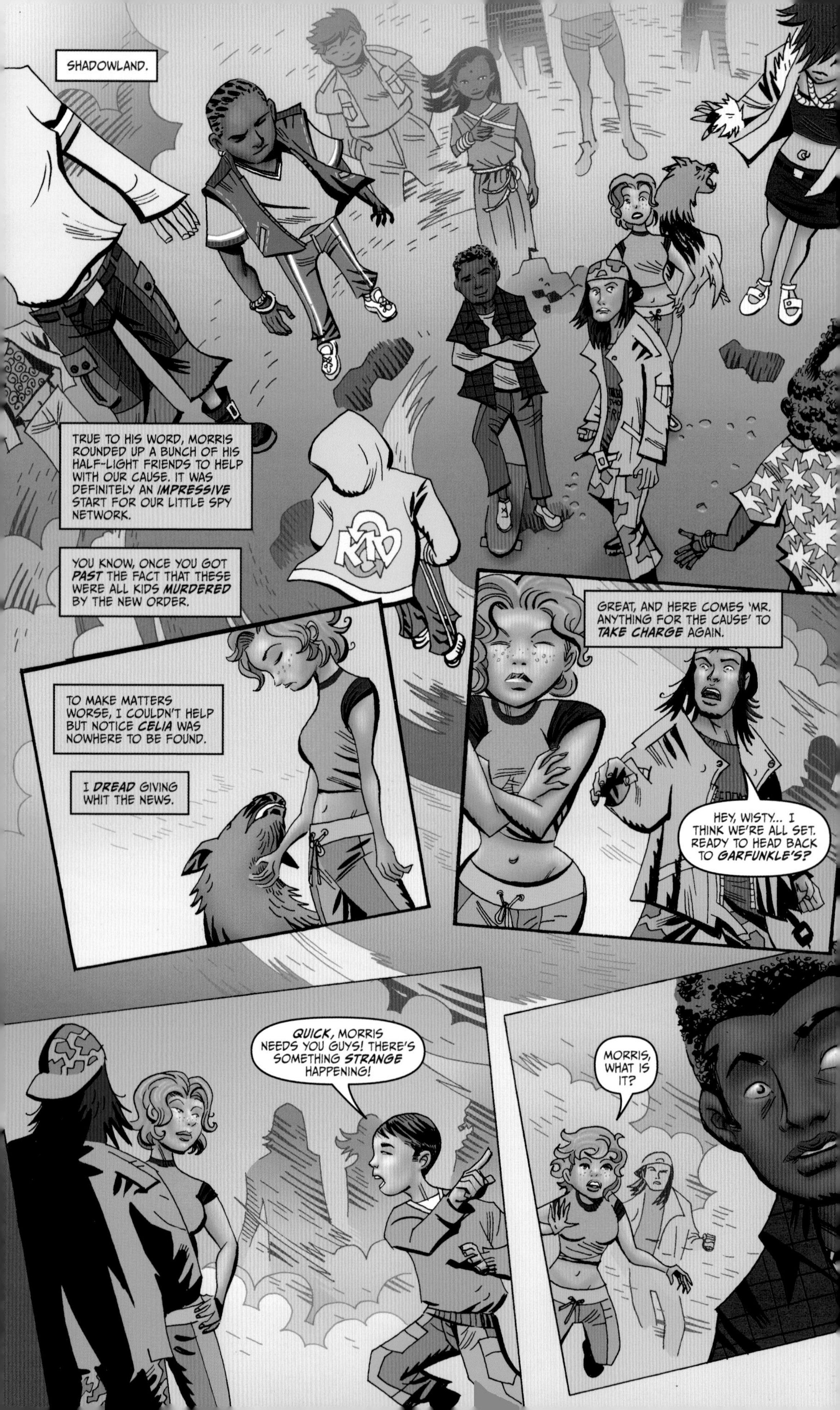
SHADOWLAND.
TRUE TO HIS WORD, MORRIS ROUNDED UP A BUNCH OF HIS HALF-LIGHT FRIENDS TO HELP WITH OUR CAUSE. IT WAS DEFINITELY AN IMPRESSIVE START FOR OUR LITTLE SPY NETWORK.
YOU KNOW, ONCE YOU GOT PAST THE FACT THAT THESE WERE ALL KIDS MURDERED BY THE NEW ORDER.
TO MAKE MATTERS WORSE, I COULDN'T HELP BUT NOTICE CELIA WAS NOWHERE TO BE FOUND.
I DREAD GIVING WHIT THE NEWS.
GREAT, AND HERE COMES 'MR. ANYTHING FOR THE CAUSE' TO TAKE CHARGE AGAIN.
HEY, WISTY... I THINK WE'RE ALL SET. READY TO HEAD BACK TO GARFUNKLE'S?
QUICK, MORRIS NEEDS YOU GUYS! THERE'S SOMETHING STRANGE HAPPENING!
MORRIS, WHAT IS IT?

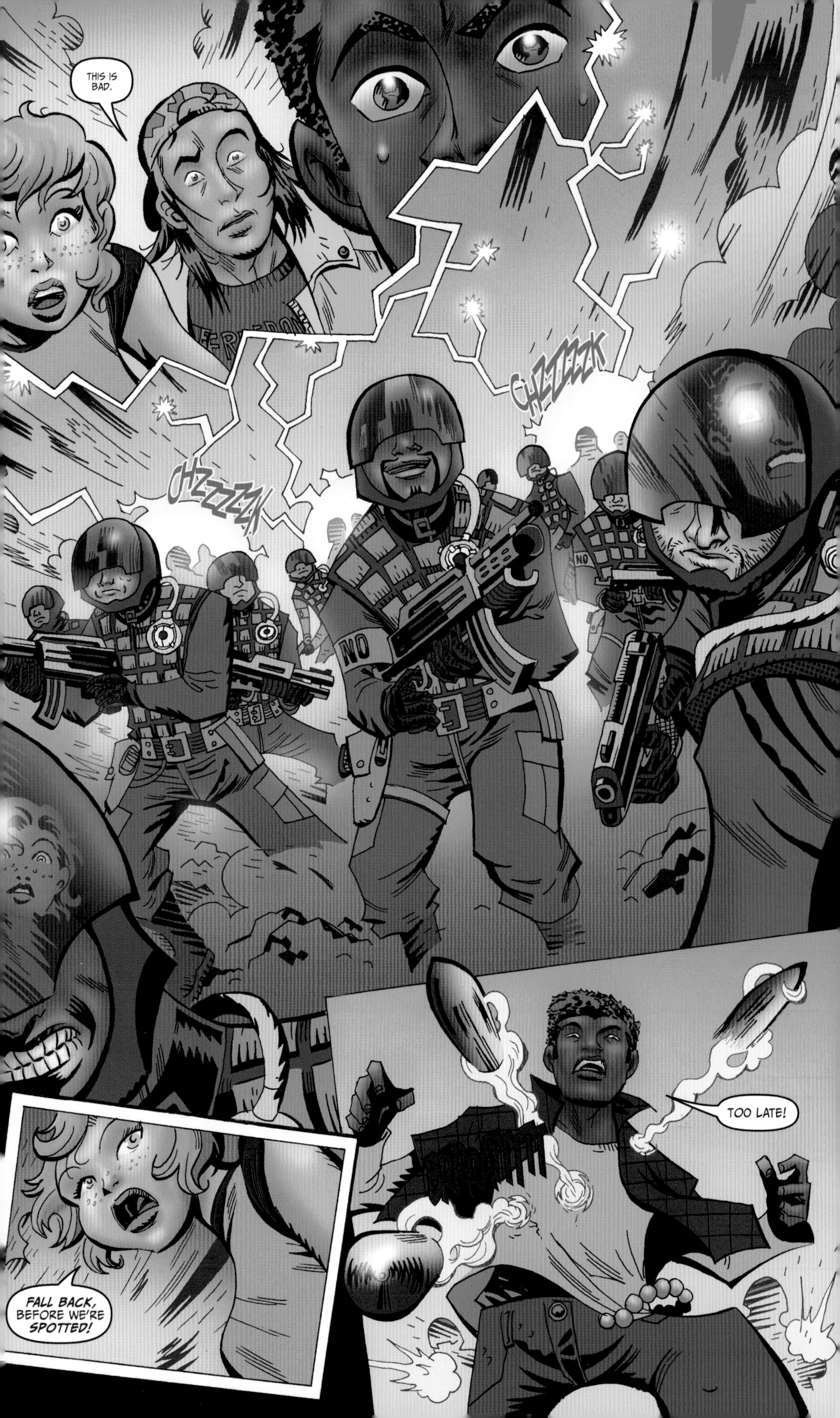
THIS IS BAD.
CHZZZZZK
CHZZZZZK
NO
NO
NO
TOO LATE!
FALL BACK, BEFORE WE'RE SPOTTED!

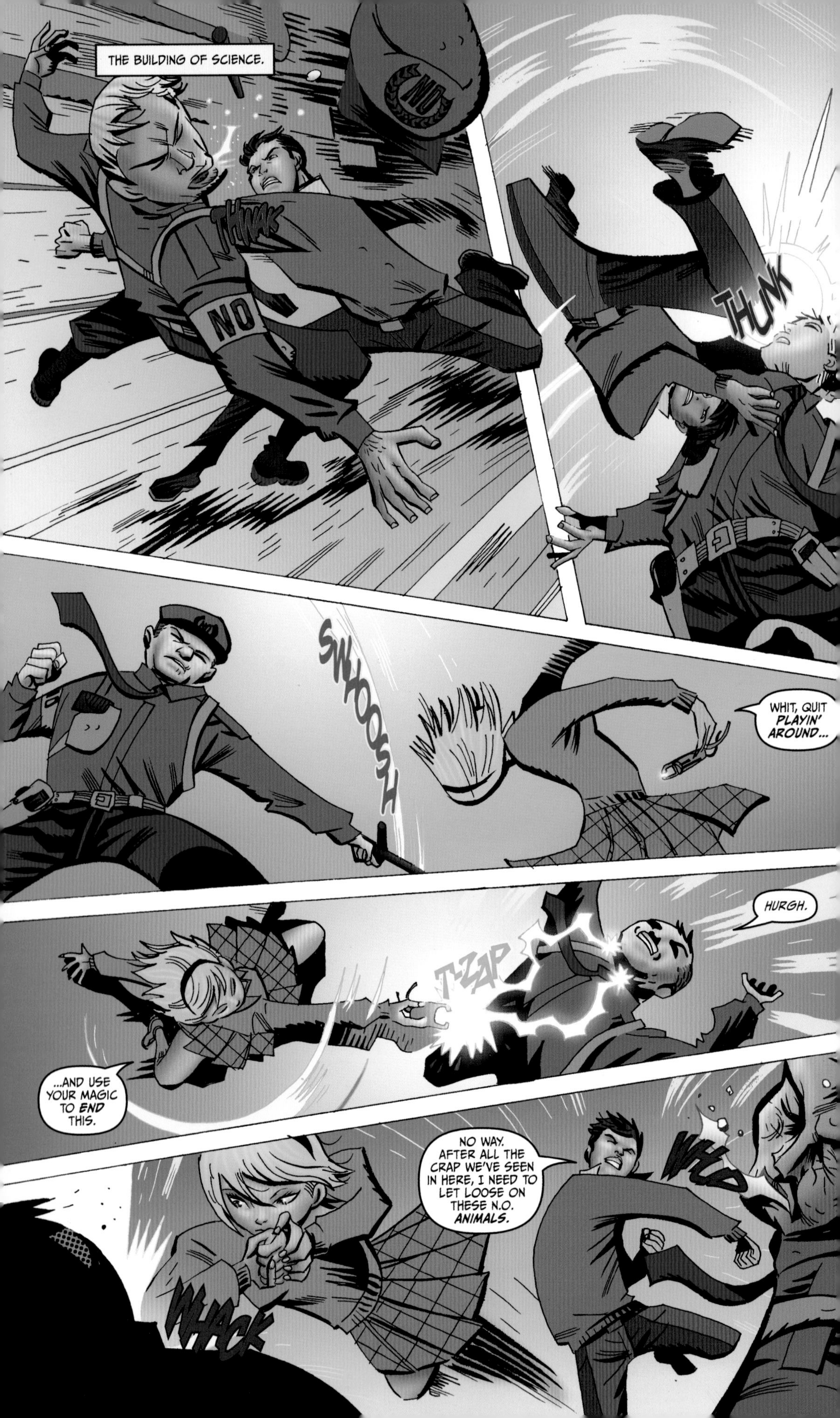
THE BUILDING OF SCIENCE.
THWAK
THUNK
SWOOOSH
WHIT, QUIT *PLAYIN'* AROUND...
HURGH.
T-ZAP
...AND USE YOUR MAGIC TO *END* THIS.
NO WAY. AFTER ALL THE CRAP WE'VE SEEN IN HERE, I NEED TO LET LOOSE ON THESE N.O. *ANIMALS*.
WHUD
WHACK

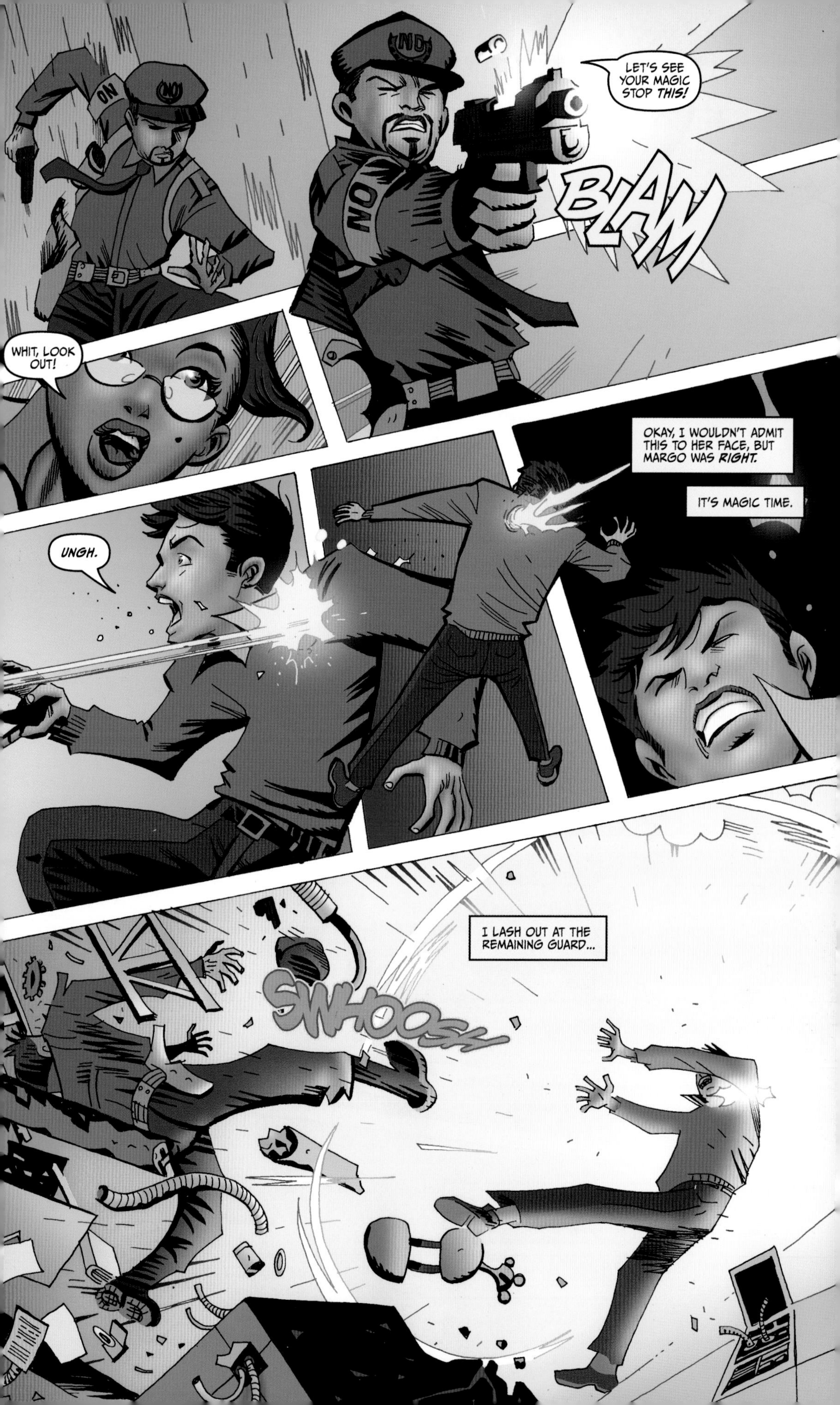
LET'S SEE YOUR MAGIC STOP THIS!
BLAM
WHIT, LOOK OUT!
OKAY, I WOULDN'T ADMIT THIS TO HER FACE, BUT MARGO WAS RIGHT.
IT'S MAGIC TIME.
UNGH.
I LASH OUT AT THE REMAINING GUARD...
SWHOOSH

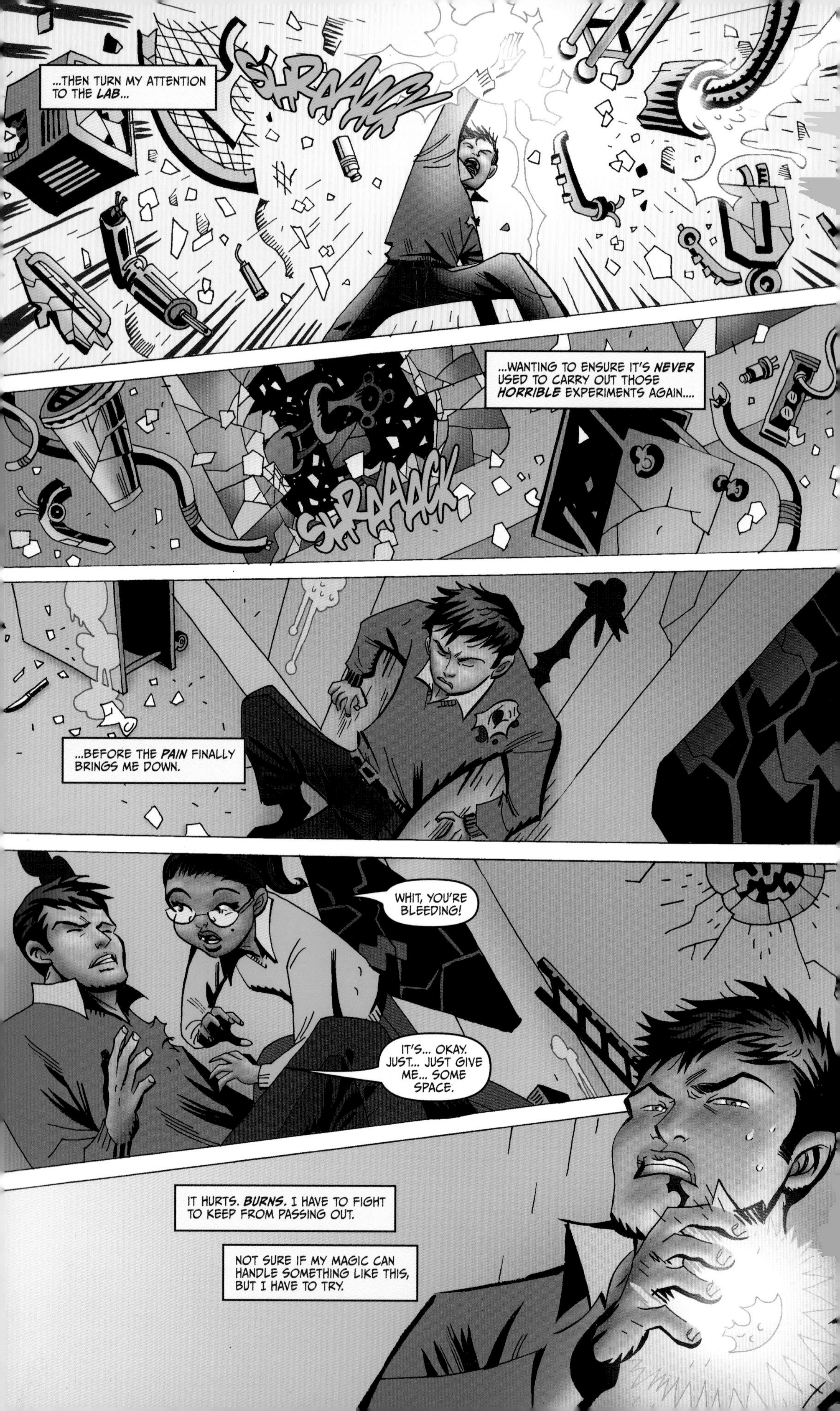

...THEN TURN MY ATTENTION TO THE *LAB*...
SKRAAACK
...WANTING TO ENSURE IT'S *NEVER* USED TO CARRY OUT THOSE *HORRIBLE* EXPERIMENTS AGAIN....
SKRAAACK
...BEFORE THE *PAIN* FINALLY BRINGS ME DOWN.
WHIT, YOU'RE BLEEDING!
IT'S... OKAY. JUST... JUST GIVE ME... SOME SPACE.
IT HURTS. *BURNS.* I HAVE TO FIGHT TO KEEP FROM PASSING OUT.
NOT SURE IF MY MAGIC CAN HANDLE SOMETHING LIKE THIS, BUT I HAVE TO TRY.

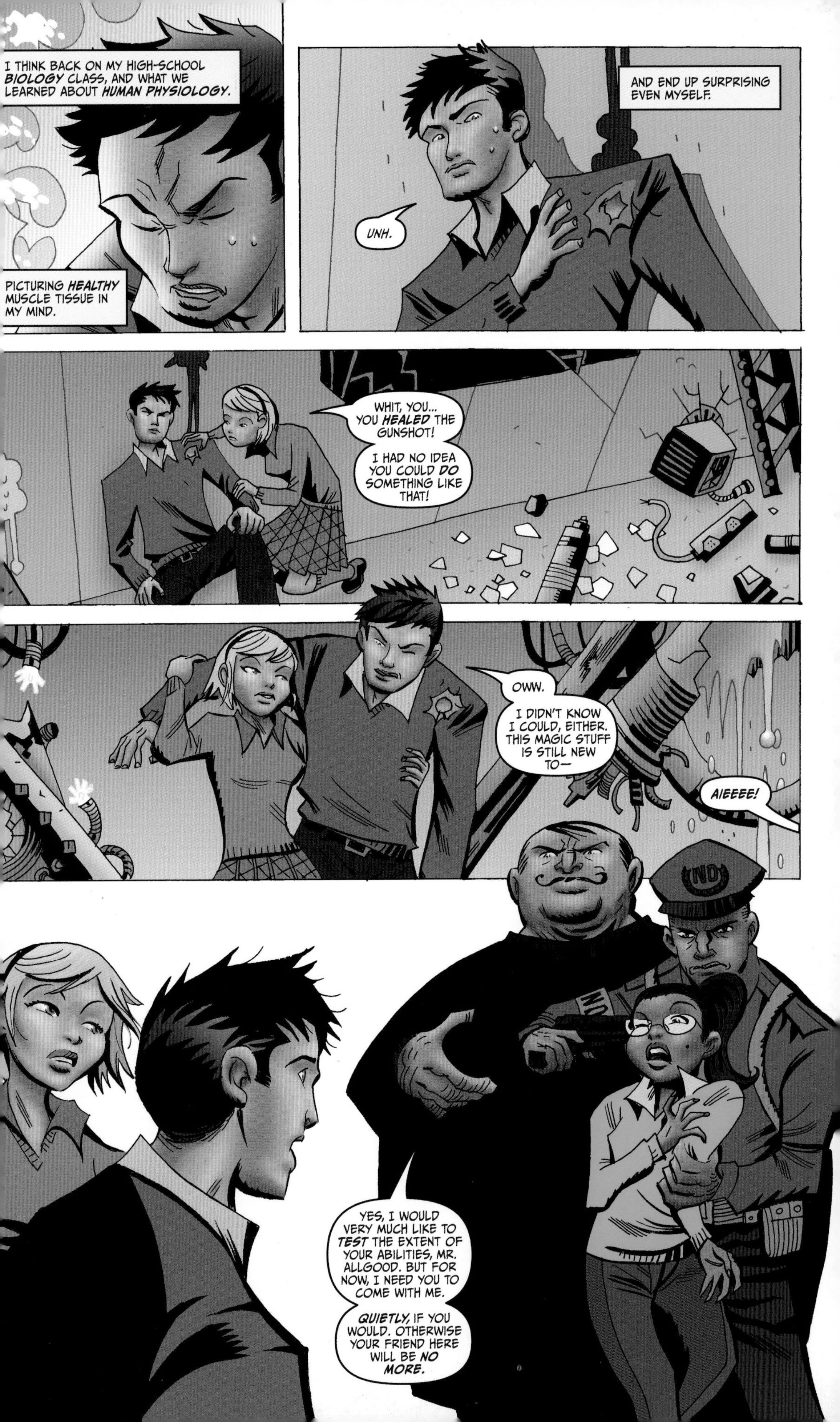

I THINK BACK ON MY HIGH-SCHOOL BIOLOGY CLASS, AND WHAT WE LEARNED ABOUT HUMAN PHYSIOLOGY.
PICTURING HEALTHY MUSCLE TISSUE IN MY MIND.
AND END UP SURPRISING EVEN MYSELF.
UNH.
WHIT, YOU... YOU HEALED THE GUNSHOT!
I HAD NO IDEA YOU COULD DO SOMETHING LIKE THAT!
OWW.
I DIDN'T KNOW I COULD, EITHER. THIS MAGIC STUFF IS STILL NEW TO—
AIEEEE!
NO
YES, I WOULD VERY MUCH LIKE TO TEST THE EXTENT OF YOUR ABILITIES, MR. ALLGOOD. BUT FOR NOW, I NEED YOU TO COME WITH ME.
QUIETLY, IF YOU WOULD. OTHERWISE YOUR FRIEND HERE WILL BE NO MORE.

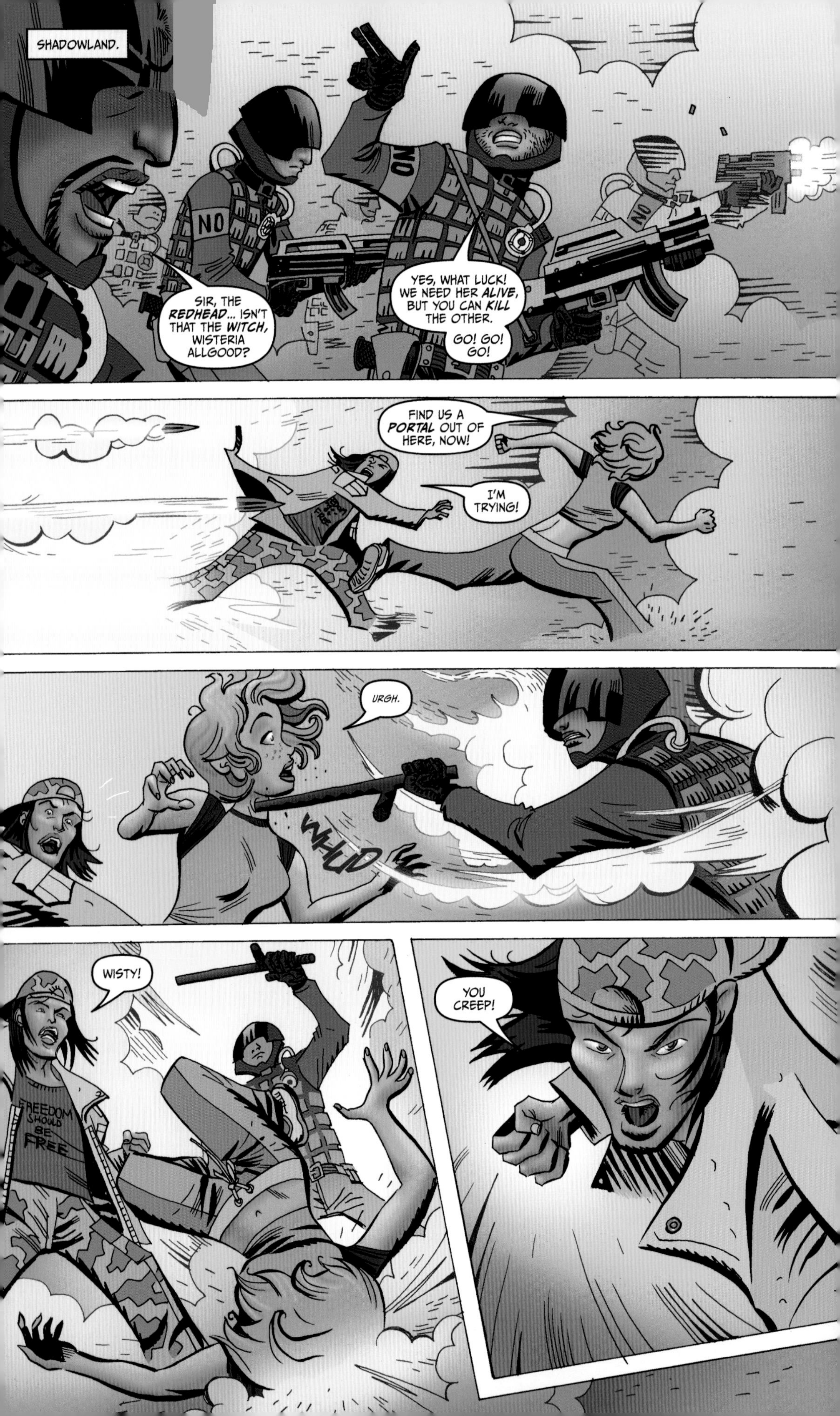
SHADOWLAND.
SIR, THE REDHEAD... ISN'T THAT THE WITCH, WISTERIA ALLGOOD?
YES, WHAT LUCK! WE NEED HER ALIVE, BUT YOU CAN KILL THE OTHER.
GO! GO! GO!
NO
FIND US A PORTAL OUT OF HERE, NOW!
I'M TRYING!
URGH.
WHUD
WISTY!
FREEDOM SHOULD BE FREE
YOU CREEP!

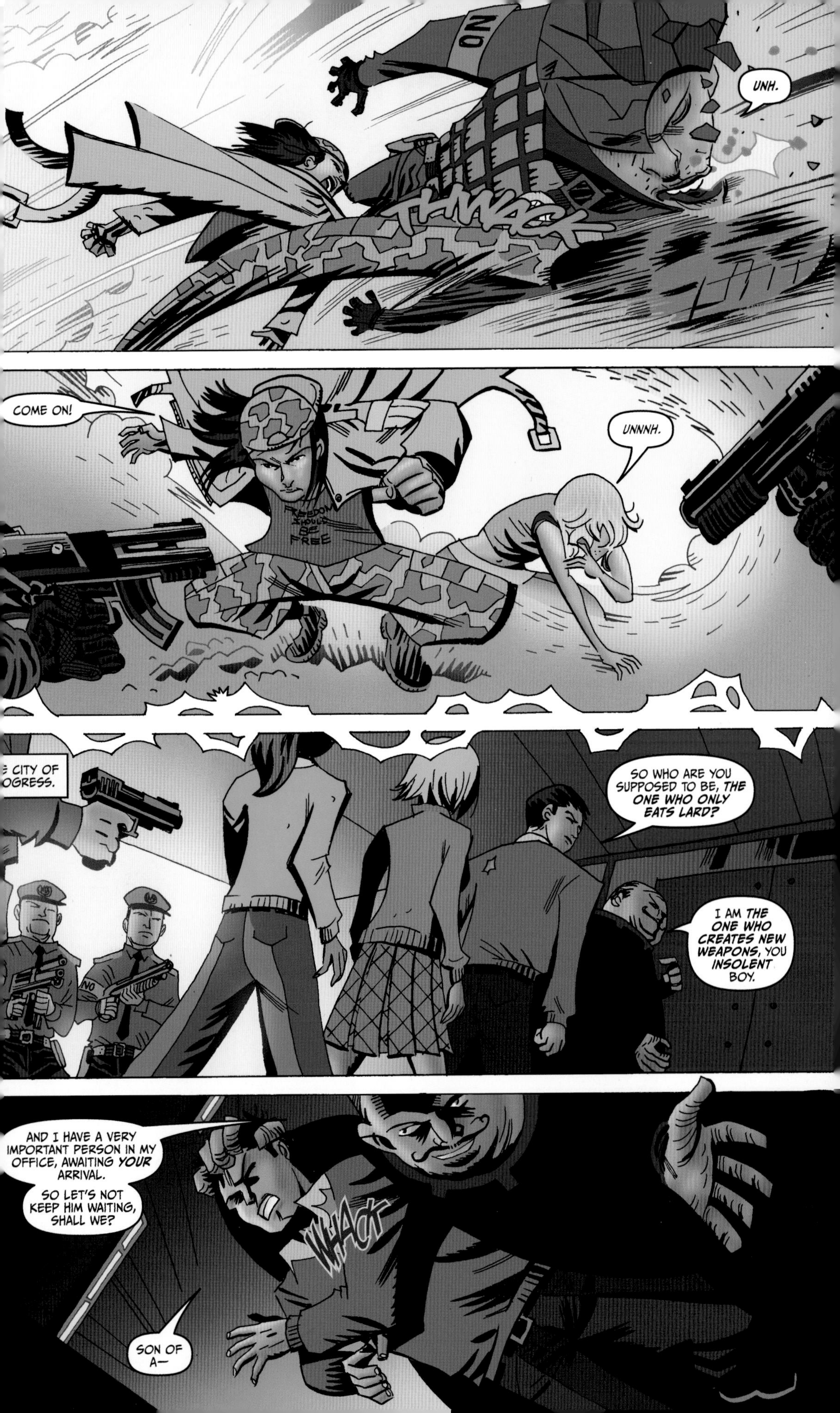
NO
UNH.
THWACK
COME ON!
UNNNH.
FREEDOM SHOULD BE FREE
CITY OF
OGRESS.
SO WHO ARE YOU SUPPOSED TO BE, THE ONE WHO ONLY EATS LARD?
I AM THE ONE WHO CREATES NEW WEAPONS, YOU INSOLENT BOY.
NO
AND I HAVE A VERY IMPORTANT PERSON IN MY OFFICE, AWAITING YOUR ARRIVAL.
SO LET'S NOT KEEP HIM WAITING, SHALL WE?
WHACK
SON OF A—

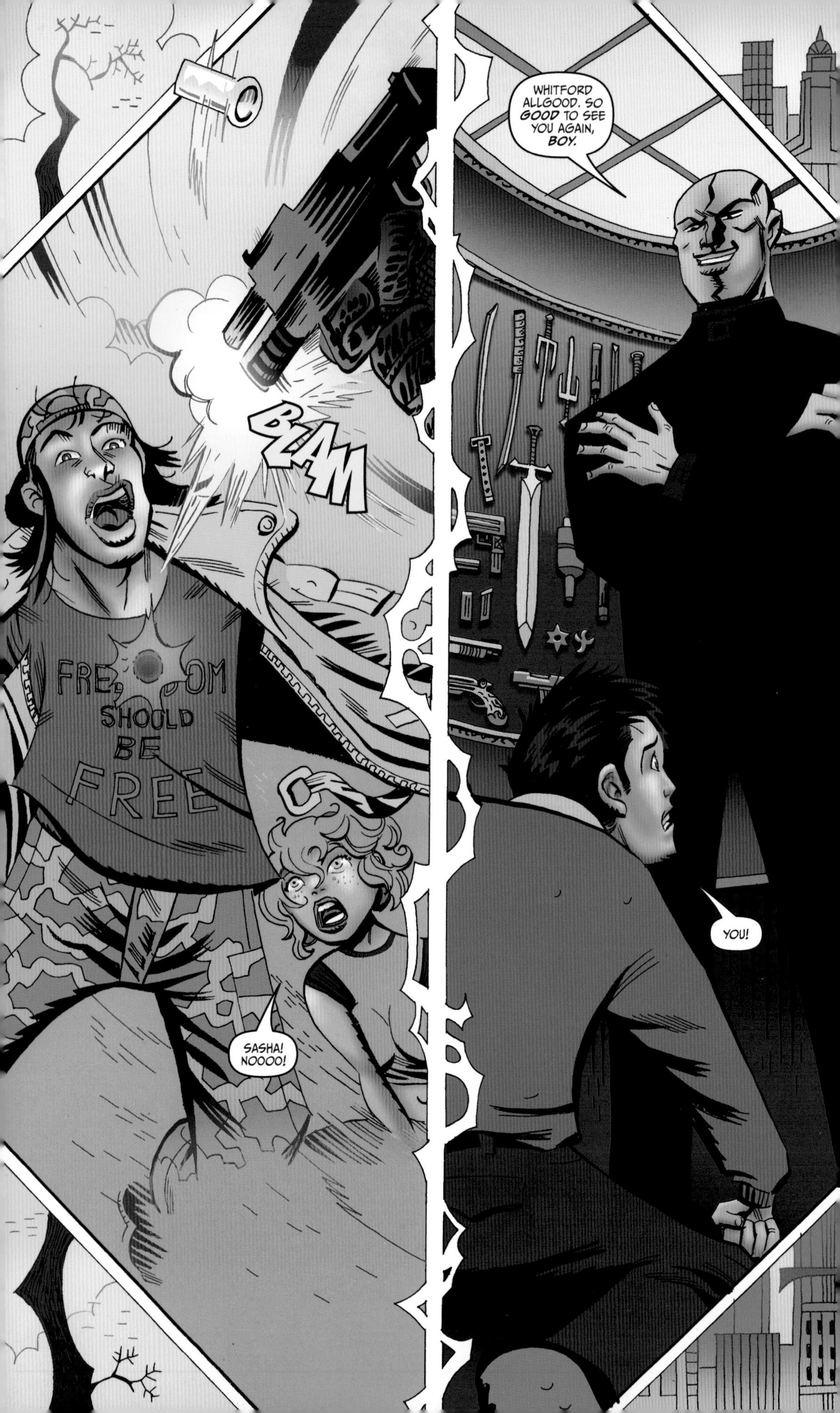
BLAM
FREEDOM SHOULD BE FREE
SASHA! NOOOO!
WHITFORD ALLGOOD. SO GOOD TO SEE YOU AGAIN, BOY.
YOU!

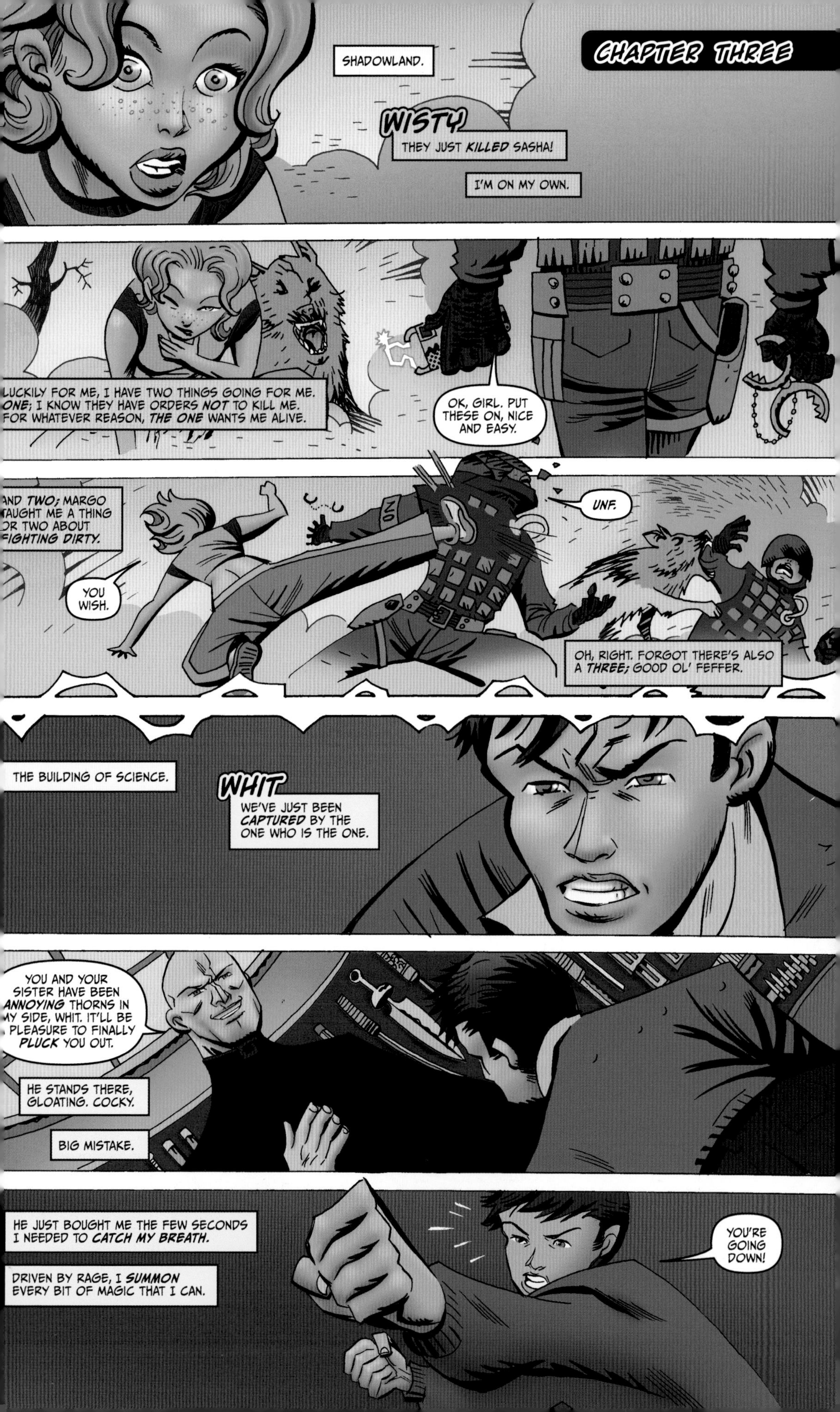
CHAPTER THREE
SHADOWLAND.
WISTY
THEY JUST KILLED SASHA!
I'M ON MY OWN.
LUCKILY FOR ME, I HAVE TWO THINGS GOING FOR ME. ONE; I KNOW THEY HAVE ORDERS NOT TO KILL ME. FOR WHATEVER REASON, THE ONE WANTS ME ALIVE.
OK, GIRL. PUT THESE ON, NICE AND EASY.
AND TWO; MARGO TAUGHT ME A THING OR TWO ABOUT FIGHTING DIRTY.
YOU WISH.
UNF.
OH, RIGHT. FORGOT THERE'S ALSO A THREE; GOOD OL' FEFFER.
THE BUILDING OF SCIENCE.
WHIT
WE'VE JUST BEEN CAPTURED BY THE ONE WHO IS THE ONE.
YOU AND YOUR SISTER HAVE BEEN ANNOYING THORNS IN MY SIDE, WHIT. IT'LL BE A PLEASURE TO FINALLY PLUCK YOU OUT.
HE STANDS THERE, GLOATING. COCKY.
BIG MISTAKE.
HE JUST BOUGHT ME THE FEW SECONDS I NEEDED TO CATCH MY BREATH.
DRIVEN BY RAGE, I SUMMON EVERY BIT OF MAGIC THAT I CAN.
YOU'RE GOING DOWN!

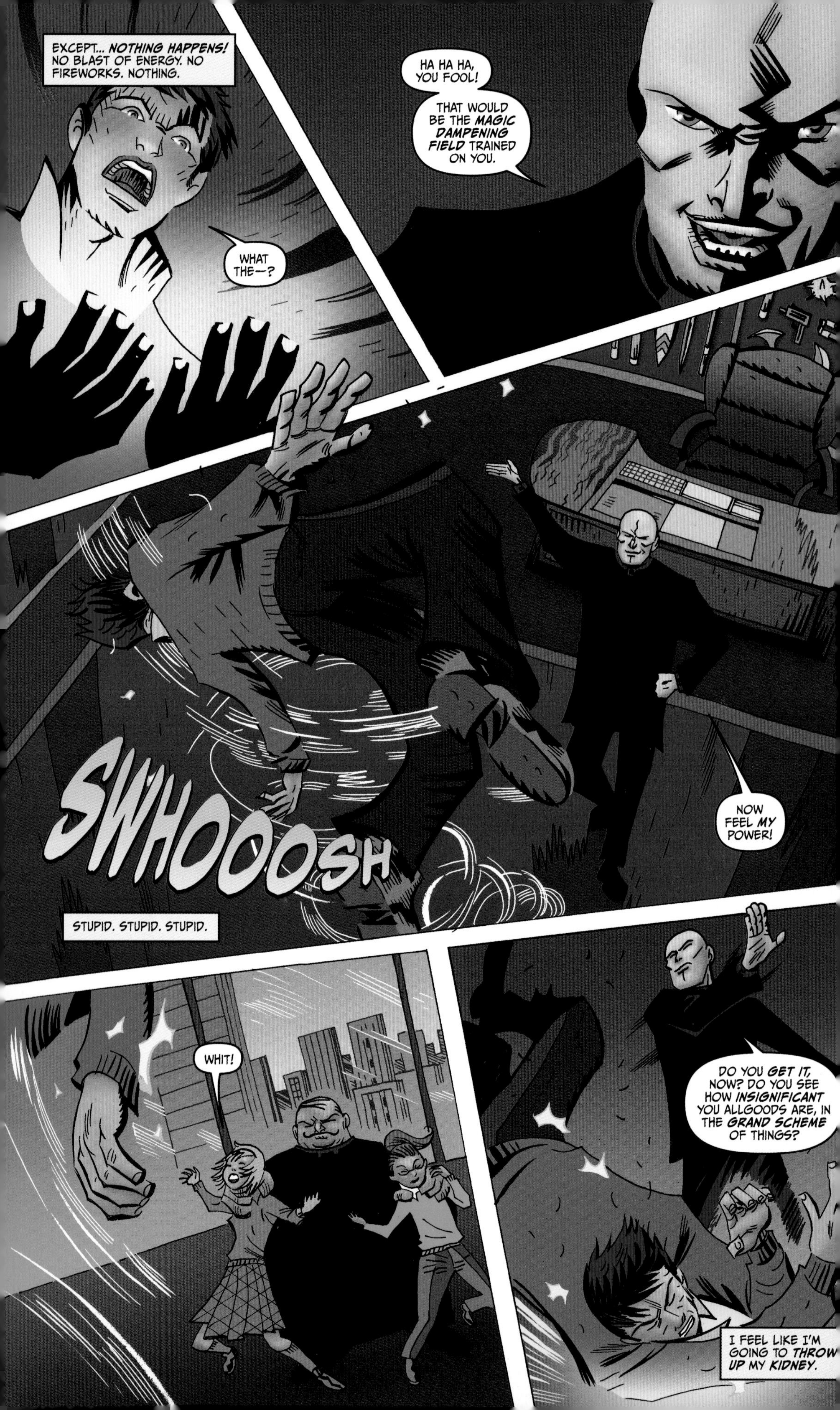
EXCEPT... NOTHING HAPPENS! NO BLAST OF ENERGY. NO FIREWORKS. NOTHING.
WHAT THE—?
HA HA HA, YOU FOOL!
THAT WOULD BE THE MAGIC DAMPENING FIELD TRAINED ON YOU.
SWHOOOSH
NOW FEEL MY POWER!
STUPID. STUPID. STUPID.
WHIT!
DO YOU GET IT, NOW? DO YOU SEE HOW INSIGNIFICANT YOU ALLGOODS ARE, IN THE GRAND SCHEME OF THINGS?
I FEEL LIKE I'M GOING TO THROW UP MY KIDNEY.

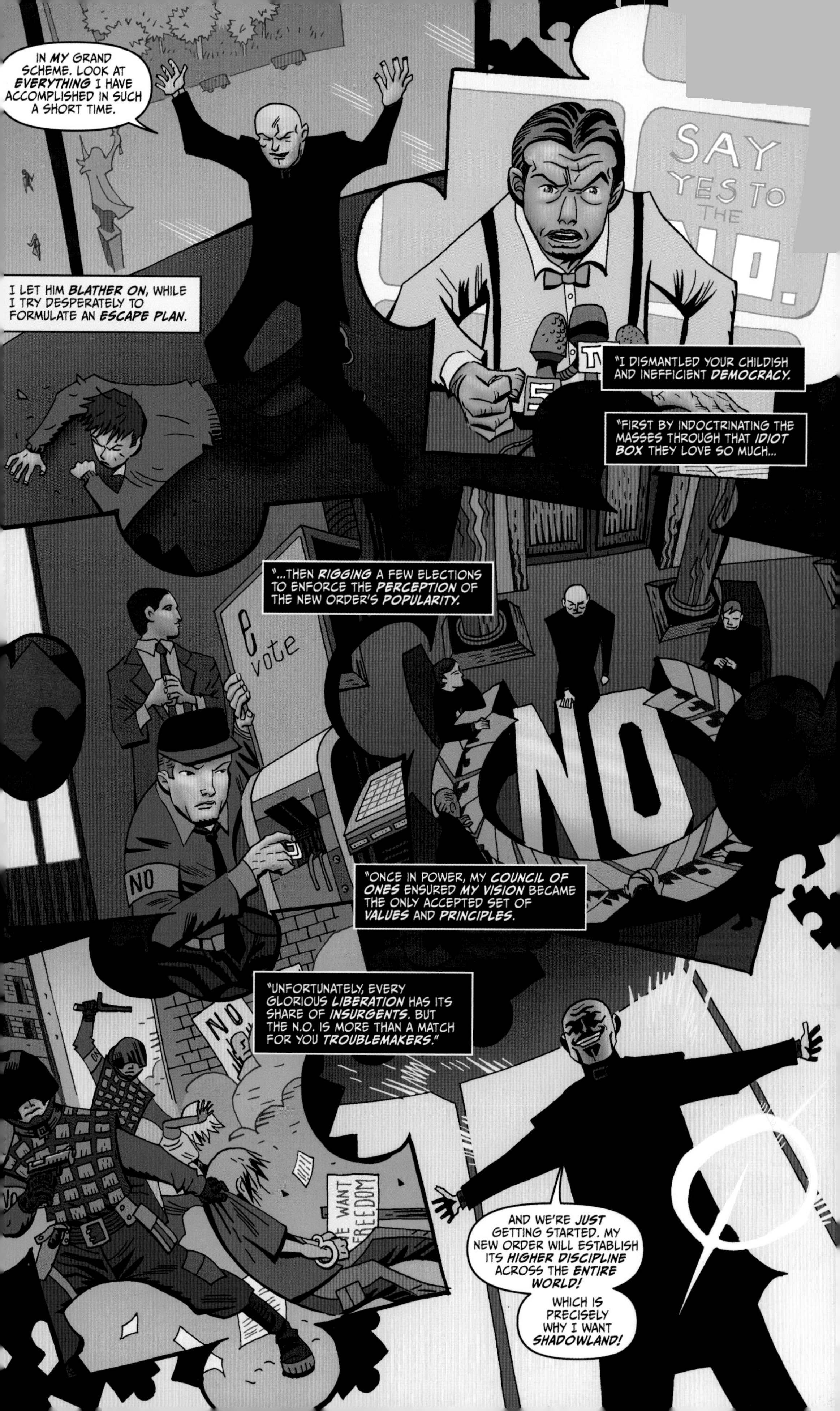

IN MY GRAND SCHEME. LOOK AT EVERYTHING I HAVE ACCOMPLISHED IN SUCH A SHORT TIME.
SAY YES TO THE N.O.
I LET HIM BLATHER ON, WHILE I TRY DESPERATELY TO FORMULATE AN ESCAPE PLAN.
"I DISMANTLED YOUR CHILDISH AND INEFFICIENT DEMOCRACY.
"FIRST BY INDOCTRINATING THE MASSES THROUGH THAT IDIOT BOX THEY LOVE SO MUCH...
"...THEN RIGGING A FEW ELECTIONS TO ENFORCE THE PERCEPTION OF THE NEW ORDER'S POPULARITY.
e vote
NO
NO
"ONCE IN POWER, MY COUNCIL OF ONES ENSURED MY VISION BECAME THE ONLY ACCEPTED SET OF VALUES AND PRINCIPLES.
"UNFORTUNATELY, EVERY GLORIOUS LIBERATION HAS ITS SHARE OF INSURGENTS. BUT THE N.O. IS MORE THAN A MATCH FOR YOU TROUBLEMAKERS."
NO
WANT FREEDOM
AND WE'RE JUST GETTING STARTED. MY NEW ORDER WILL ESTABLISH ITS HIGHER DISCIPLINE ACROSS THE ENTIRE WORLD!
WHICH IS PRECISELY WHY I WANT SHADOWLAND!

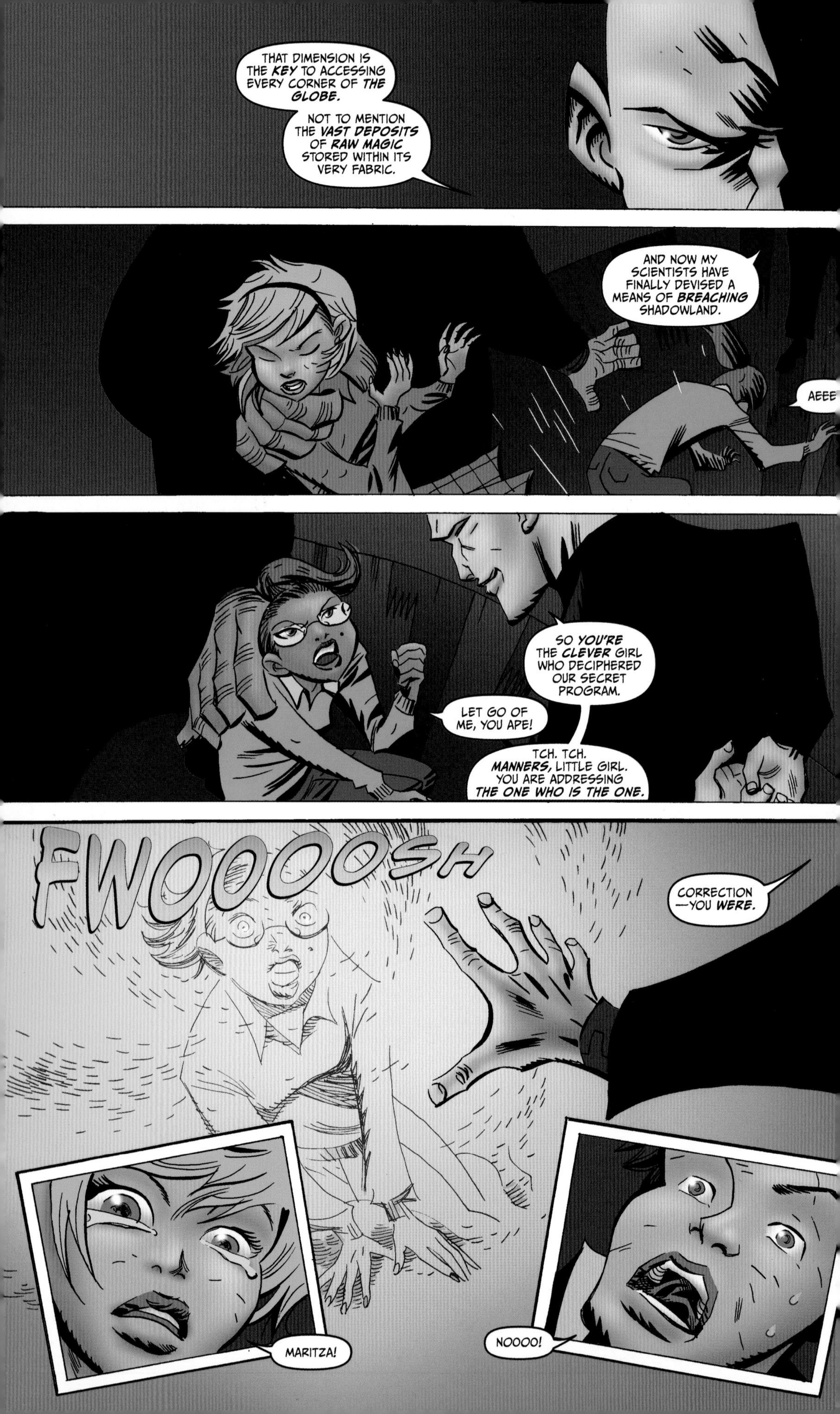
THAT DIMENSION IS THE KEY TO ACCESSING EVERY CORNER OF THE GLOBE.
NOT TO MENTION THE VAST DEPOSITS OF RAW MAGIC STORED WITHIN ITS VERY FABRIC.
AND NOW MY SCIENTISTS HAVE FINALLY DEVISED A MEANS OF BREACHING SHADOWLAND.
AEEE
SO YOU'RE THE CLEVER GIRL WHO DECIPHERED OUR SECRET PROGRAM.
LET GO OF ME, YOU APE!
TCH. TCH. MANNERS, LITTLE GIRL. YOU ARE ADDRESSING THE ONE WHO IS THE ONE.
FWOOOOSH
CORRECTION —YOU WERE.
MARITZA!
NOOOO!

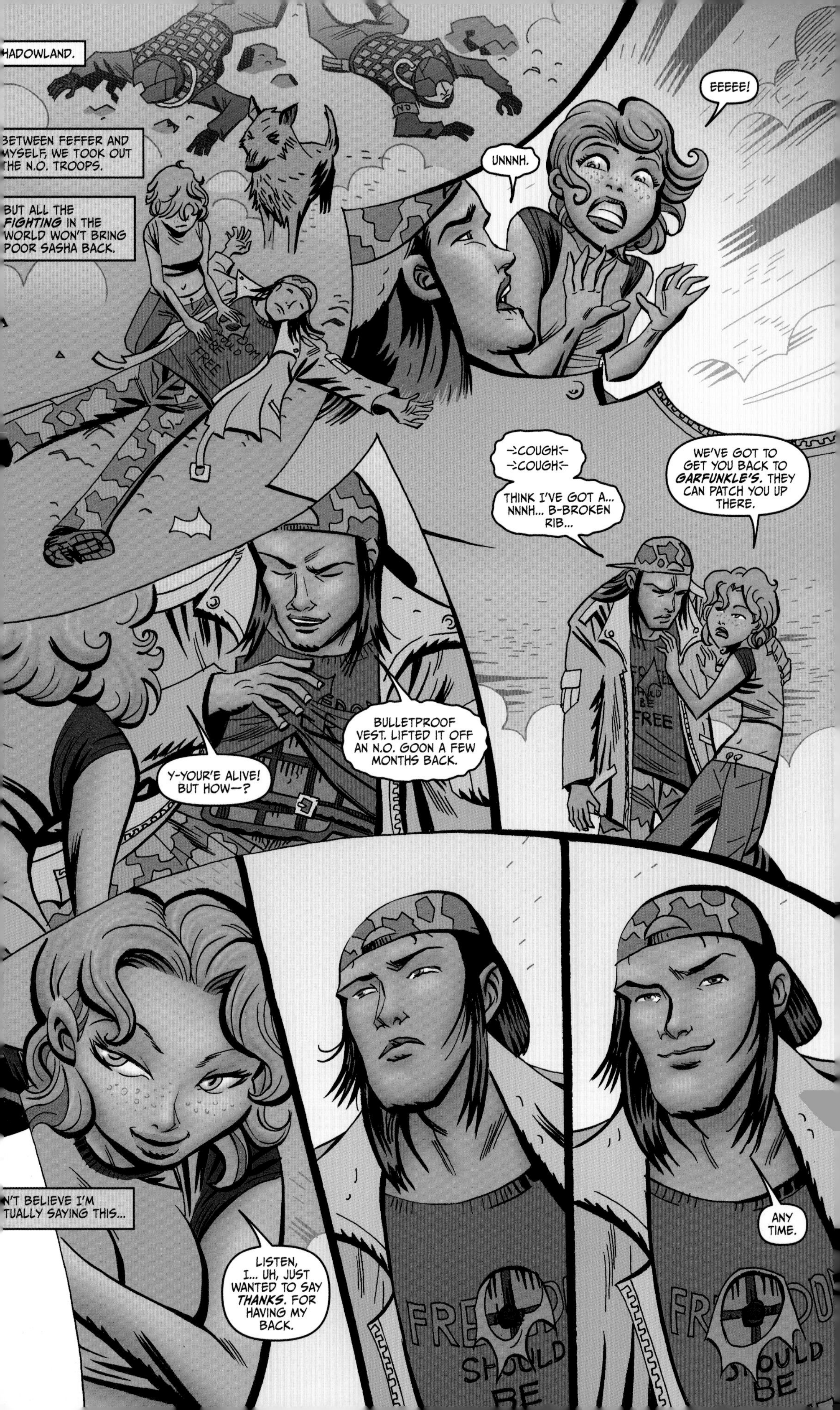
HADOWLAND.
BETWEEN FEFFER AND MYSELF, WE TOOK OUT THE N.O. TROOPS.
BUT ALL THE FIGHTING IN THE WORLD WON'T BRING POOR SASHA BACK.
UNNNH.
EEEEE!
Y-YOUR'E ALIVE! BUT HOW—?
BULLETPROOF VEST. LIFTED IT OFF AN N.O. GOON A FEW MONTHS BACK.
COUGH
COUGH
THINK I'VE GOT A... NNNH... B-BROKEN RIB...
WE'VE GOT TO GET YOU BACK TO GARFUNKLE'S. THEY CAN PATCH YOU UP THERE.
N'T BELIEVE I'M TUALLY SAYING THIS...
LISTEN, I... UH, JUST WANTED TO SAY THANKS. FOR HAVING MY BACK.
ANY TIME.

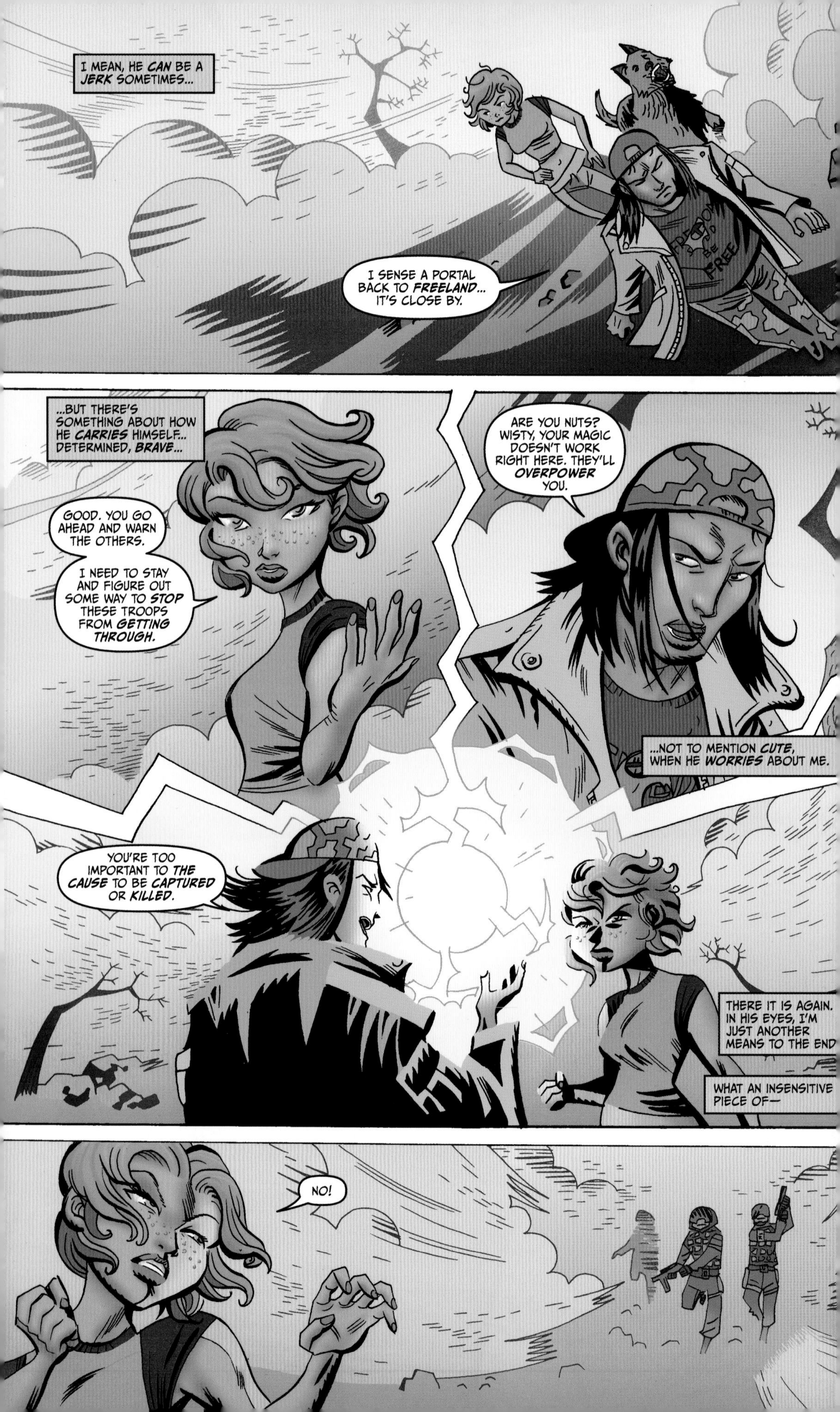
I MEAN, HE CAN BE A JERK SOMETIMES...
I SENSE A PORTAL BACK TO FREELAND... IT'S CLOSE BY.
...BUT THERE'S SOMETHING ABOUT HOW HE CARRIES HIMSELF... DETERMINED, BRAVE...
GOOD. YOU GO AHEAD AND WARN THE OTHERS.
I NEED TO STAY AND FIGURE OUT SOME WAY TO STOP THESE TROOPS FROM GETTING THROUGH.
ARE YOU NUTS? WISTY, YOUR MAGIC DOESN'T WORK RIGHT HERE. THEY'LL OVERPOWER YOU.
...NOT TO MENTION CUTE, WHEN HE WORRIES ABOUT ME.
YOU'RE TOO IMPORTANT TO THE CAUSE TO BE CAPTURED OR KILLED.
THERE IT IS AGAIN. IN HIS EYES, I'M JUST ANOTHER MEANS TO THE END
WHAT AN INSENSITIVE PIECE OF—
NO!

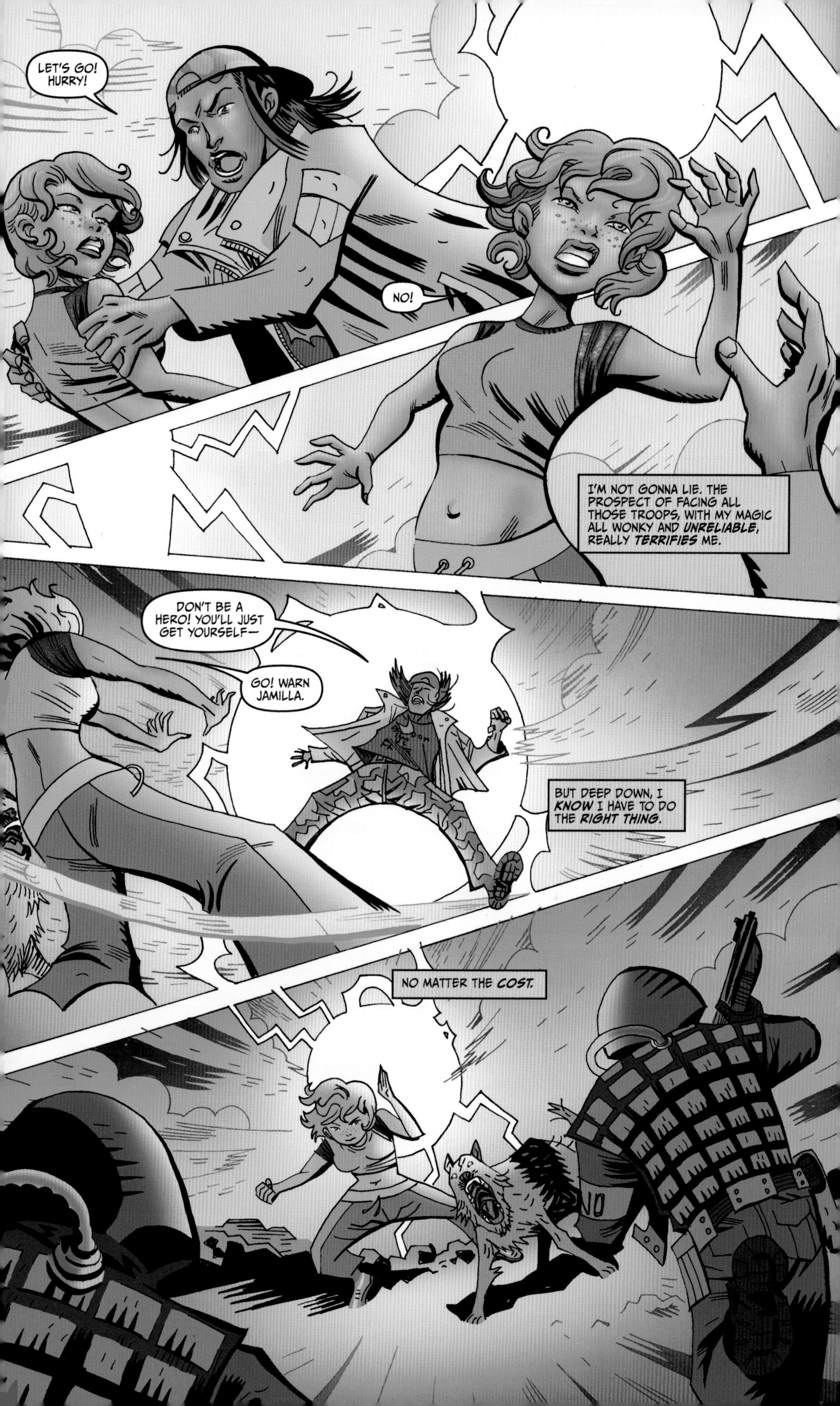
LET'S GO! HURRY!
NO!
I'M NOT GONNA LIE. THE PROSPECT OF FACING ALL THOSE TROOPS, WITH MY MAGIC ALL WONKY AND UNRELIABLE, REALLY TERRIFIES ME.
DON'T BE A HERO! YOU'LL JUST GET YOURSELF—
GO! WARN JAMILLA.
BUT DEEP DOWN, I KNOW I HAVE TO DO THE RIGHT THING.
NO MATTER THE COST.

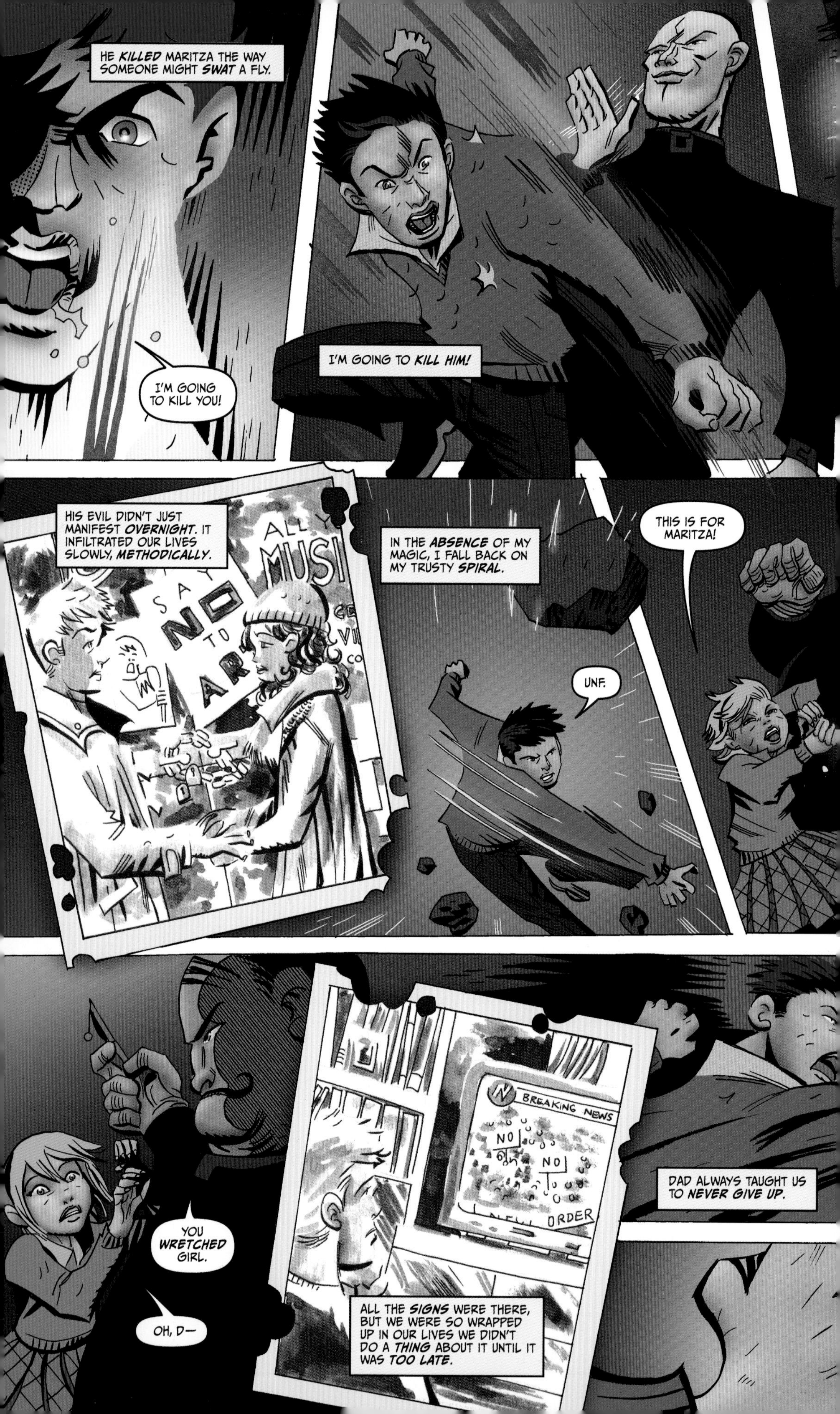
HE KILLED MARITZA THE WAY SOMEONE MIGHT SWAT A FLY.
I'M GOING TO KILL YOU!
I'M GOING TO KILL HIM!
HIS EVIL DIDN'T JUST MANIFEST OVERNIGHT. IT INFILTRATED OUR LIVES SLOWLY, METHODICALLY.
SAY NO TO ART
IN THE ABSENCE OF MY MAGIC, I FALL BACK ON MY TRUSTY SPIRAL.
THIS IS FOR MARITZA!
UNF.
YOU WRETCHED GIRL.
OH, D—
BREAKING NEWS
NO
NO
NEW ORDER
ALL THE SIGNS WERE THERE, BUT WE WERE SO WRAPPED UP IN OUR LIVES WE DIDN'T DO A THING ABOUT IT UNTIL IT WAS TOO LATE.
DAD ALWAYS TAUGHT US TO NEVER GIVE UP.

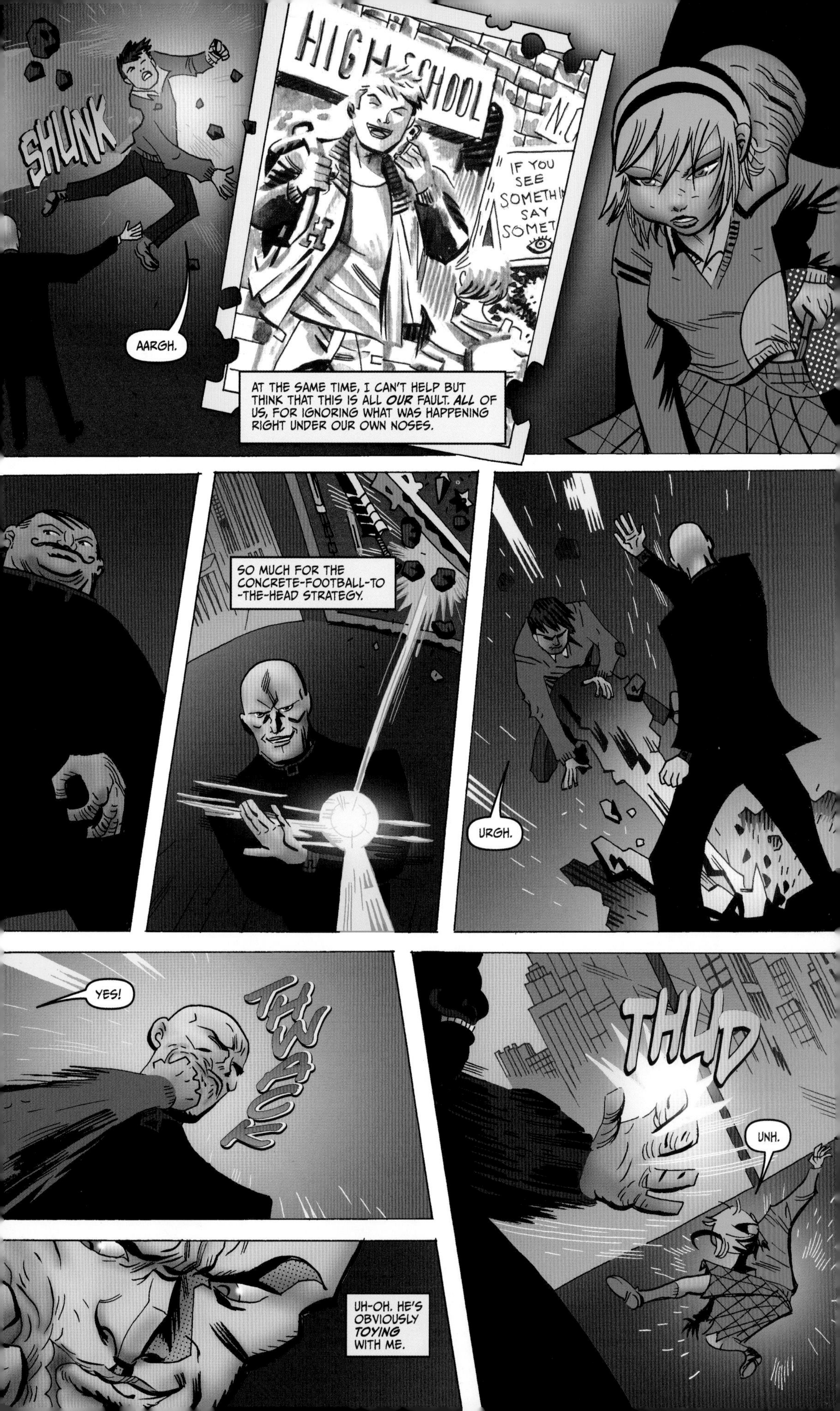
SHUNK
HIGH SCHOOL
IF YOU SEE SOMETHI SAY SOMET
AARGH.
AT THE SAME TIME, I CAN'T HELP BUT THINK THAT THIS IS ALL *OUR* FAULT. *ALL* OF US, FOR IGNORING WHAT WAS HAPPENING RIGHT UNDER OUR OWN NOSES.
SO MUCH FOR THE CONCRETE-FOOTBALL-TO-THE-HEAD STRATEGY.
URGH.
YES!
THWACK
THUD
UNH.
UH-OH. HE'S OBVIOUSLY *TOYING* WITH ME.

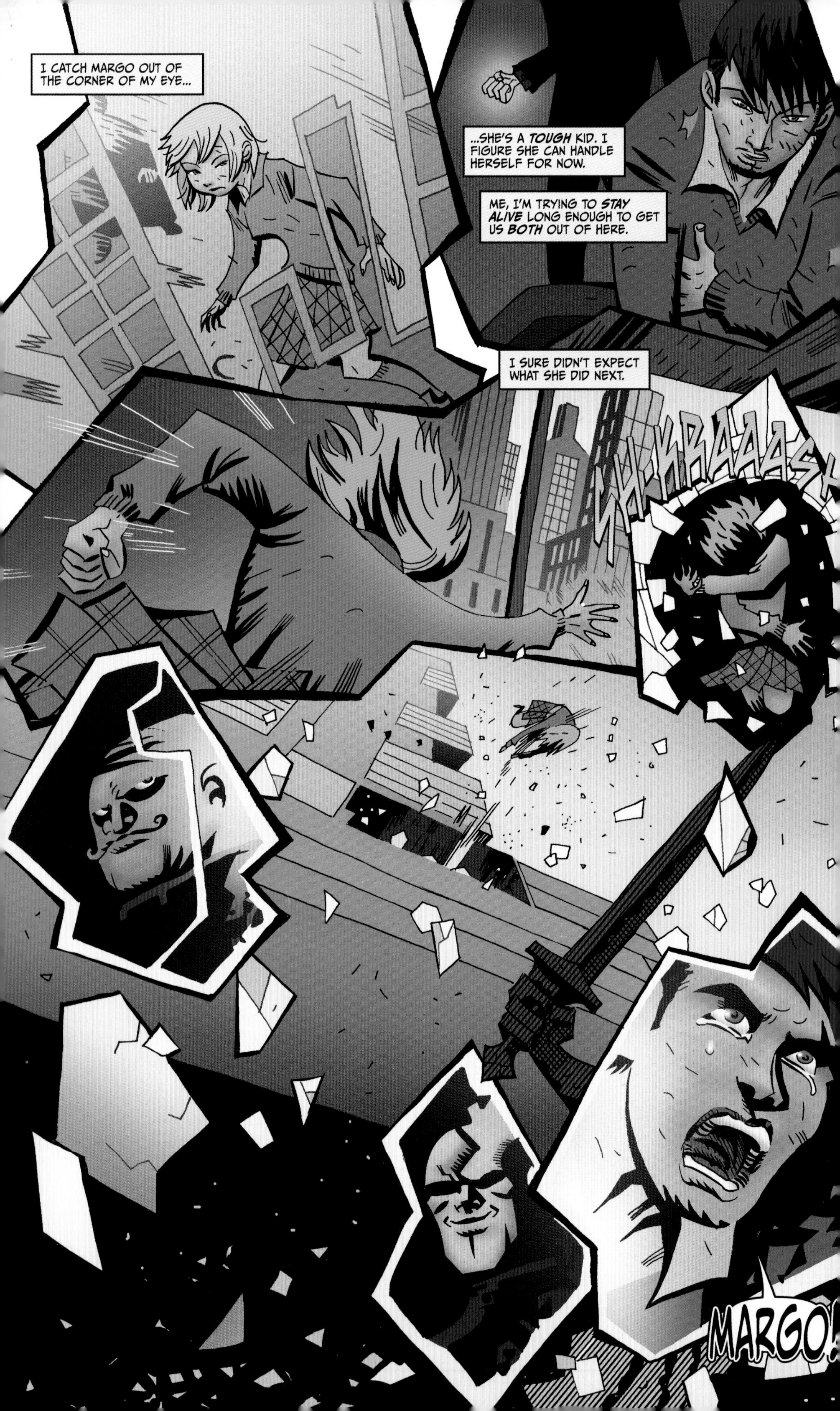

I CATCH MARGO OUT OF THE CORNER OF MY EYE...
...SHE'S A *TOUGH* KID. I FIGURE SHE CAN HANDLE HERSELF FOR NOW.
ME, I'M TRYING TO *STAY ALIVE* LONG ENOUGH TO GET US *BOTH* OUT OF HERE.
I SURE DIDN'T EXPECT WHAT SHE DID NEXT.
SKKRAAASH
MARGO!

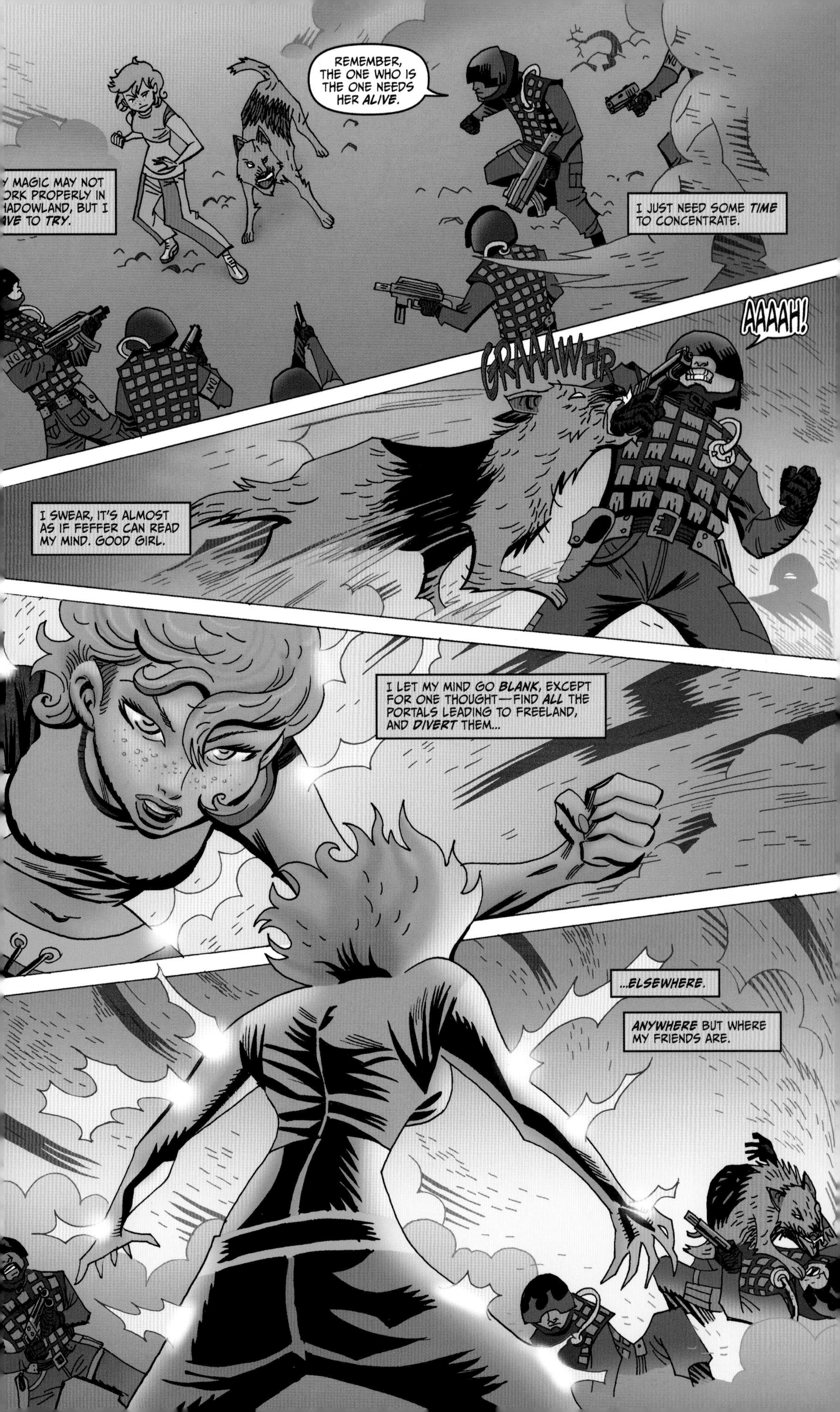

REMEMBER, THE ONE WHO IS THE ONE NEEDS HER *ALIVE*.
Y MAGIC MAY NOT ORK PROPERLY IN HADOWLAND, BUT I AVE TO *TRY*.
I JUST NEED SOME *TIME* TO CONCENTRATE.
AAAAH!
GRAAAWHR
I SWEAR, IT'S ALMOST AS IF FEFFER CAN READ MY MIND. GOOD GIRL.
I LET MY MIND GO *BLANK*, EXCEPT FOR ONE THOUGHT—FIND *ALL* THE PORTALS LEADING TO FREELAND, AND *DIVERT* THEM...
...ELSEWHERE.
ANYWHERE BUT WHERE MY FRIENDS ARE.

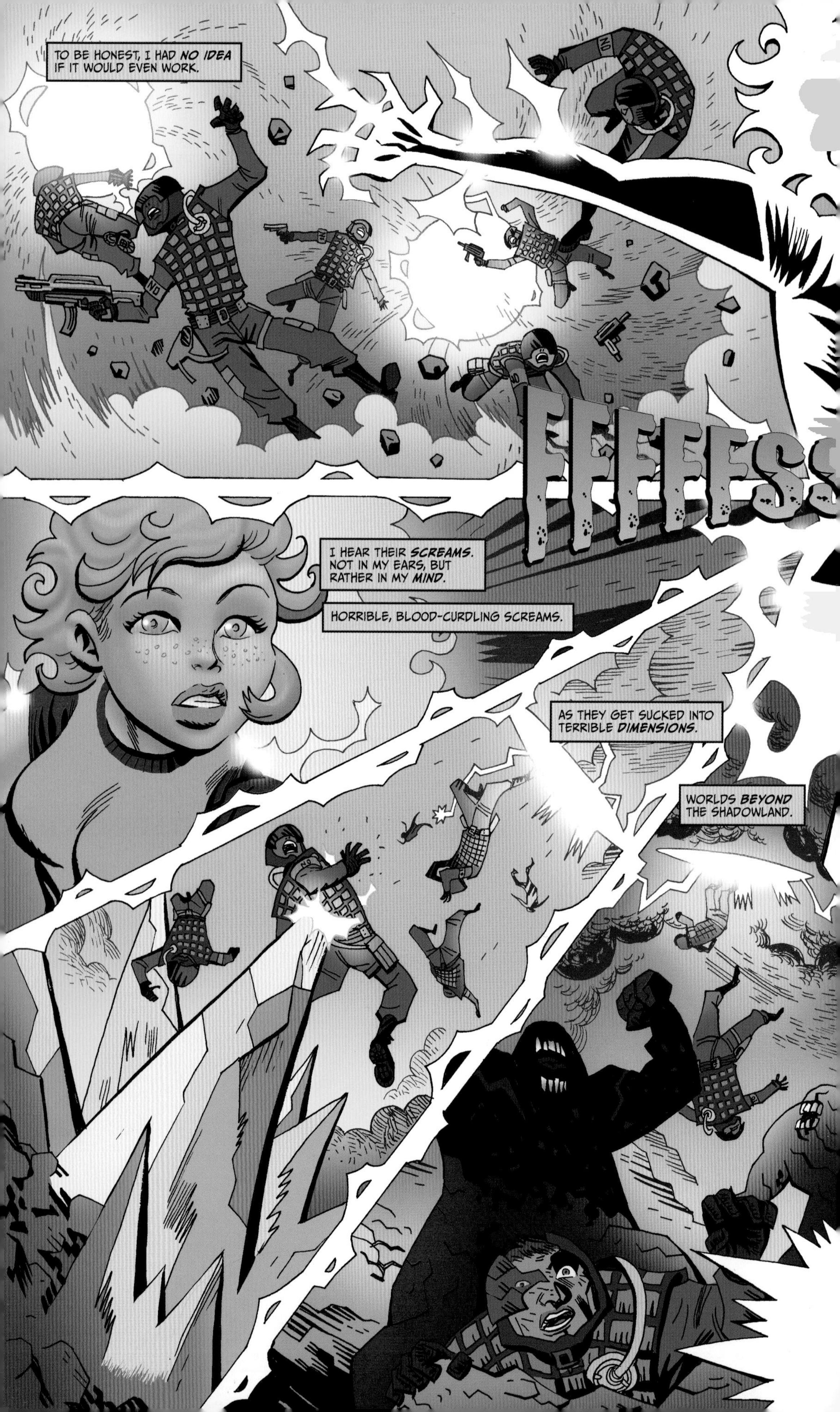

TO BE HONEST, I HAD NO IDEA IF IT WOULD EVEN WORK.
EFFFSS
I HEAR THEIR SCREAMS. NOT IN MY EARS, BUT RATHER IN MY MIND.
HORRIBLE, BLOOD-CURDLING SCREAMS.
AS THEY GET SUCKED INTO TERRIBLE DIMENSIONS.
WORLDS BEYOND THE SHADOWLAND.

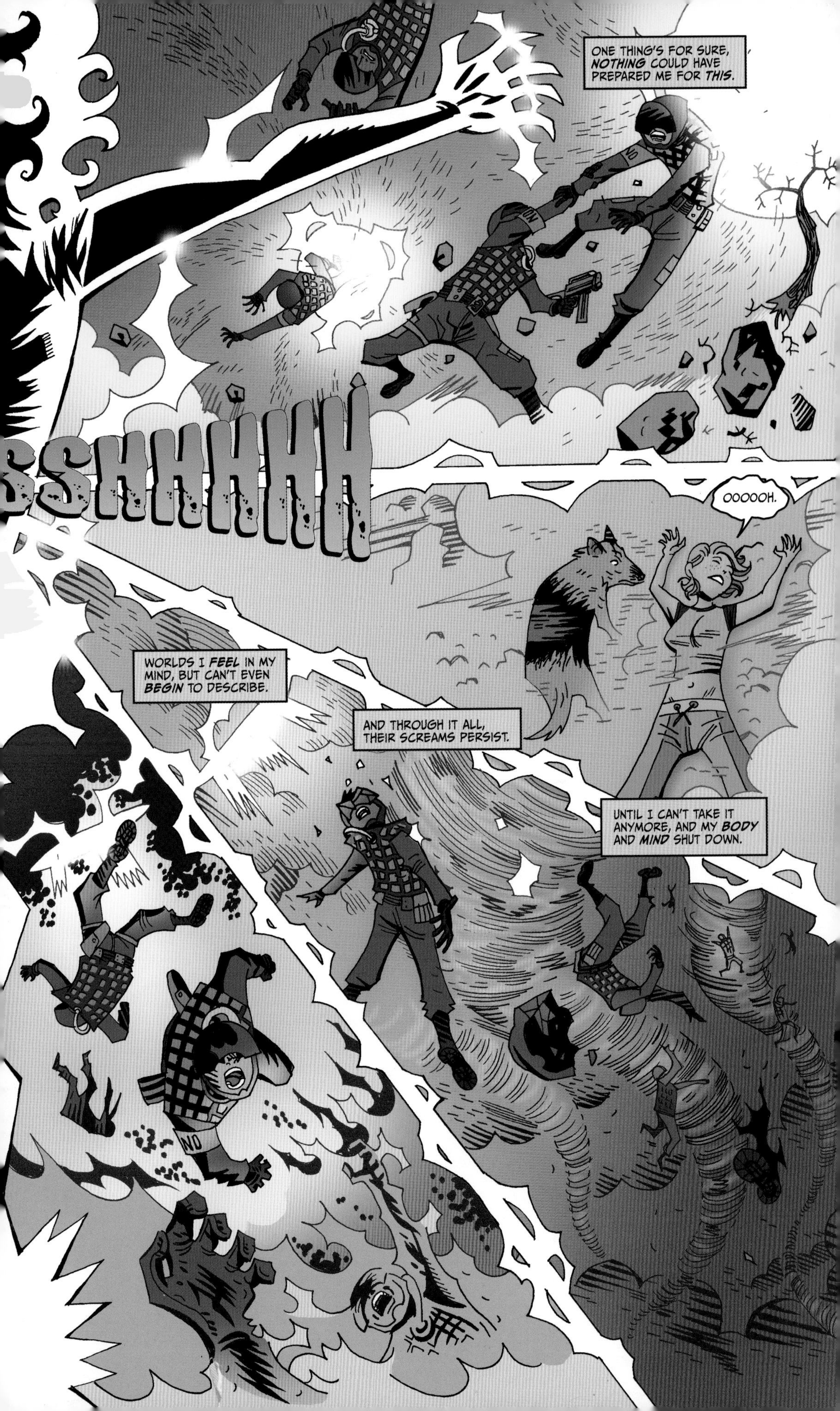
ONE THING'S FOR SURE, NOTHING COULD HAVE PREPARED ME FOR THIS.
SSHHHHH
OOOOOH.
WORLDS I FEEL IN MY MIND, BUT CAN'T EVEN BEGIN TO DESCRIBE.
AND THROUGH IT ALL, THEIR SCREAMS PERSIST.
UNTIL I CAN'T TAKE IT ANYMORE, AND MY BODY AND MIND SHUT DOWN.
NO

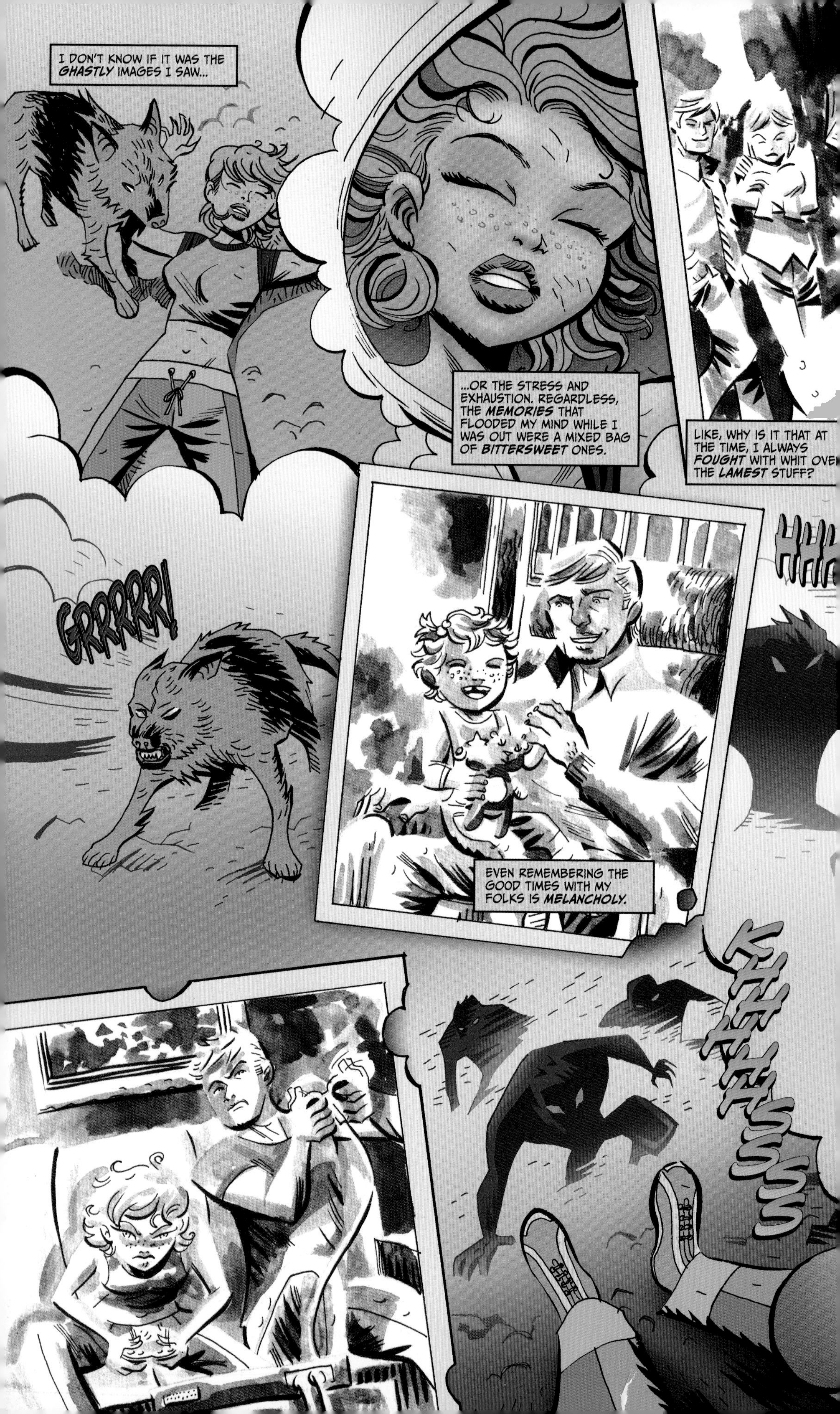
I DON'T KNOW IF IT WAS THE GHASTLY IMAGES I SAW...
...OR THE STRESS AND EXHAUSTION. REGARDLESS, THE MEMORIES THAT FLOODED MY MIND WHILE I WAS OUT WERE A MIXED BAG OF BITTERSWEET ONES.
LIKE, WHY IS IT THAT AT THE TIME, I ALWAYS FOUGHT WITH WHIT OVE THE LAMEST STUFF?
GRRRRR!
EVEN REMEMBERING THE GOOD TIMES WITH MY FOLKS IS MELANCHOLY.
KHHHHSSSS

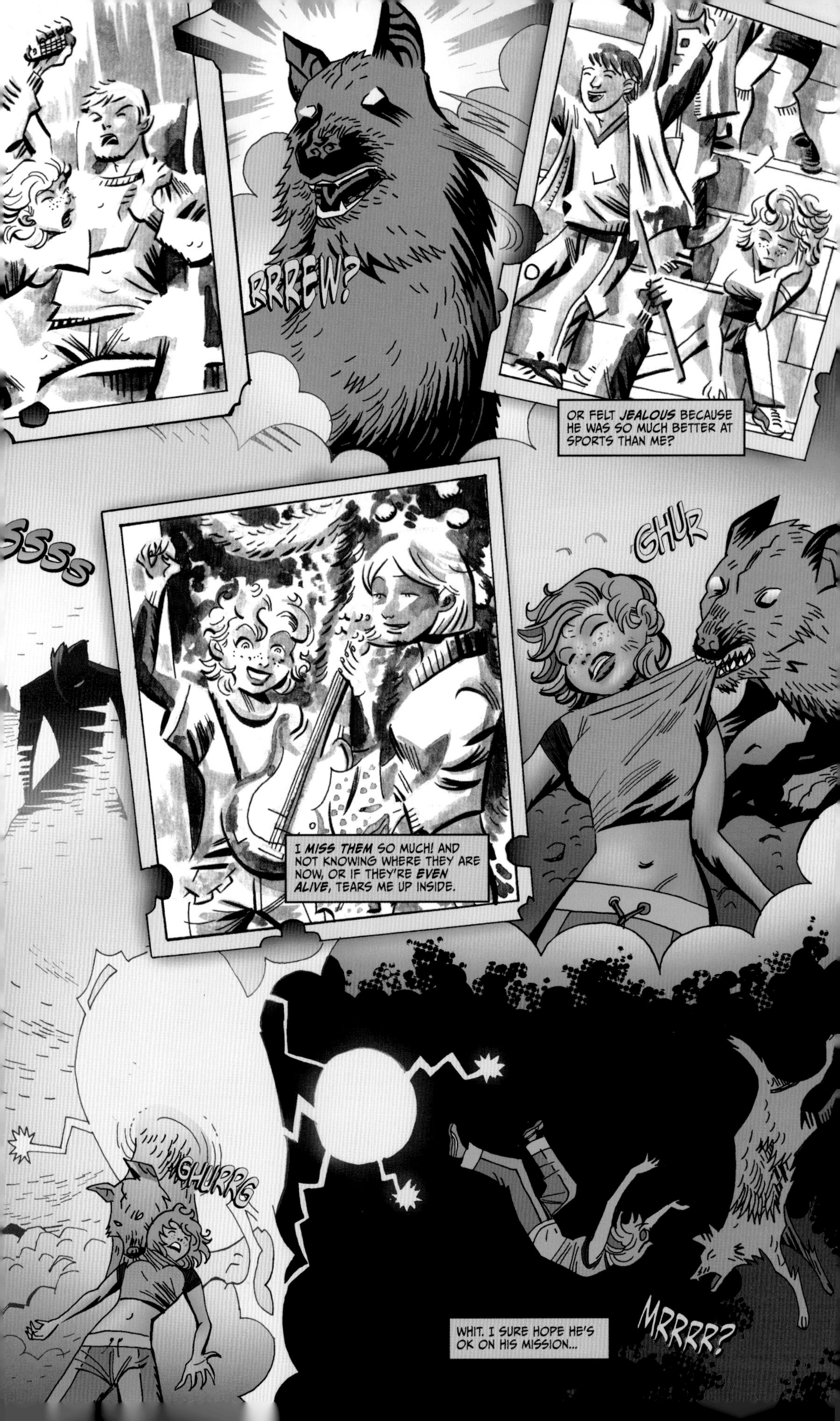
RRREW?
OR FELT JEALOUS BECAUSE HE WAS SO MUCH BETTER AT SPORTS THAN ME?
SSSS
I MISS THEM SO MUCH! AND NOT KNOWING WHERE THEY ARE NOW, OR IF THEY'RE EVEN ALIVE, TEARS ME UP INSIDE.
GHUR
GHURRG
WHIT. I SURE HOPE HE'S OK ON HIS MISSION...
MRRRR?

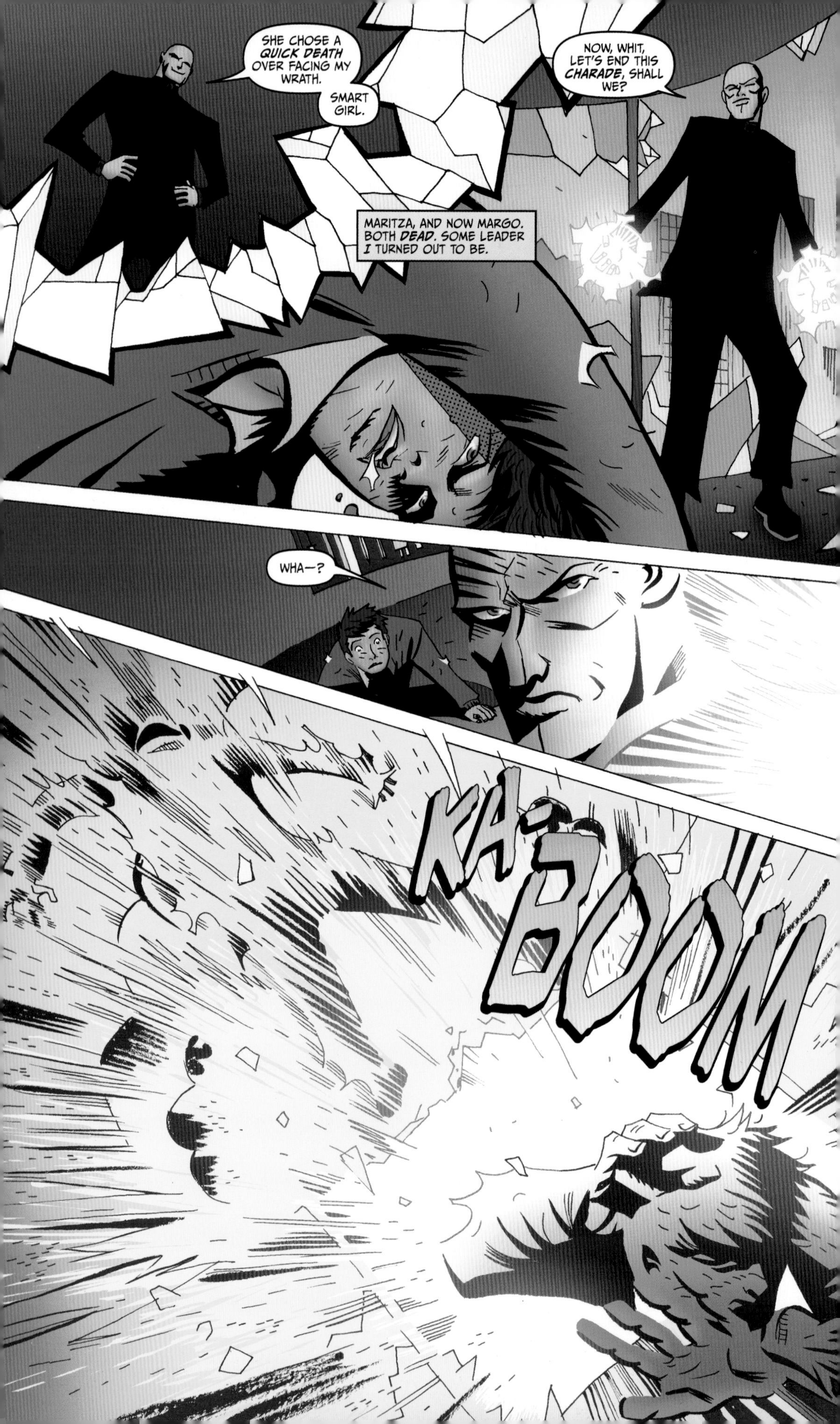
SHE CHOSE A QUICK DEATH OVER FACING MY WRATH.
SMART GIRL.
NOW, WHIT, LET'S END THIS CHARADE, SHALL WE?
MARITZA, AND NOW MARGO. BOTH DEAD. SOME LEADER I TURNED OUT TO BE.
WHA—?
KA-BOOM

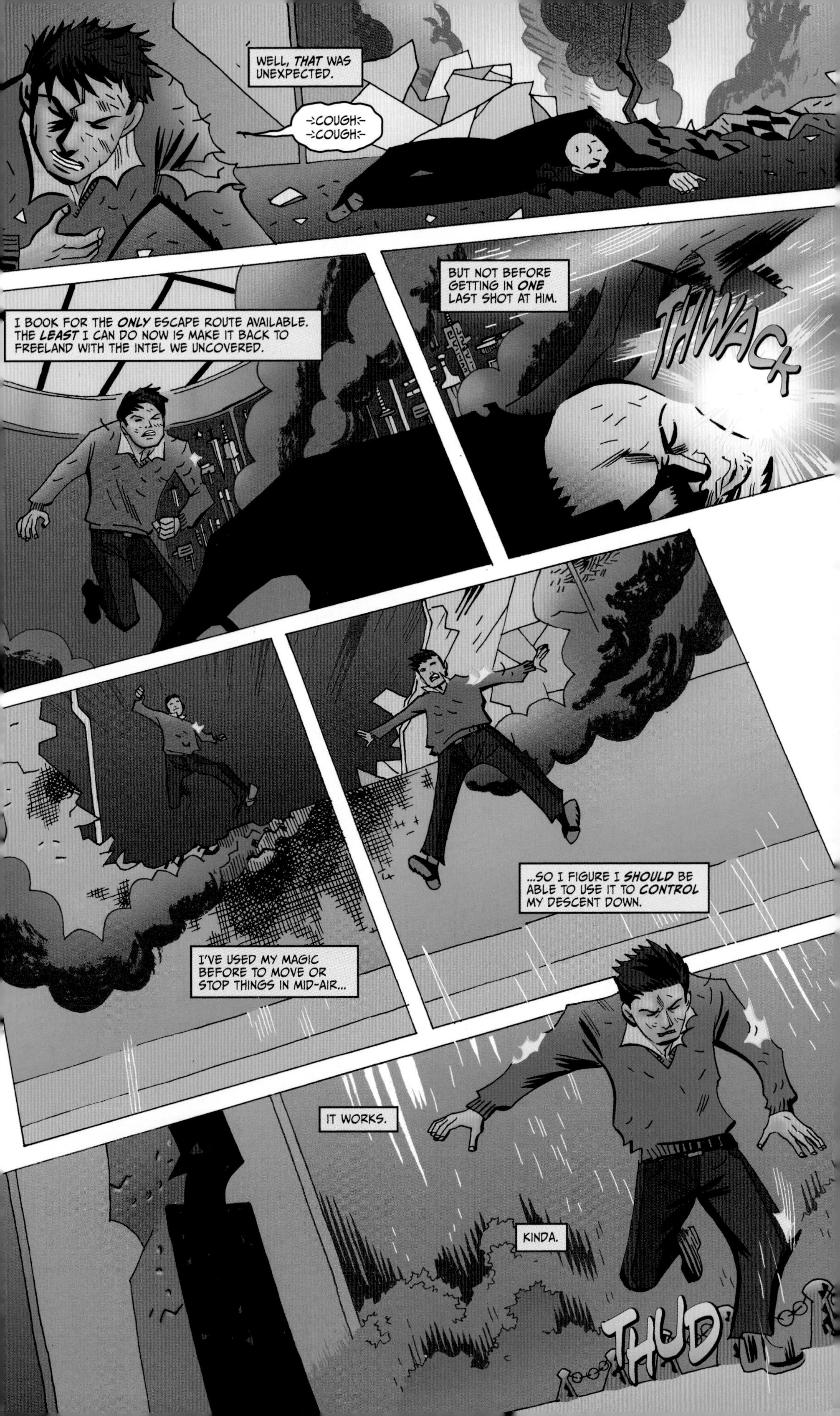
WELL, *THAT* WAS UNEXPECTED.
-COUGH- -COUGH-
I BOOK FOR THE *ONLY* ESCAPE ROUTE AVAILABLE. THE *LEAST* I CAN DO NOW IS MAKE IT BACK TO FREELAND WITH THE INTEL WE UNCOVERED.
BUT NOT BEFORE GETTING IN *ONE* LAST SHOT AT HIM.
THWACK
I'VE USED MY MAGIC BEFORE TO MOVE OR STOP THINGS IN MID-AIR...
...SO I FIGURE I *SHOULD* BE ABLE TO USE IT TO *CONTROL* MY DESCENT DOWN.
IT WORKS.
KINDA.
THUD

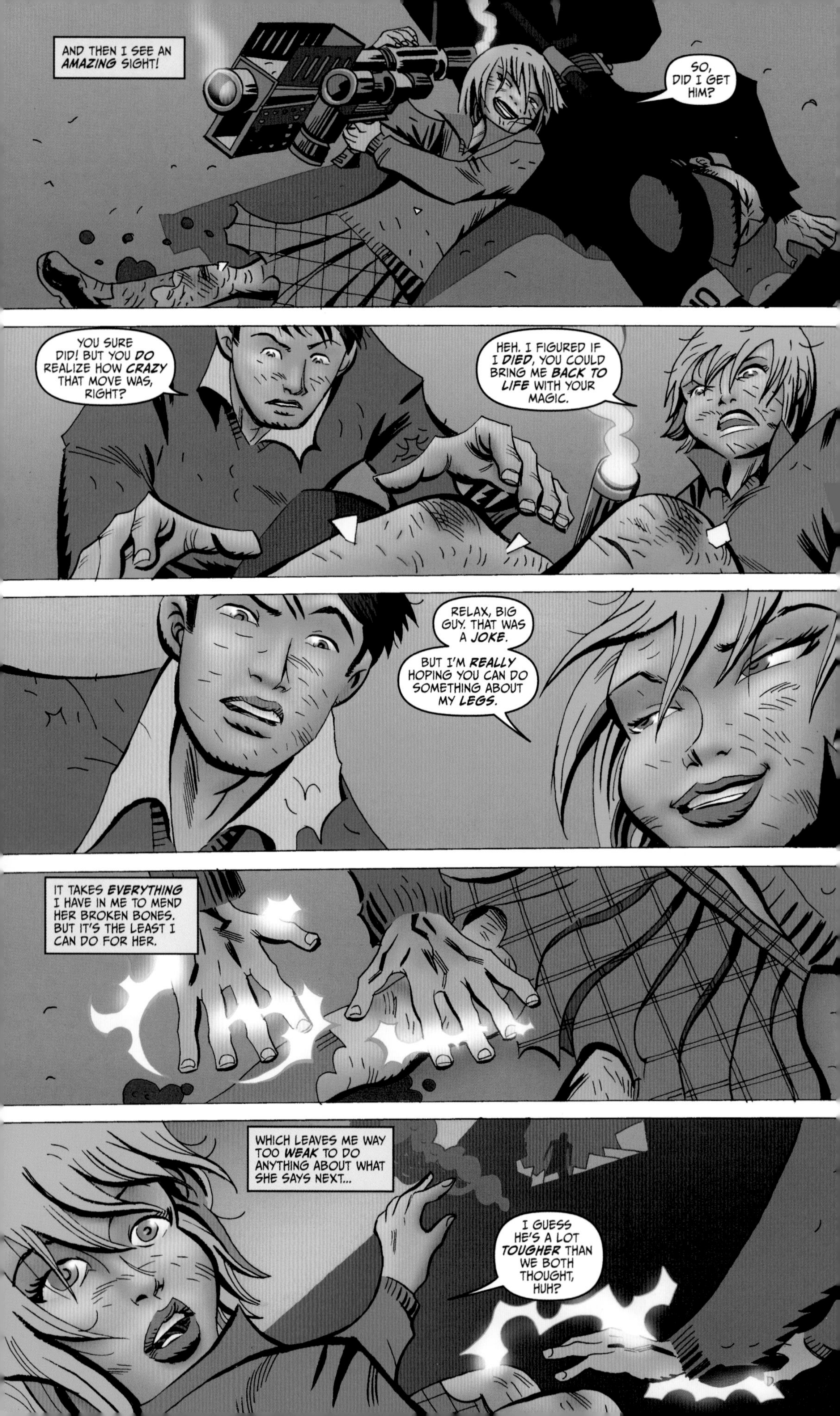
AND THEN I SEE AN AMAZING SIGHT!
SO, DID I GET HIM?
YOU SURE DID! BUT YOU DO REALIZE HOW CRAZY THAT MOVE WAS, RIGHT?
HEH. I FIGURED IF I DIED, YOU COULD BRING ME BACK TO LIFE WITH YOUR MAGIC.
RELAX, BIG GUY. THAT WAS A JOKE.
BUT I'M REALLY HOPING YOU CAN DO SOMETHING ABOUT MY LEGS.
IT TAKES EVERYTHING I HAVE IN ME TO MEND HER BROKEN BONES. BUT IT'S THE LEAST I CAN DO FOR HER.
WHICH LEAVES ME WAY TOO WEAK TO DO ANYTHING ABOUT WHAT SHE SAYS NEXT...
I GUESS HE'S A LOT TOUGHER THAN WE BOTH THOUGHT, HUH?

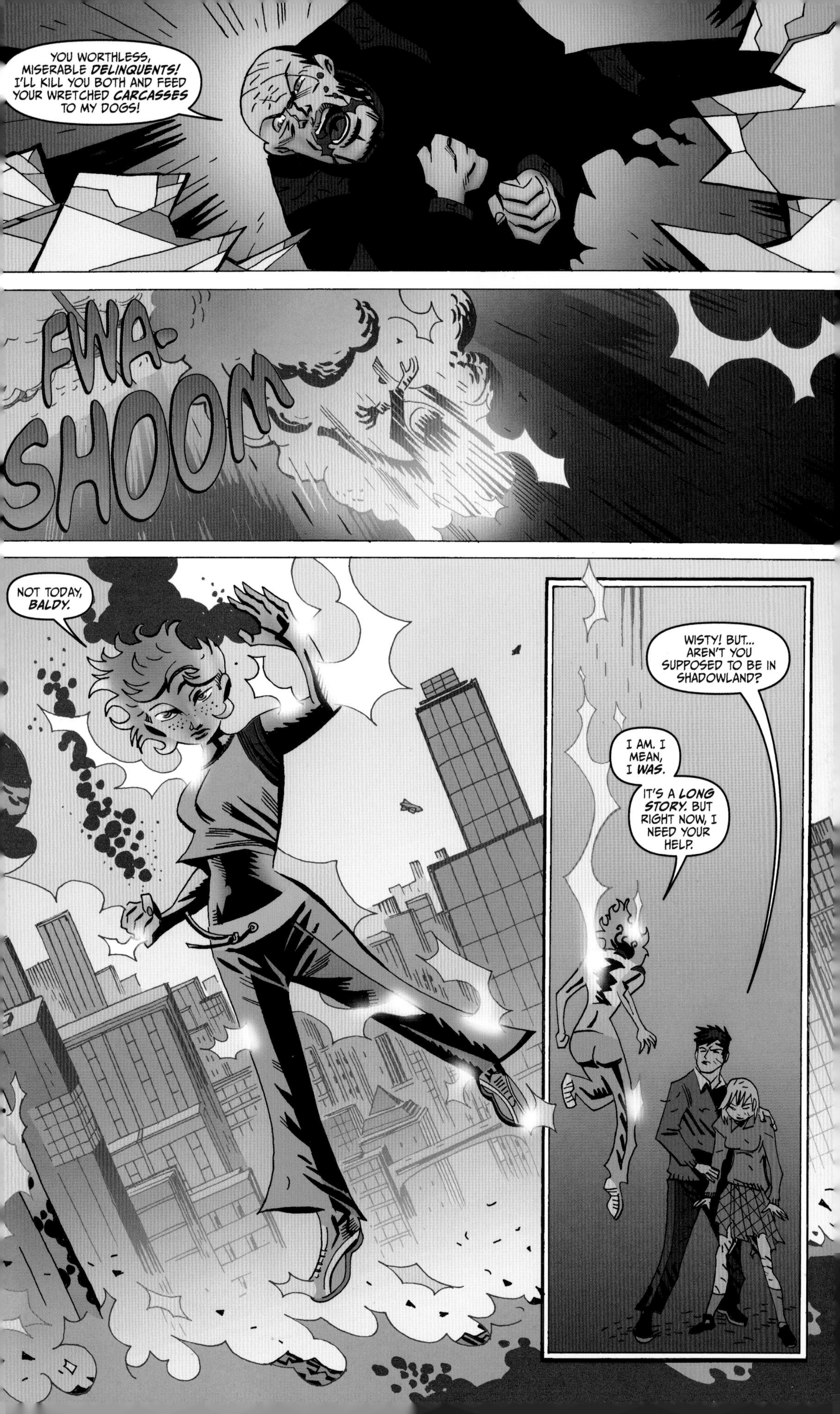
YOU WORTHLESS, MISERABLE DELINQUENTS! I'LL KILL YOU BOTH AND FEED YOUR WRETCHED CARCASSES TO MY DOGS!
FWA-SHOOM
NOT TODAY, BALDY.
WISTY! BUT... AREN'T YOU SUPPOSED TO BE IN SHADOWLAND?
I AM. I MEAN, I WAS.
IT'S A LONG STORY. BUT RIGHT NOW, I NEED YOUR HELP.

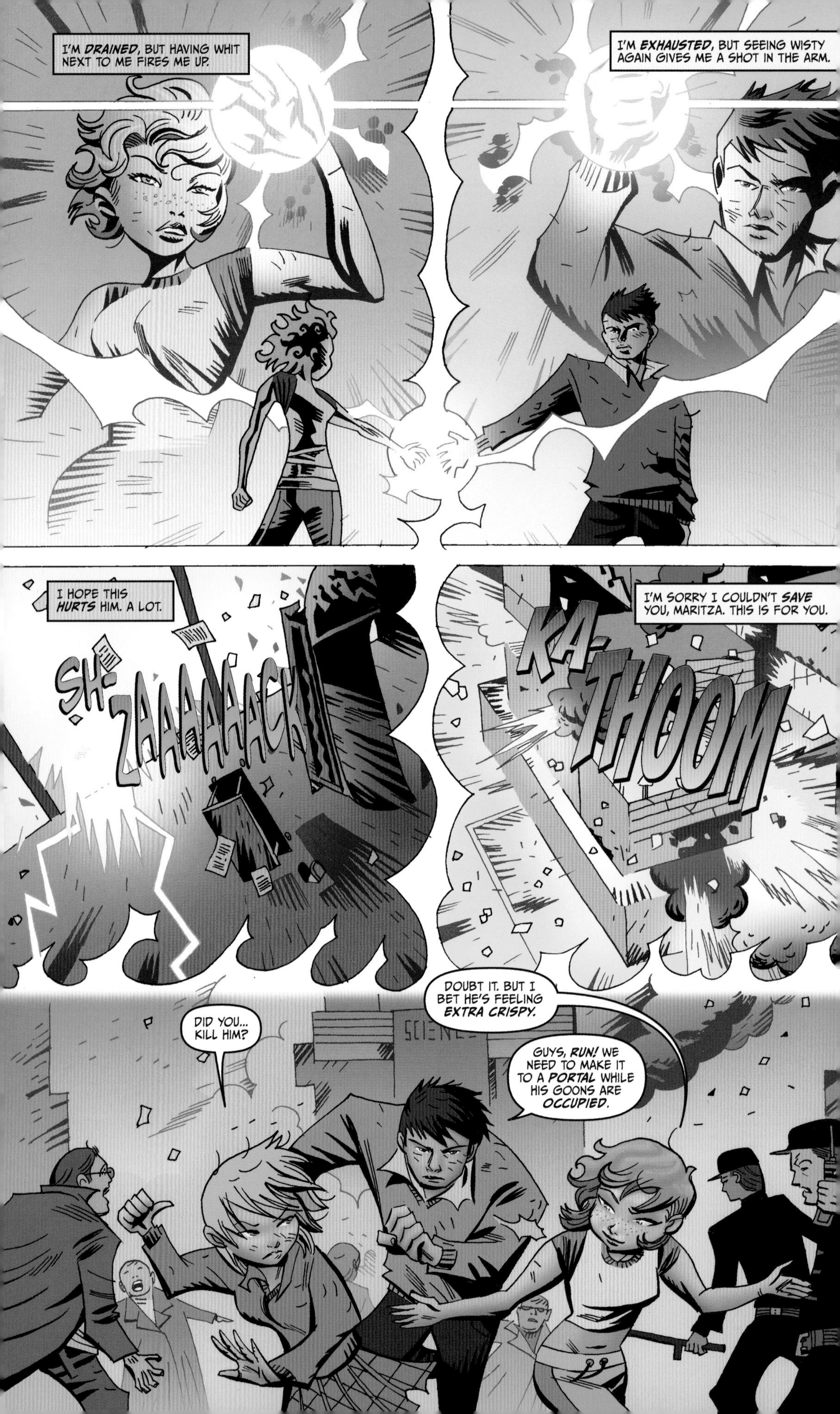

I'M DRAINED, BUT HAVING WHIT NEXT TO ME FIRES ME UP.
I'M EXHAUSTED, BUT SEEING WISTY AGAIN GIVES ME A SHOT IN THE ARM.
I HOPE THIS HURTS HIM. A LOT.
SH-ZAAAAAACK!
I'M SORRY I COULDN'T SAVE YOU, MARITZA. THIS IS FOR YOU.
KA-THOOM
DID YOU... KILL HIM?
DOUBT IT. BUT I BET HE'S FEELING EXTRA CRISPY.
GUYS, RUN! WE NEED TO MAKE IT TO A PORTAL WHILE HIS GOONS ARE OCCUPIED.

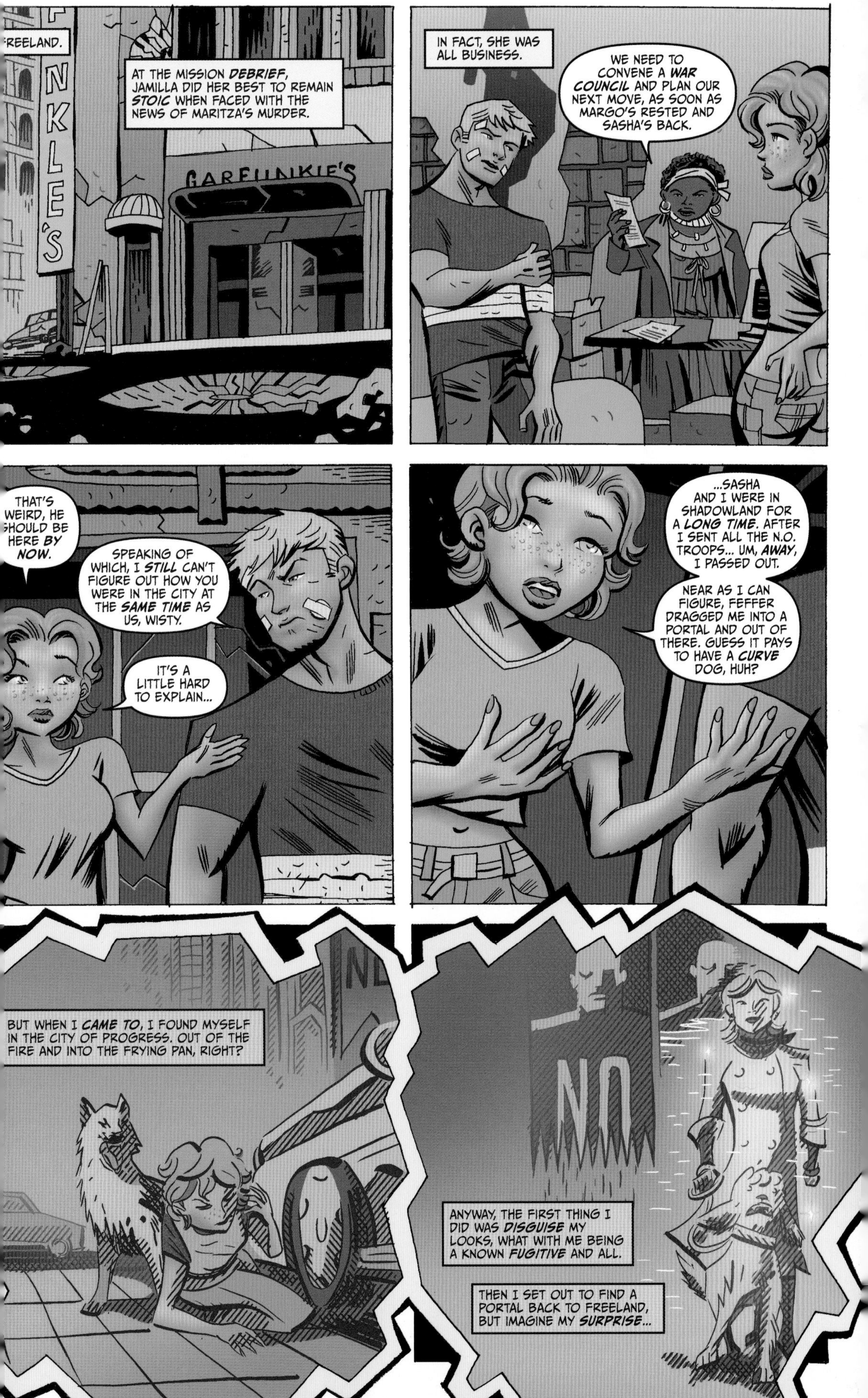
FREELAND.
AT THE MISSION DEBRIEF, JAMILLA DID HER BEST TO REMAIN STOIC WHEN FACED WITH THE NEWS OF MARITZA'S MURDER.
GARFUNKLE'S
IN FACT, SHE WAS ALL BUSINESS.
WE NEED TO CONVENE A WAR COUNCIL AND PLAN OUR NEXT MOVE, AS SOON AS MARGO'S RESTED AND SASHA'S BACK.
THAT'S WEIRD, HE SHOULD BE HERE BY NOW.
SPEAKING OF WHICH, I STILL CAN'T FIGURE OUT HOW YOU WERE IN THE CITY AT THE SAME TIME AS US, WISTY.
IT'S A LITTLE HARD TO EXPLAIN...
...SASHA AND I WERE IN SHADOWLAND FOR A LONG TIME. AFTER I SENT ALL THE N.O. TROOPS... UM, AWAY, I PASSED OUT.
NEAR AS I CAN FIGURE, FEFFER DRAGGED ME INTO A PORTAL AND OUT OF THERE. GUESS IT PAYS TO HAVE A CURVE DOG, HUH?
BUT WHEN I CAME TO, I FOUND MYSELF IN THE CITY OF PROGRESS. OUT OF THE FIRE AND INTO THE FRYING PAN, RIGHT?
NO
ANYWAY, THE FIRST THING I DID WAS DISGUISE MY LOOKS, WHAT WITH ME BEING A KNOWN FUGITIVE AND ALL.
THEN I SET OUT TO FIND A PORTAL BACK TO FREELAND, BUT IMAGINE MY SURPRISE...

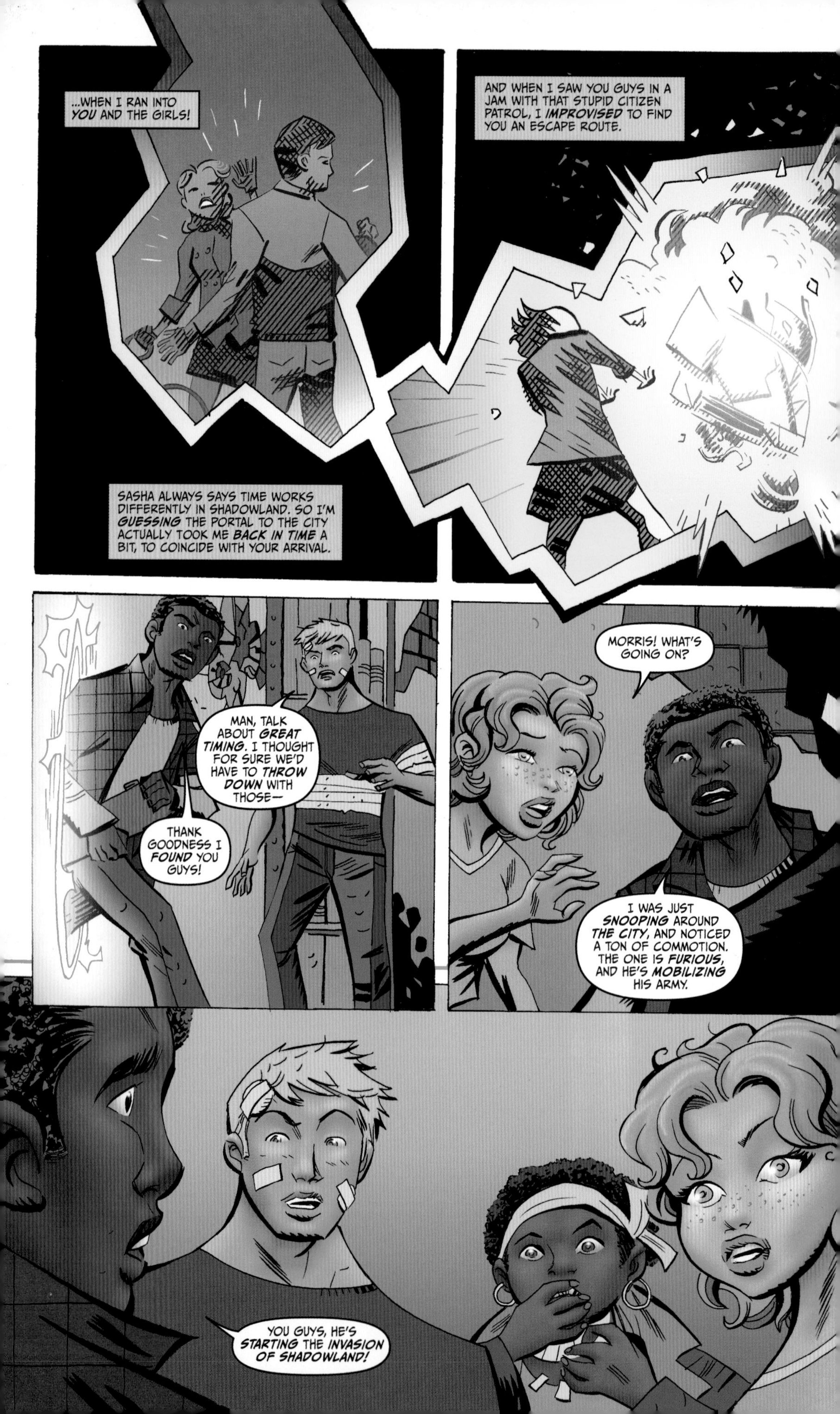
...WHEN I RAN INTO YOU AND THE GIRLS!
AND WHEN I SAW YOU GUYS IN A JAM WITH THAT STUPID CITIZEN PATROL, I IMPROVISED TO FIND YOU AN ESCAPE ROUTE.
SASHA ALWAYS SAYS TIME WORKS DIFFERENTLY IN SHADOWLAND. SO I'M GUESSING THE PORTAL TO THE CITY ACTUALLY TOOK ME BACK IN TIME A BIT, TO COINCIDE WITH YOUR ARRIVAL.
MAN, TALK ABOUT GREAT TIMING. I THOUGHT FOR SURE WE'D HAVE TO THROW DOWN WITH THOSE—
THANK GOODNESS I FOUND YOU GUYS!
MORRIS! WHAT'S GOING ON?
I WAS JUST SNOOPING AROUND THE CITY, AND NOTICED A TON OF COMMOTION. THE ONE IS FURIOUS, AND HE'S MOBILIZING HIS ARMY.
YOU GUYS, HE'S STARTING THE INVASION OF SHADOWLAND!

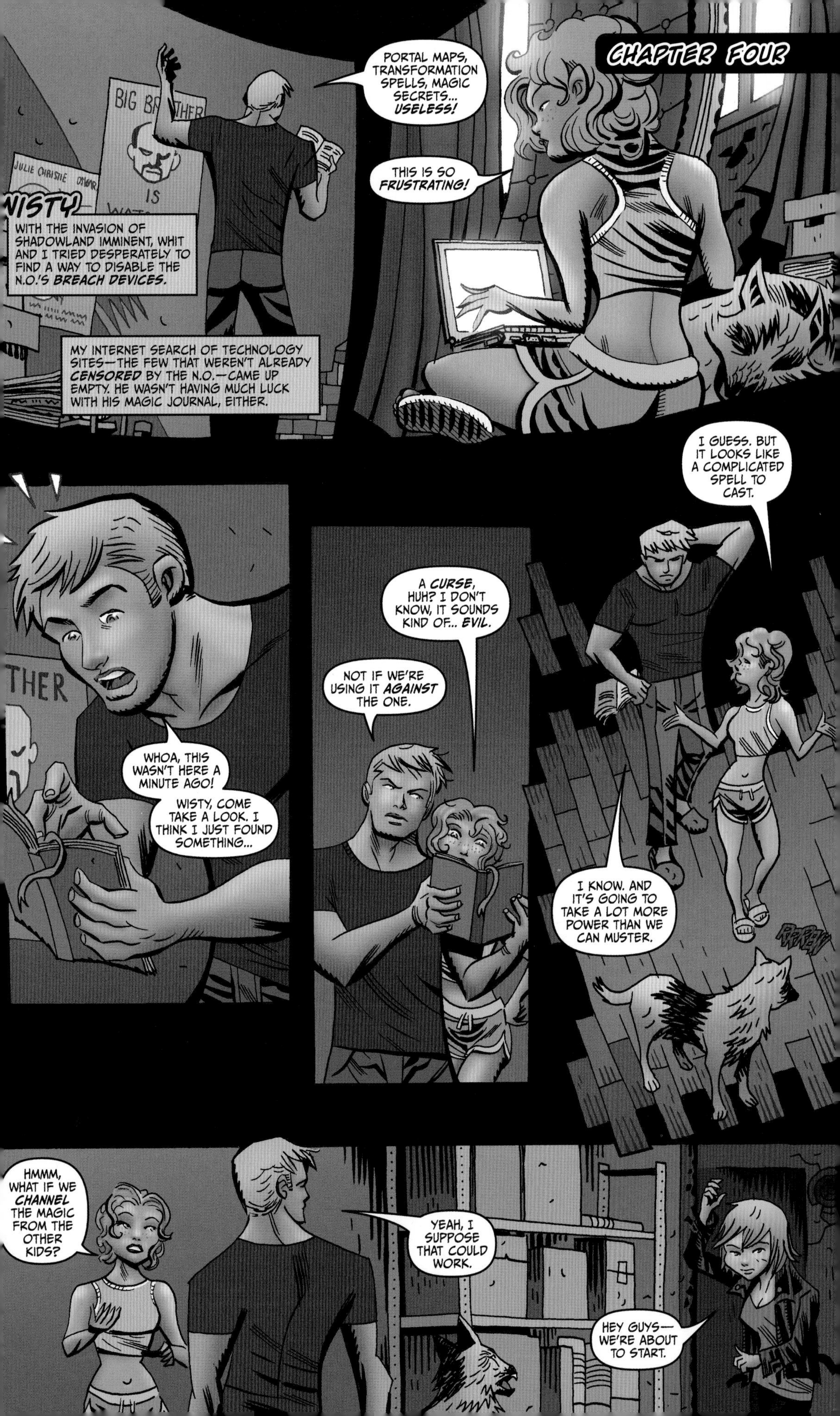
CHAPTER FOUR
BIG BROTHER IS WATCHING
JULIE CHRISTIE
WISTY
WITH THE INVASION OF SHADOWLAND IMMINENT, WHIT AND I TRIED DESPERATELY TO FIND A WAY TO DISABLE THE N.O.'S BREACH DEVICES.
MY INTERNET SEARCH OF TECHNOLOGY SITES—THE FEW THAT WEREN'T ALREADY CENSORED BY THE N.O.—CAME UP EMPTY. HE WASN'T HAVING MUCH LUCK WITH HIS MAGIC JOURNAL, EITHER.
PORTAL MAPS, TRANSFORMATION SPELLS, MAGIC SECRETS... USELESS!
THIS IS SO FRUSTRATING!
WHOA, THIS WASN'T HERE A MINUTE AGO!
WISTY, COME TAKE A LOOK. I THINK I JUST FOUND SOMETHING...
THER
A CURSE, HUH? I DON'T KNOW, IT SOUNDS KIND OF... EVIL.
NOT IF WE'RE USING IT AGAINST THE ONE.
I GUESS. BUT IT LOOKS LIKE A COMPLICATED SPELL TO CAST.
I KNOW. AND IT'S GOING TO TAKE A LOT MORE POWER THAN WE CAN MUSTER.
RRRAOW
HMMM, WHAT IF WE CHANNEL THE MAGIC FROM THE OTHER KIDS?
YEAH, I SUPPOSE THAT COULD WORK.
HEY GUYS— WE'RE ABOUT TO START.

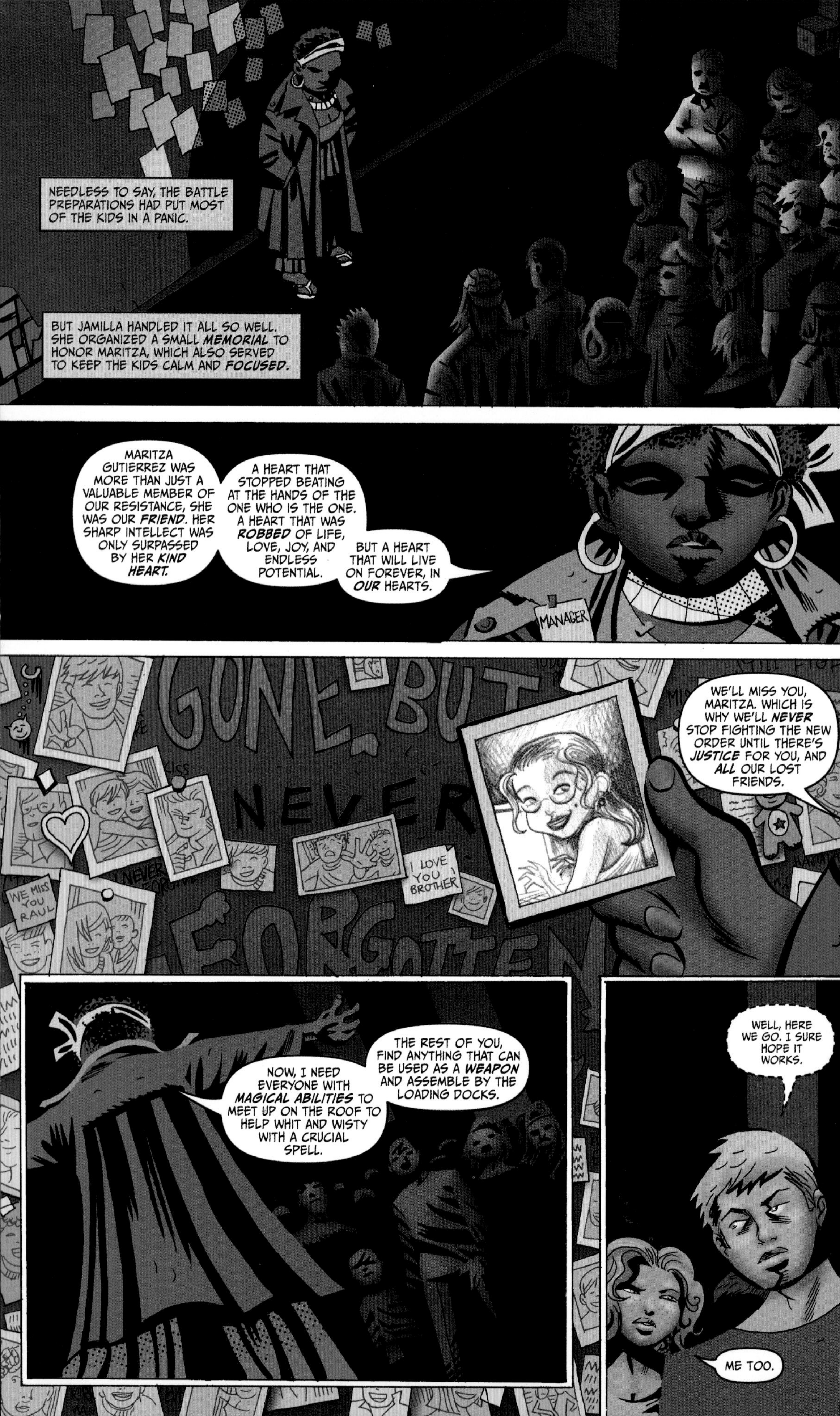
NEEDLESS TO SAY, THE BATTLE PREPARATIONS HAD PUT MOST OF THE KIDS IN A PANIC.
BUT JAMILLA HANDLED IT ALL SO WELL. SHE ORGANIZED A SMALL MEMORIAL TO HONOR MARITZA, WHICH ALSO SERVED TO KEEP THE KIDS CALM AND FOCUSED.
MARITZA GUTIERREZ WAS MORE THAN JUST A VALUABLE MEMBER OF OUR RESISTANCE, SHE WAS OUR FRIEND. HER SHARP INTELLECT WAS ONLY SURPASSED BY HER KIND HEART.
A HEART THAT STOPPED BEATING AT THE HANDS OF THE ONE WHO IS THE ONE. A HEART THAT WAS ROBBED OF LIFE, LOVE, JOY, AND ENDLESS POTENTIAL.
BUT A HEART THAT WILL LIVE ON FOREVER, IN OUR HEARTS.
MANAGER
GONE BUT NEVER FORGOTTEN
WE MISS YOU RAUL
I LOVE YOU BROTHER
WE'LL MISS YOU, MARITZA. WHICH IS WHY WE'LL NEVER STOP FIGHTING THE NEW ORDER UNTIL THERE'S JUSTICE FOR YOU, AND ALL OUR LOST FRIENDS.
NOW, I NEED EVERYONE WITH MAGICAL ABILITIES TO MEET UP ON THE ROOF TO HELP WHIT AND WISTY WITH A CRUCIAL SPELL.
THE REST OF YOU, FIND ANYTHING THAT CAN BE USED AS A WEAPON AND ASSEMBLE BY THE LOADING DOCKS.
WELL, HERE WE GO. I SURE HOPE IT WORKS.
ME TOO.

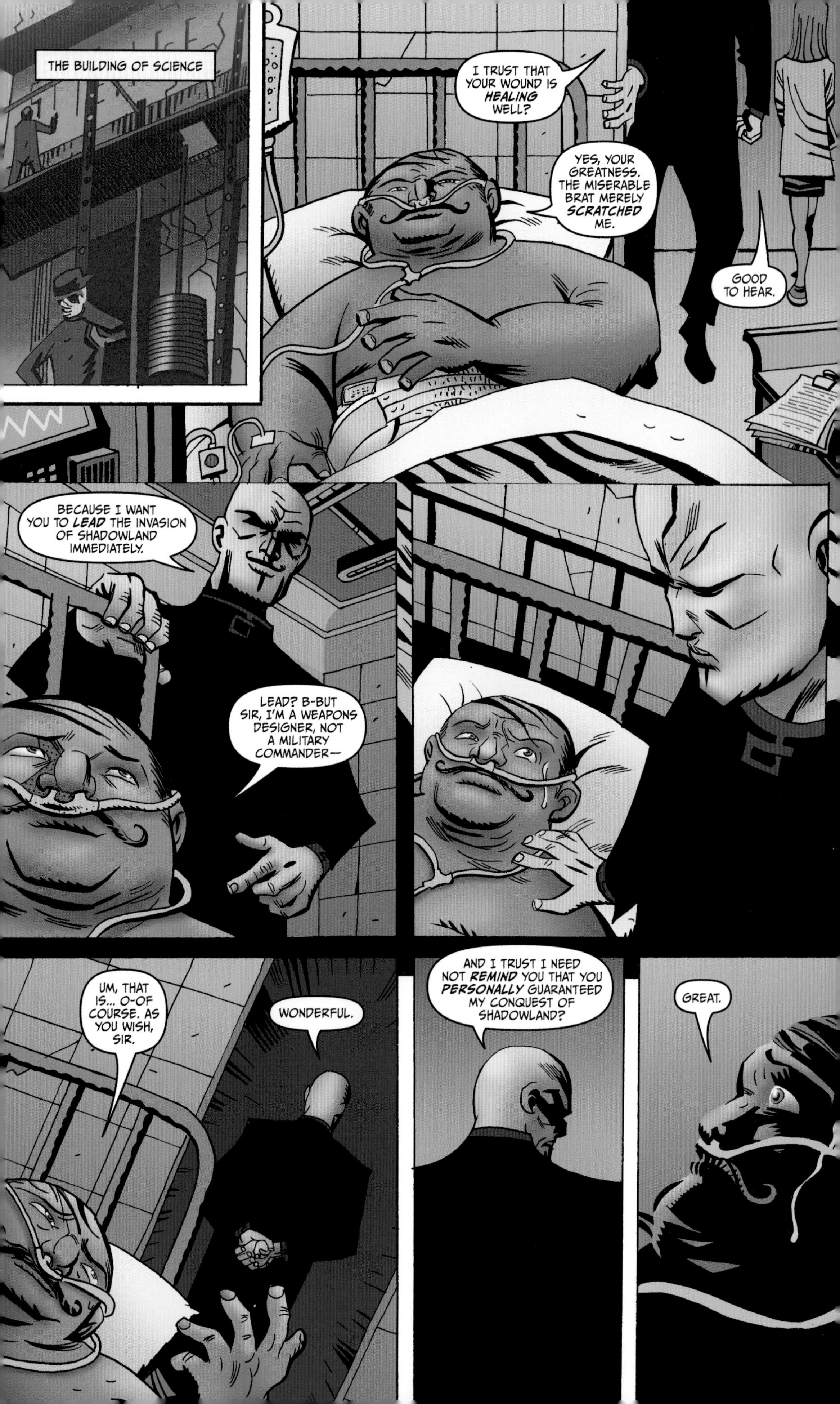

THE BUILDING OF SCIENCE
I TRUST THAT YOUR WOUND IS HEALING WELL?
YES, YOUR GREATNESS. THE MISERABLE BRAT MERELY SCRATCHED ME.
GOOD TO HEAR.
BECAUSE I WANT YOU TO LEAD THE INVASION OF SHADOWLAND IMMEDIATELY.
LEAD? B-BUT SIR, I'M A WEAPONS DESIGNER, NOT A MILITARY COMMANDER—
UM, THAT IS... O-OF COURSE. AS YOU WISH, SIR.
WONDERFUL.
AND I TRUST I NEED NOT REMIND YOU THAT YOU PERSONALLY GUARANTEED MY CONQUEST OF SHADOWLAND?
GREAT.

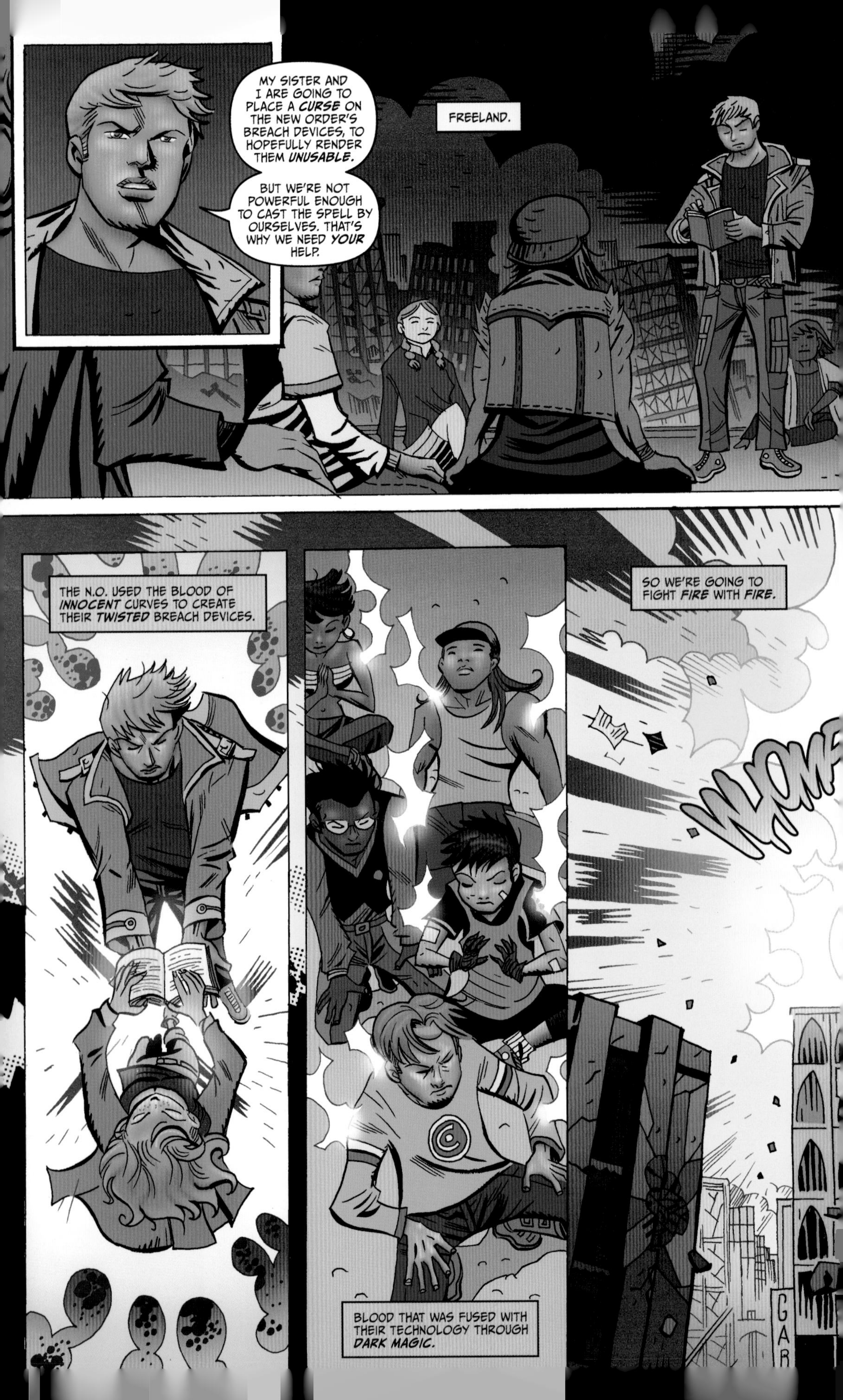
MY SISTER AND I ARE GOING TO PLACE A *CURSE* ON THE NEW ORDER'S BREACH DEVICES, TO HOPEFULLY RENDER THEM *UNUSABLE.*
BUT WE'RE NOT POWERFUL ENOUGH TO CAST THE SPELL BY OURSELVES. THAT'S WHY WE NEED *YOUR* HELP.
FREELAND.
THE N.O. USED THE BLOOD OF *INNOCENT* CURVES TO CREATE THEIR *TWISTED* BREACH DEVICES.
BLOOD THAT WAS FUSED WITH THEIR TECHNOLOGY THROUGH *DARK MAGIC.*
SO WE'RE GOING TO FIGHT *FIRE* WITH *FIRE.*

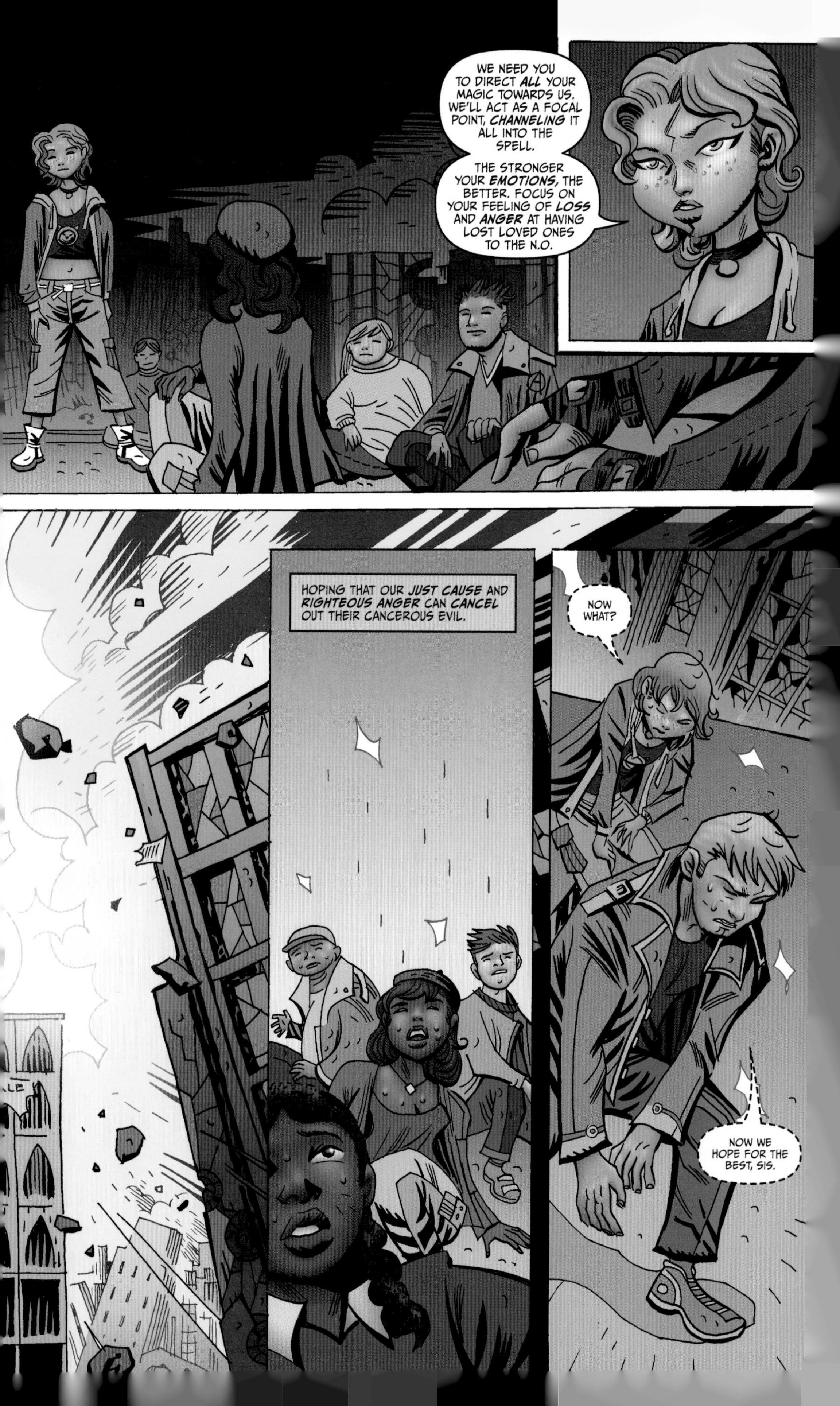
WE NEED YOU TO DIRECT ALL YOUR MAGIC TOWARDS US. WE'LL ACT AS A FOCAL POINT, CHANNELING IT ALL INTO THE SPELL.
THE STRONGER YOUR EMOTIONS, THE BETTER. FOCUS ON YOUR FEELING OF LOSS AND ANGER AT HAVING LOST LOVED ONES TO THE N.O.
HOPING THAT OUR JUST CAUSE AND RIGHTEOUS ANGER CAN CANCEL OUT THEIR CANCEROUS EVIL.
NOW WHAT?
NOW WE HOPE FOR THE BEST, SIS.

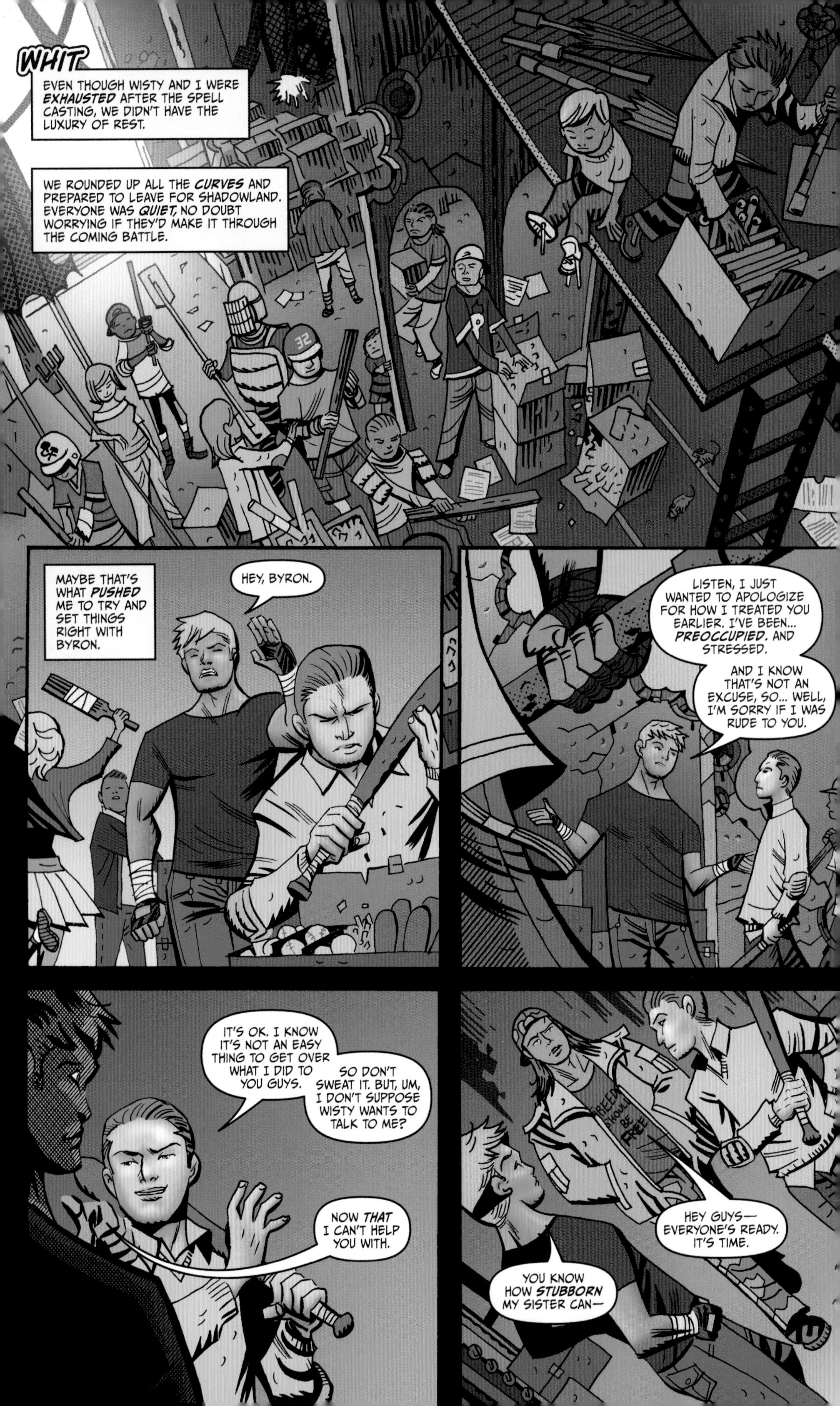
WHIT
EVEN THOUGH WISTY AND I WERE EXHAUSTED AFTER THE SPELL CASTING, WE DIDN'T HAVE THE LUXURY OF REST.
WE ROUNDED UP ALL THE CURVES AND PREPARED TO LEAVE FOR SHADOWLAND. EVERYONE WAS QUIET, NO DOUBT WORRYING IF THEY'D MAKE IT THROUGH THE COMING BATTLE.
MAYBE THAT'S WHAT PUSHED ME TO TRY AND SET THINGS RIGHT WITH BYRON.
HEY, BYRON.
LISTEN, I JUST WANTED TO APOLOGIZE FOR HOW I TREATED YOU EARLIER. I'VE BEEN... PREOCCUPIED. AND STRESSED.
AND I KNOW THAT'S NOT AN EXCUSE, SO... WELL, I'M SORRY IF I WAS RUDE TO YOU.
IT'S OK. I KNOW IT'S NOT AN EASY THING TO GET OVER WHAT I DID TO YOU GUYS.
SO DON'T SWEAT IT. BUT, UM, I DON'T SUPPOSE WISTY WANTS TO TALK TO ME?
NOW THAT I CAN'T HELP YOU WITH.
YOU KNOW HOW STUBBORN MY SISTER CAN—
HEY GUYS— EVERYONE'S READY. IT'S TIME.
FREEDOM SHOULD BE FREE

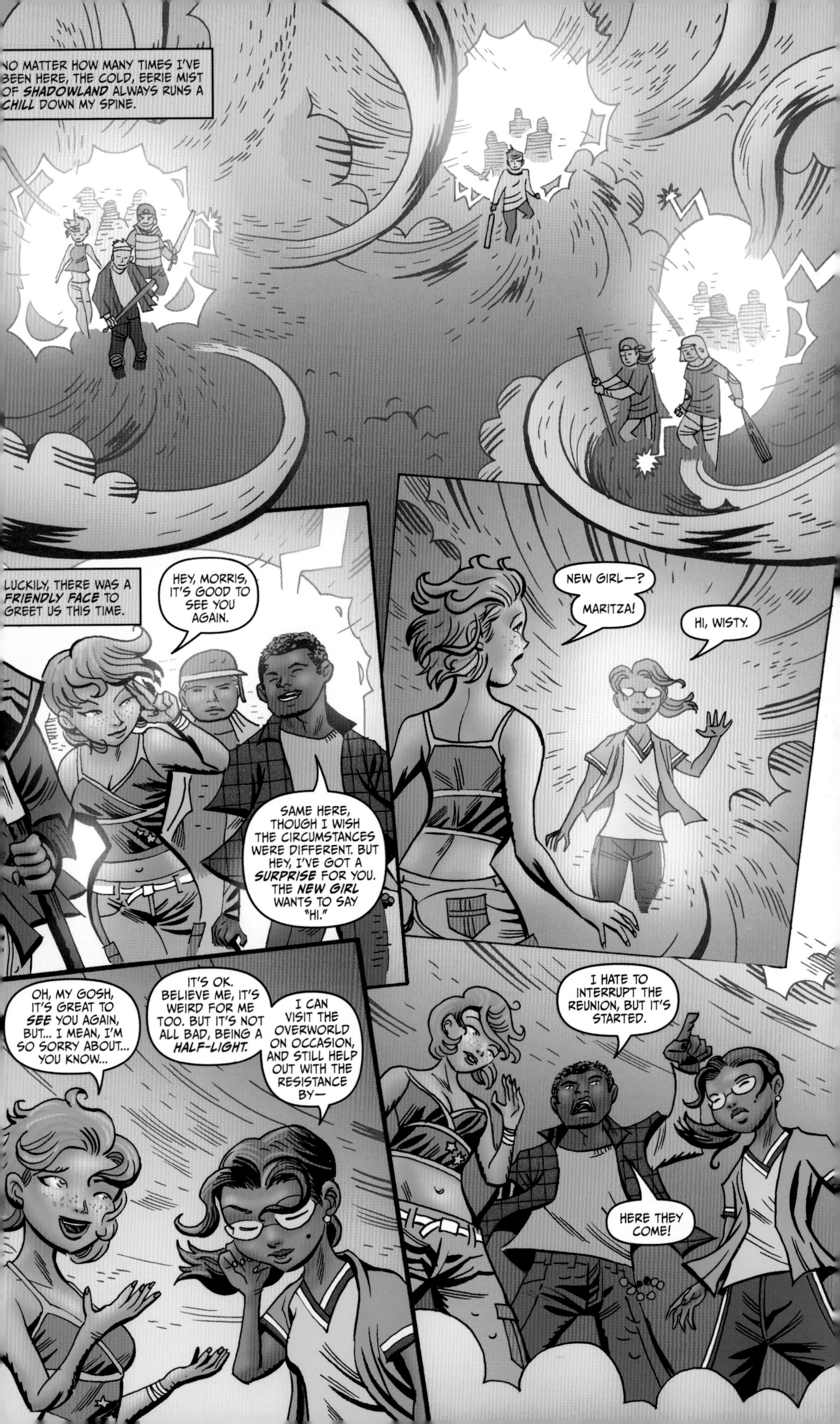
NO MATTER HOW MANY TIMES I'VE BEEN HERE, THE COLD, EERIE MIST OF SHADOWLAND ALWAYS RUNS A CHILL DOWN MY SPINE.
LUCKILY, THERE WAS A FRIENDLY FACE TO GREET US THIS TIME.
HEY, MORRIS, IT'S GOOD TO SEE YOU AGAIN.
SAME HERE, THOUGH I WISH THE CIRCUMSTANCES WERE DIFFERENT. BUT HEY, I'VE GOT A SURPRISE FOR YOU. THE NEW GIRL WANTS TO SAY "HI."
NEW GIRL—? MARITZA!
HI, WISTY.
OH, MY GOSH, IT'S GREAT TO SEE YOU AGAIN, BUT... I MEAN, I'M SO SORRY ABOUT... YOU KNOW...
IT'S OK. BELIEVE ME, IT'S WEIRD FOR ME TOO. BUT IT'S NOT ALL BAD, BEING A HALF-LIGHT.
I CAN VISIT THE OVERWORLD ON OCCASION, AND STILL HELP OUT WITH THE RESISTANCE BY—
I HATE TO INTERRUPT THE REUNION, BUT IT'S STARTED.
HERE THEY COME!

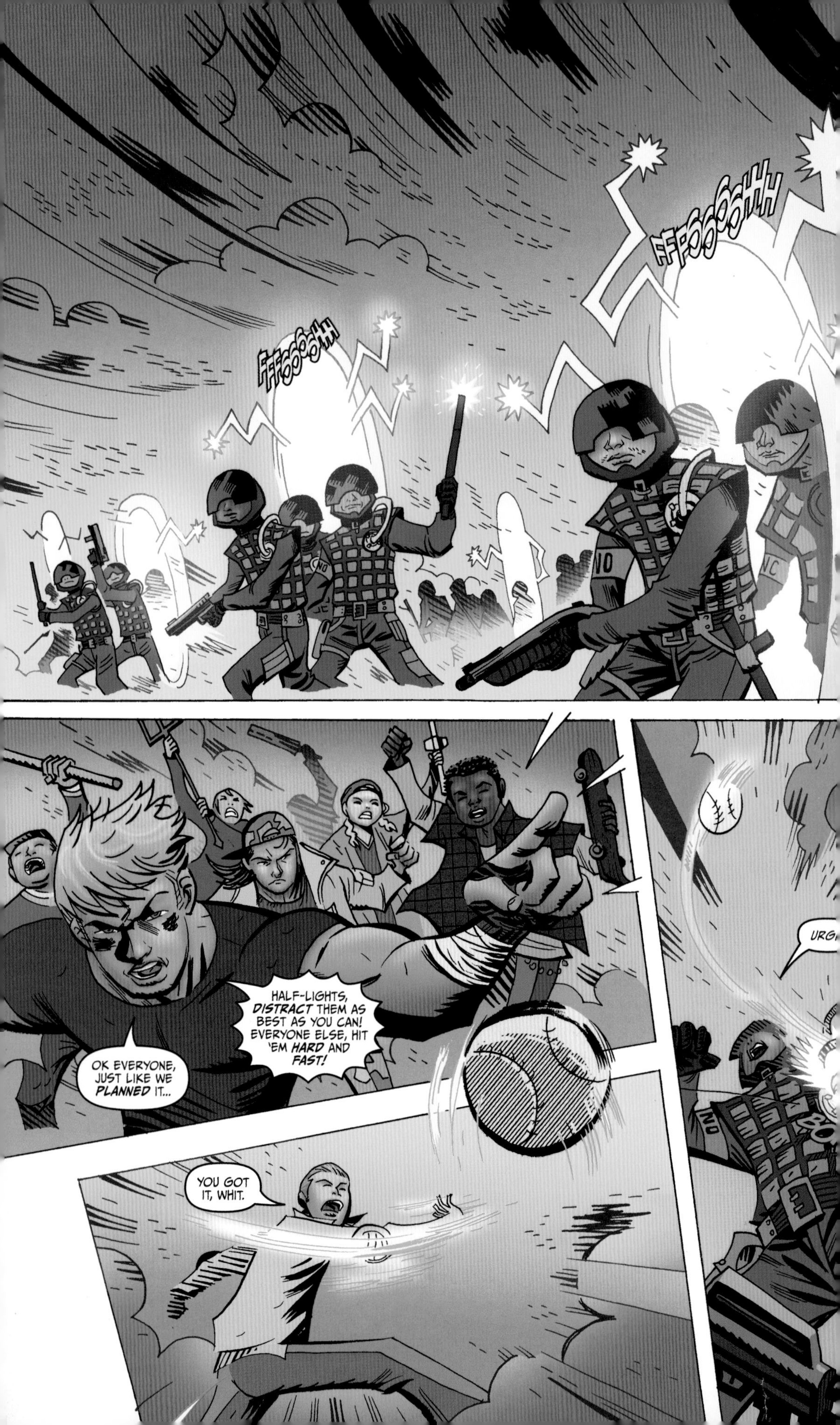
FFFSSSSHHH
FFFSSSSHHH
OK EVERYONE, JUST LIKE WE PLANNED IT...
HALF-LIGHTS, DISTRACT THEM AS BEST AS YOU CAN! EVERYONE ELSE, HIT 'EM HARD AND FAST!
YOU GOT IT, WHIT.
URG

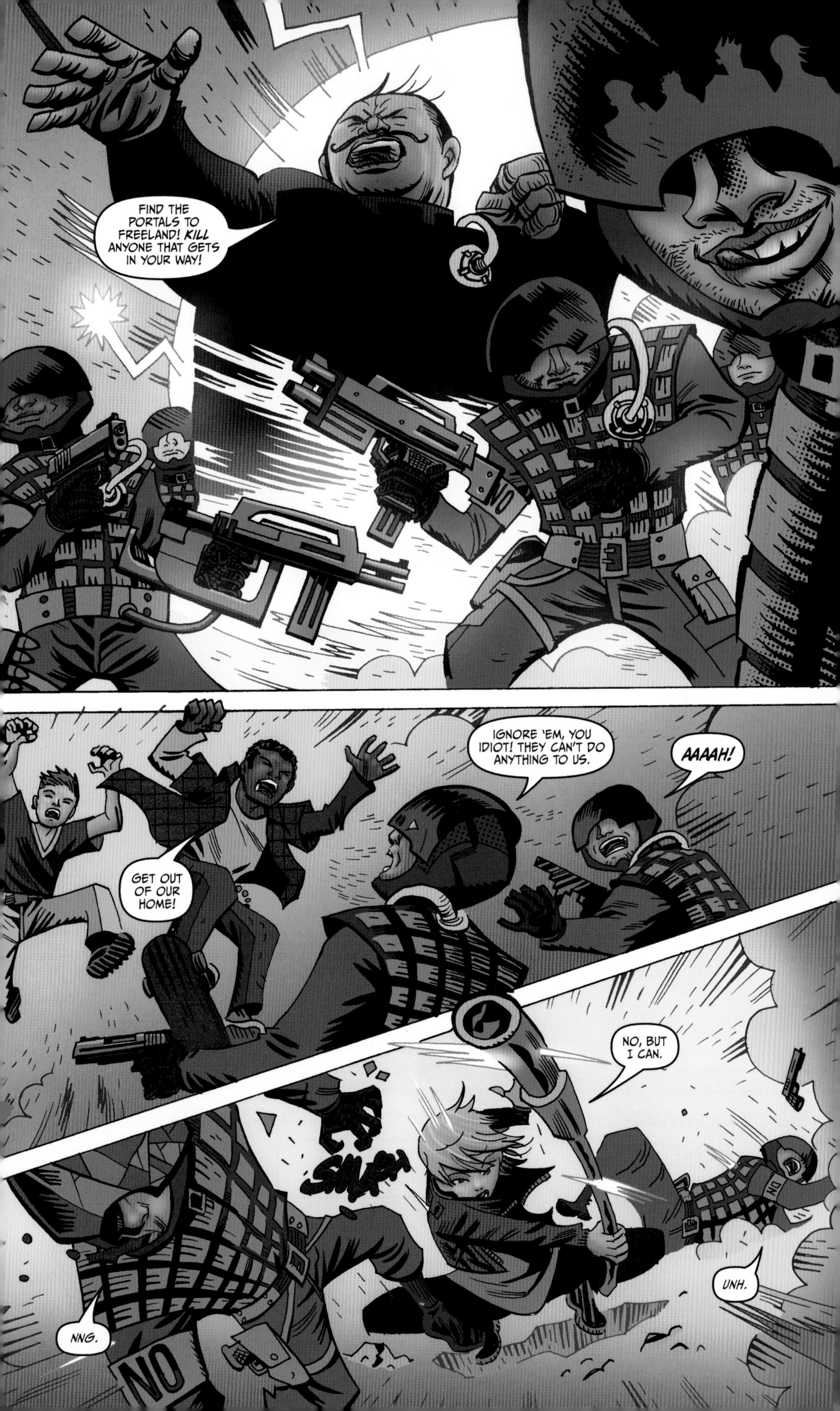

FIND THE PORTALS TO FREELAND! KILL ANYONE THAT GETS IN YOUR WAY!
GET OUT OF OUR HOME!
IGNORE 'EM, YOU IDIOT! THEY CAN'T DO ANYTHING TO US.
AAAAH!
NO, BUT I CAN.
NNG.
UNH.

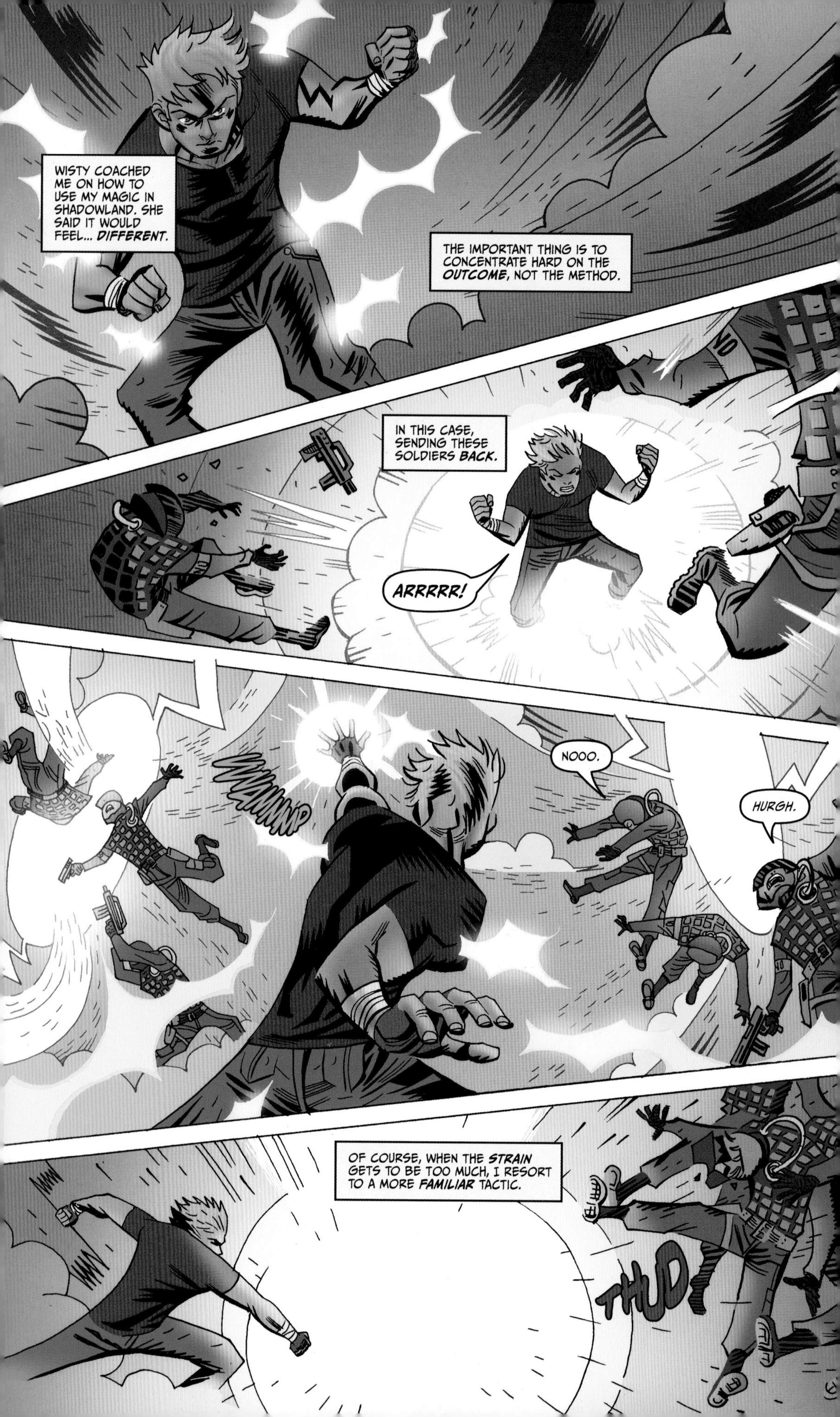

WISTY COACHED ME ON HOW TO USE MY MAGIC IN SHADOWLAND. SHE SAID IT WOULD FEEL... *DIFFERENT*.
THE IMPORTANT THING IS TO CONCENTRATE HARD ON THE *OUTCOME*, NOT THE METHOD.
IN THIS CASE, SENDING THESE SOLDIERS *BACK*.
ARRRRR!
WHAAAAMP
NOOO.
HURGH.
OF COURSE, WHEN THE *STRAIN* GETS TO BE TOO MUCH, I RESORT TO A MORE *FAMILIAR* TACTIC.
THUD

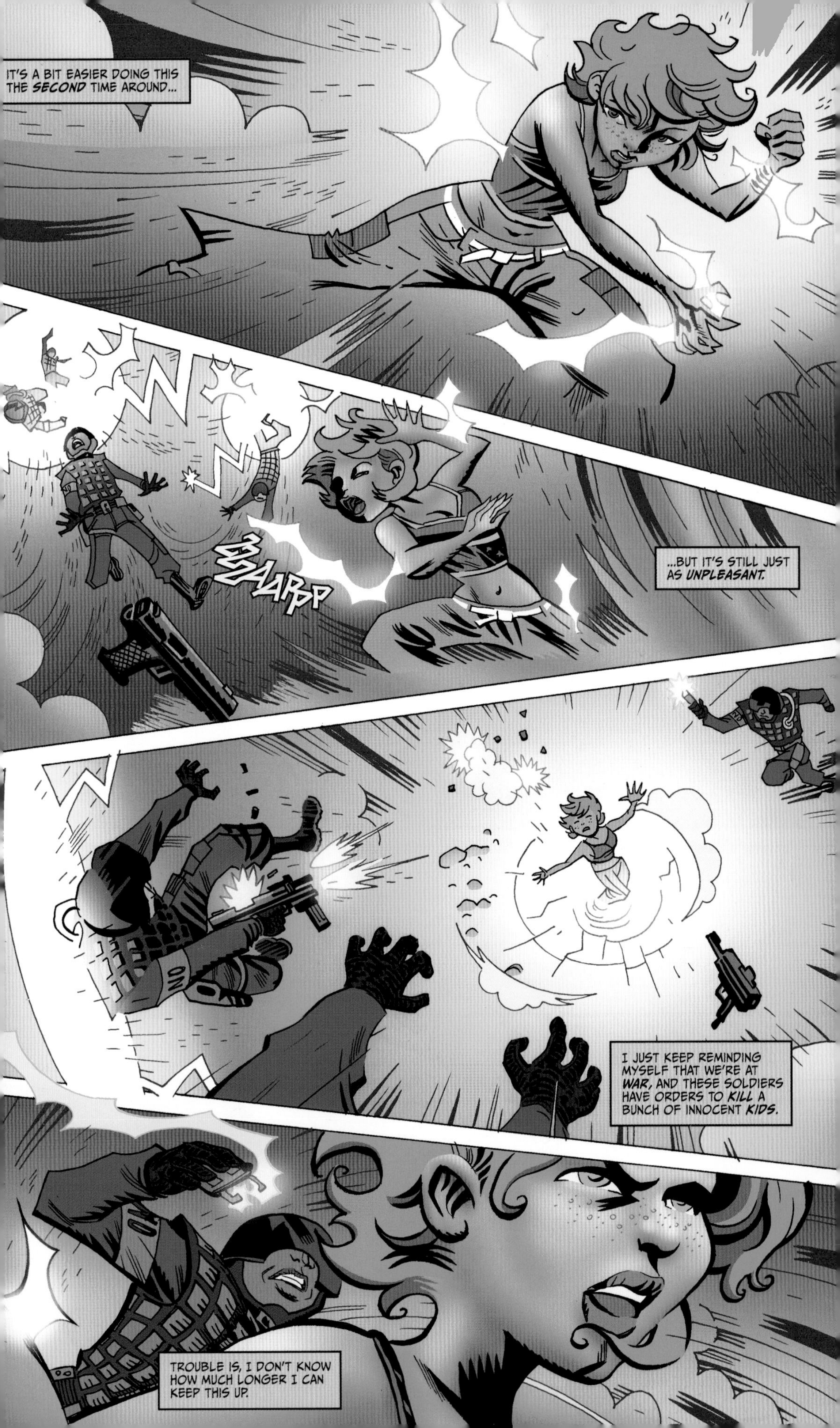
IT'S A BIT EASIER DOING THIS THE *SECOND* TIME AROUND...
ZZAARPP
...BUT IT'S STILL JUST AS *UNPLEASANT.*
I JUST KEEP REMINDING MYSELF THAT WE'RE AT *WAR,* AND THESE SOLDIERS HAVE ORDERS TO *KILL* A BUNCH OF INNOCENT *KIDS.*
TROUBLE IS, I DON'T KNOW HOW MUCH LONGER I CAN KEEP THIS UP.

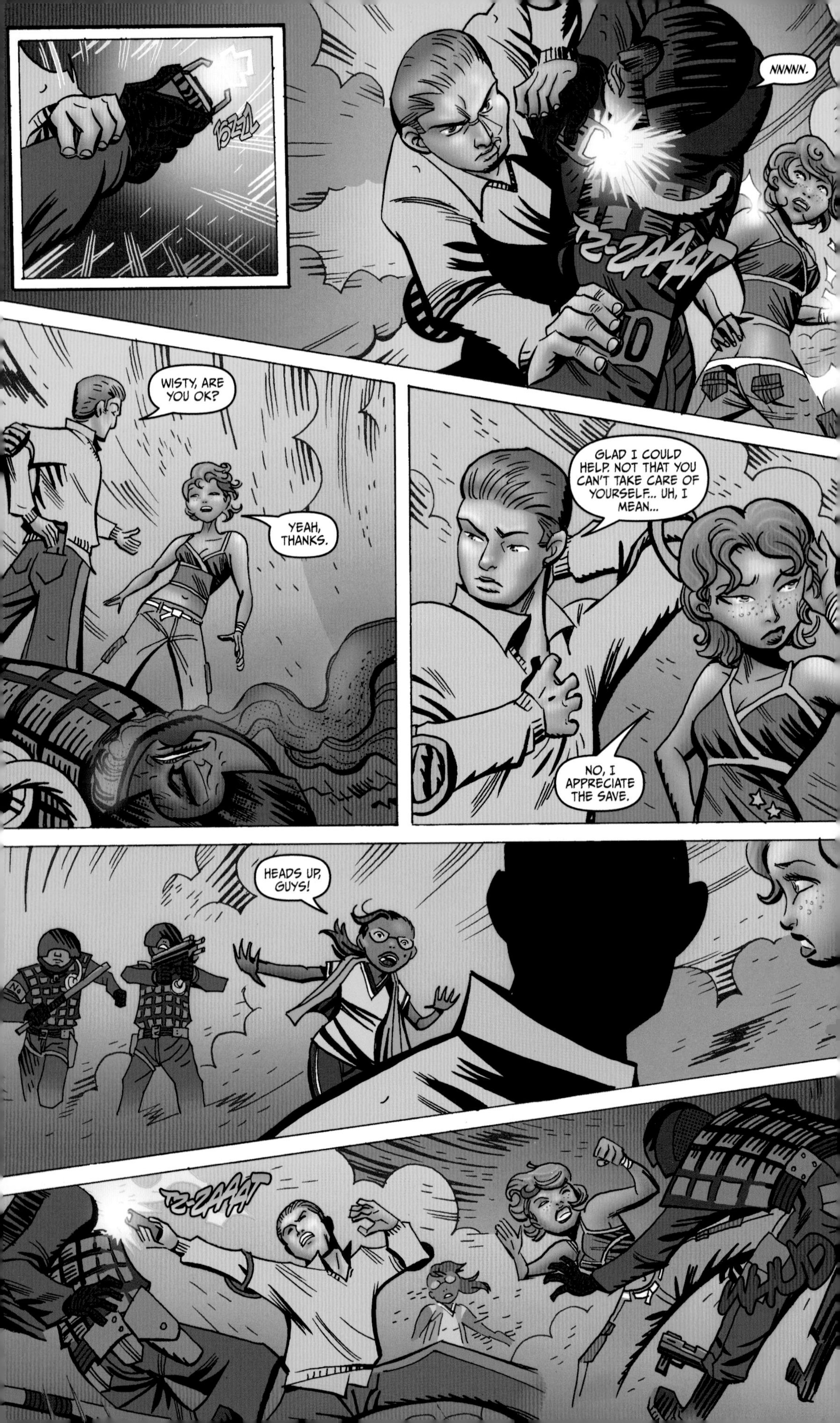

ISZZZ
NNNNN.
TZ-ZAAAT
WISTY, ARE YOU OK?
YEAH, THANKS.
GLAD I COULD HELP. NOT THAT YOU CAN'T TAKE CARE OF YOURSELF... UH, I MEAN...
NO, I APPRECIATE THE SAVE.
HEADS UP, GUYS!
TZ-ZAAAT
WHUD

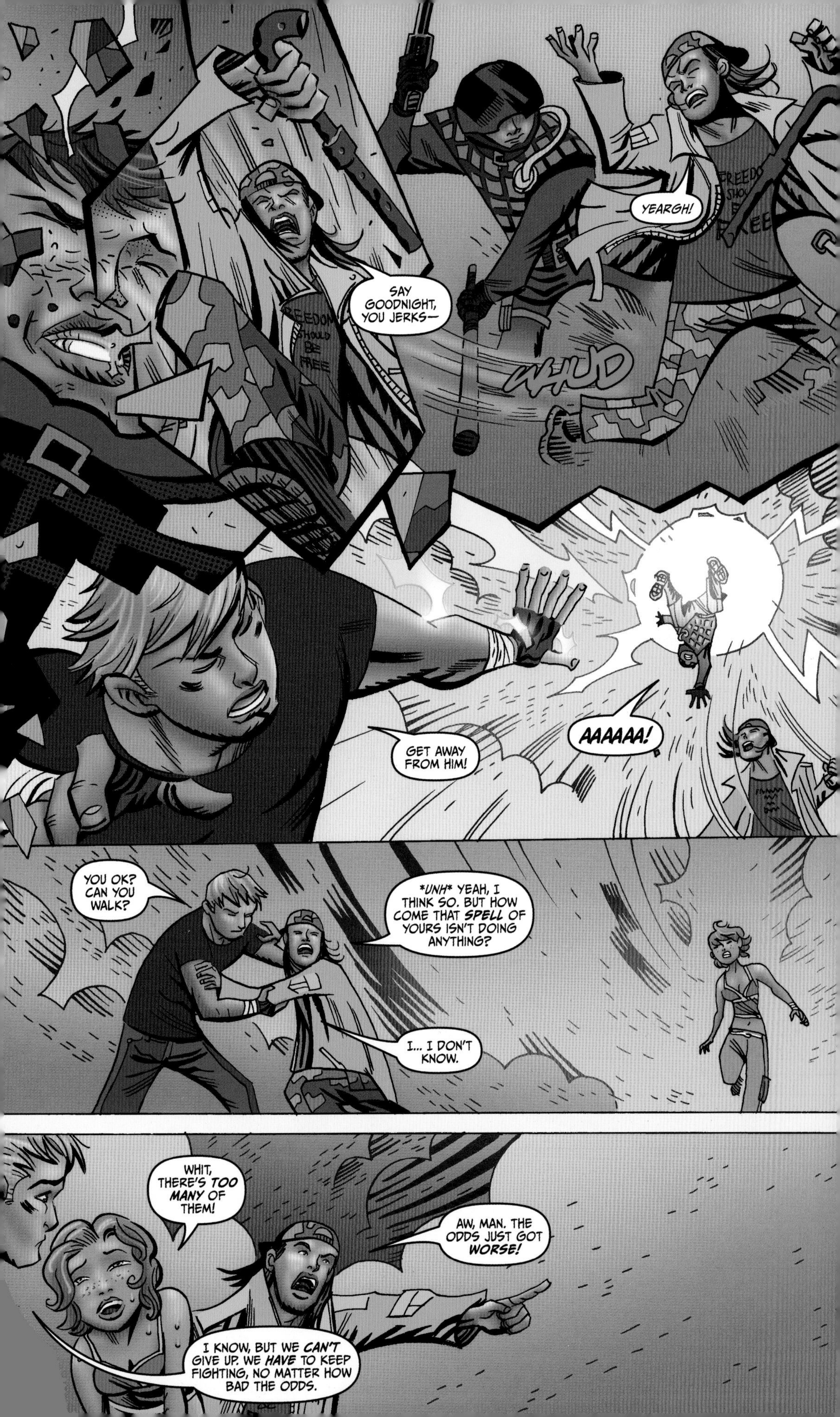

YEARGH!
SAY GOODNIGHT, YOU JERKS—
WHUD
FREEDOM SHOULD BE FREE
GET AWAY FROM HIM!
AAAAAA!
YOU OK? CAN YOU WALK?
UNH YEAH, I THINK SO. BUT HOW COME THAT SPELL OF YOURS ISN'T DOING ANYTHING?
I... I DON'T KNOW.
WHIT, THERE'S TOO MANY OF THEM!
AW, MAN. THE ODDS JUST GOT WORSE!
I KNOW, BUT WE CAN'T GIVE UP. WE HAVE TO KEEP FIGHTING, NO MATTER HOW BAD THE ODDS.

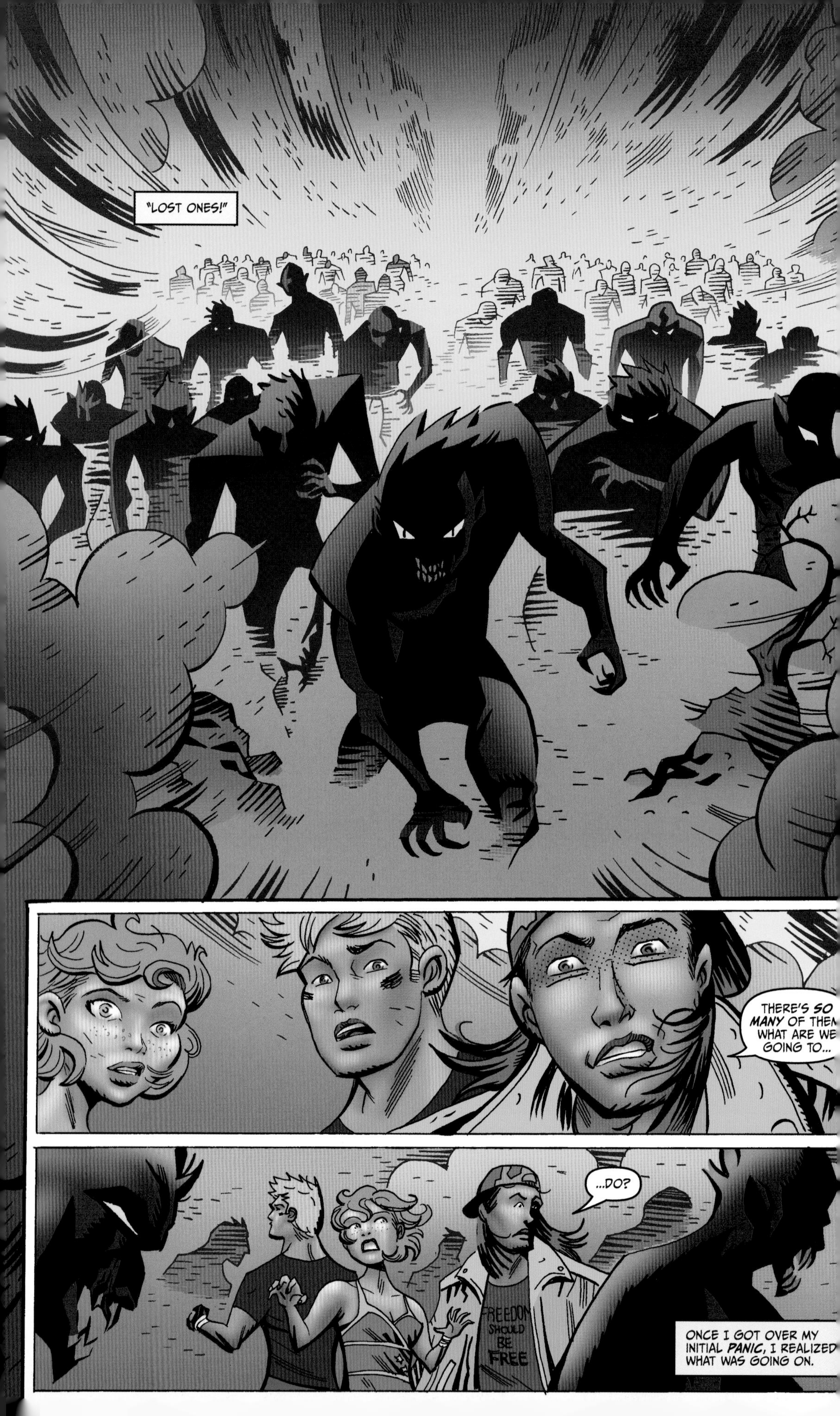
"LOST ONES!"
THERE'S SO MANY OF THEM WHAT ARE WE GOING TO...
...DO?
ONCE I GOT OVER MY INITIAL PANIC, I REALIZED WHAT WAS GOING ON.
FREEDOM SHOULD BE FREE

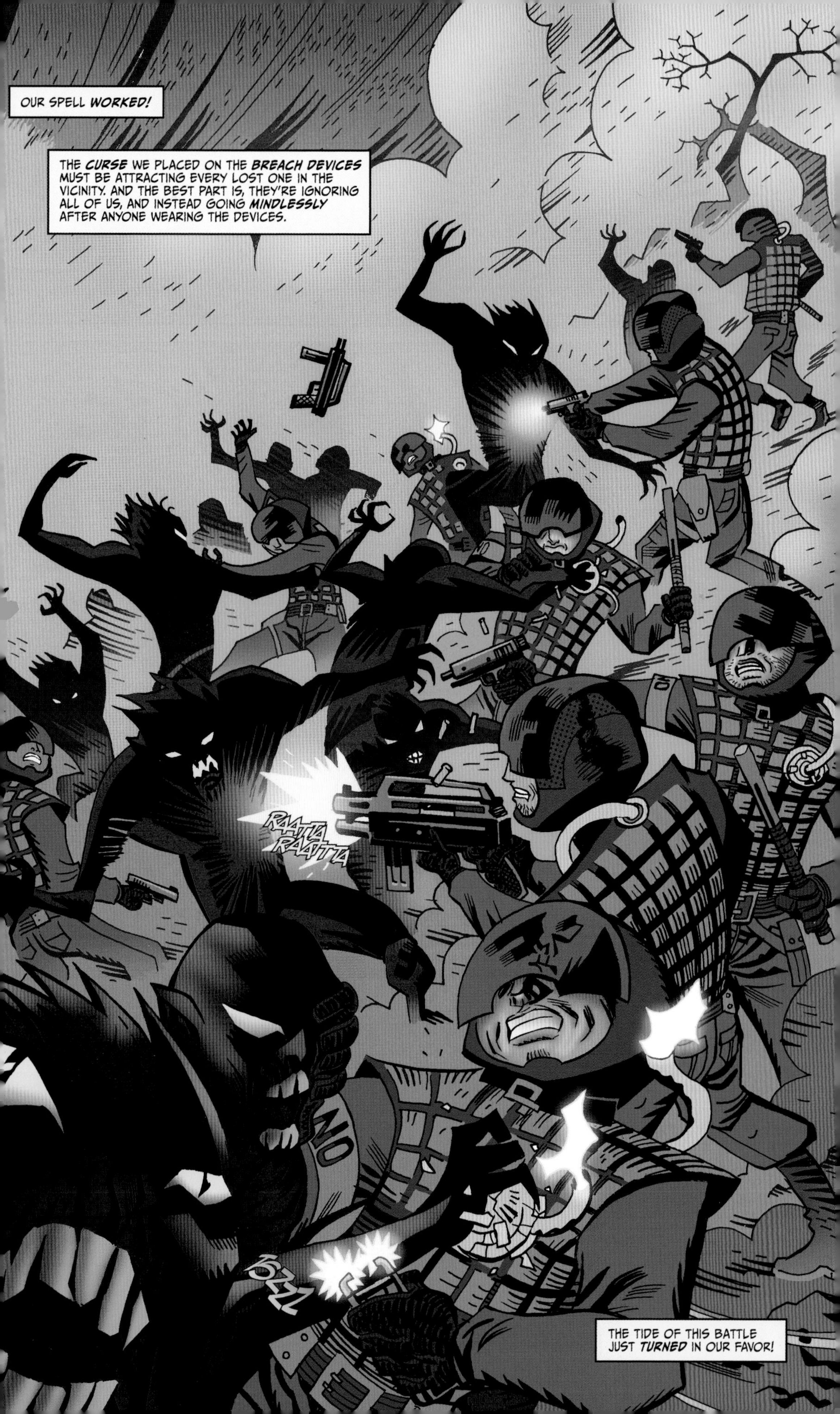
OUR SPELL **WORKED!**
THE **CURSE** WE PLACED ON THE **BREACH DEVICES** MUST BE ATTRACTING EVERY LOST ONE IN THE VICINITY. AND THE BEST PART IS, THEY'RE IGNORING ALL OF US, AND INSTEAD GOING **MINDLESSLY** AFTER ANYONE WEARING THE DEVICES.
RAATTA RAATTA
ZZZT
THE TIDE OF THIS BATTLE JUST **TURNED** IN OUR FAVOR!

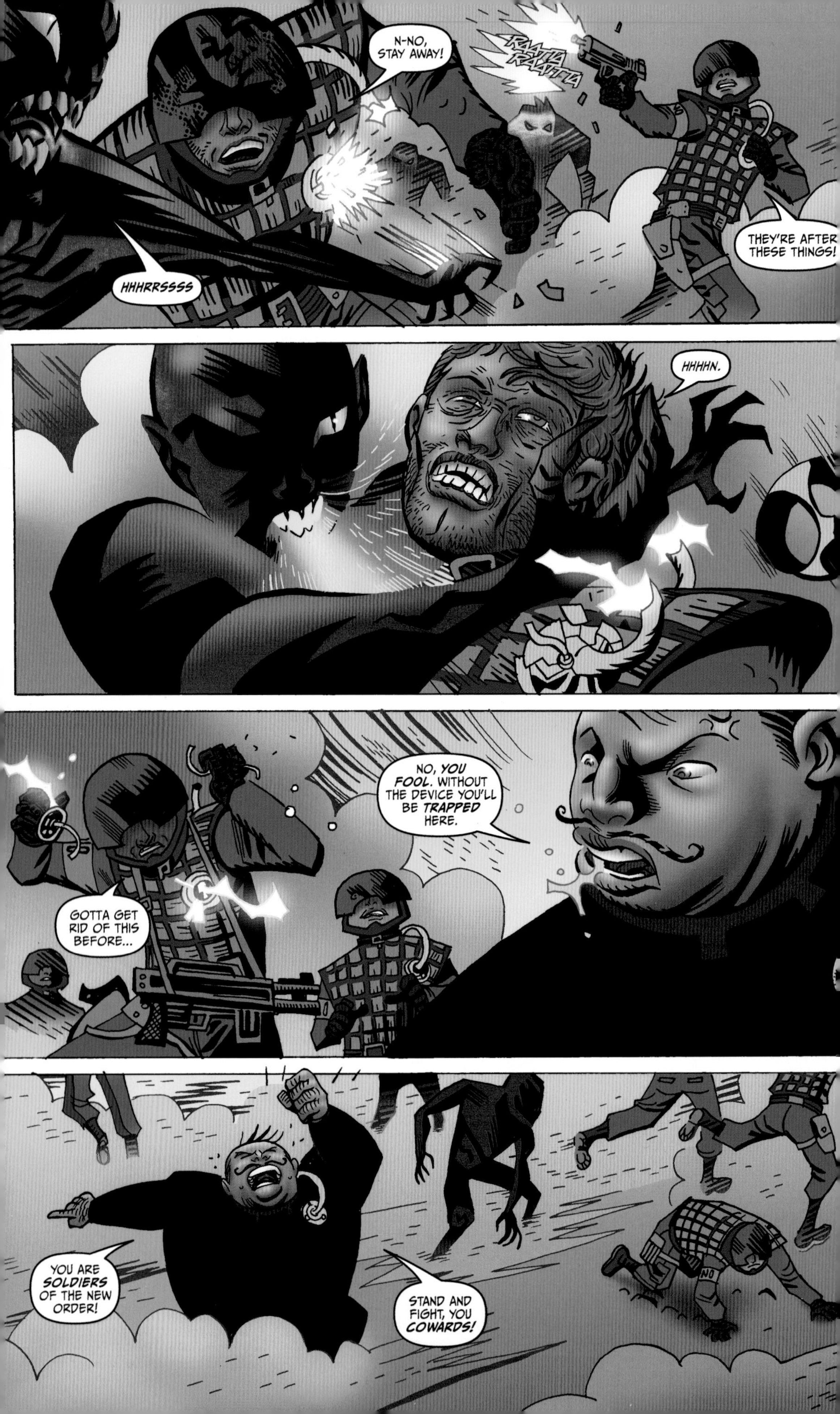
N-NO, STAY AWAY!
RAATTA RAATTA
THEY'RE AFTER THESE THINGS!
HHHRRSSSS
HHHHN.
NO, *YOU FOOL*. WITHOUT THE DEVICE YOU'LL BE *TRAPPED* HERE.
GOTTA GET RID OF THIS BEFORE...
YOU ARE *SOLDIERS* OF THE NEW ORDER!
STAND AND FIGHT, YOU *COWARDS!*

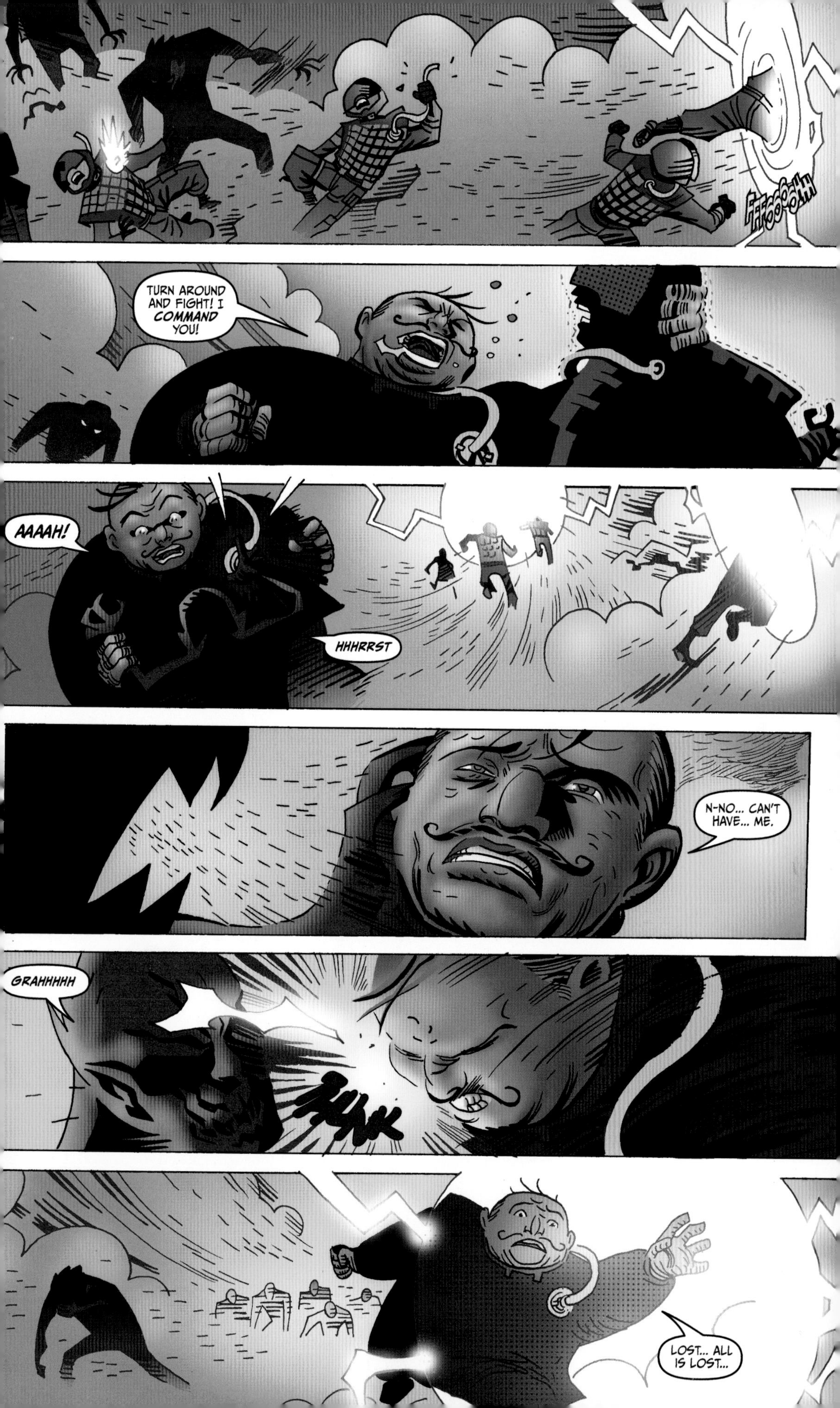
FFFSSSSHH
TURN AROUND AND FIGHT! I **COMMAND** YOU!
AAAAH!
HHHRRST
N-NO... CAN'T HAVE... ME.
GRAHHHHH
LOST... ALL IS LOST...

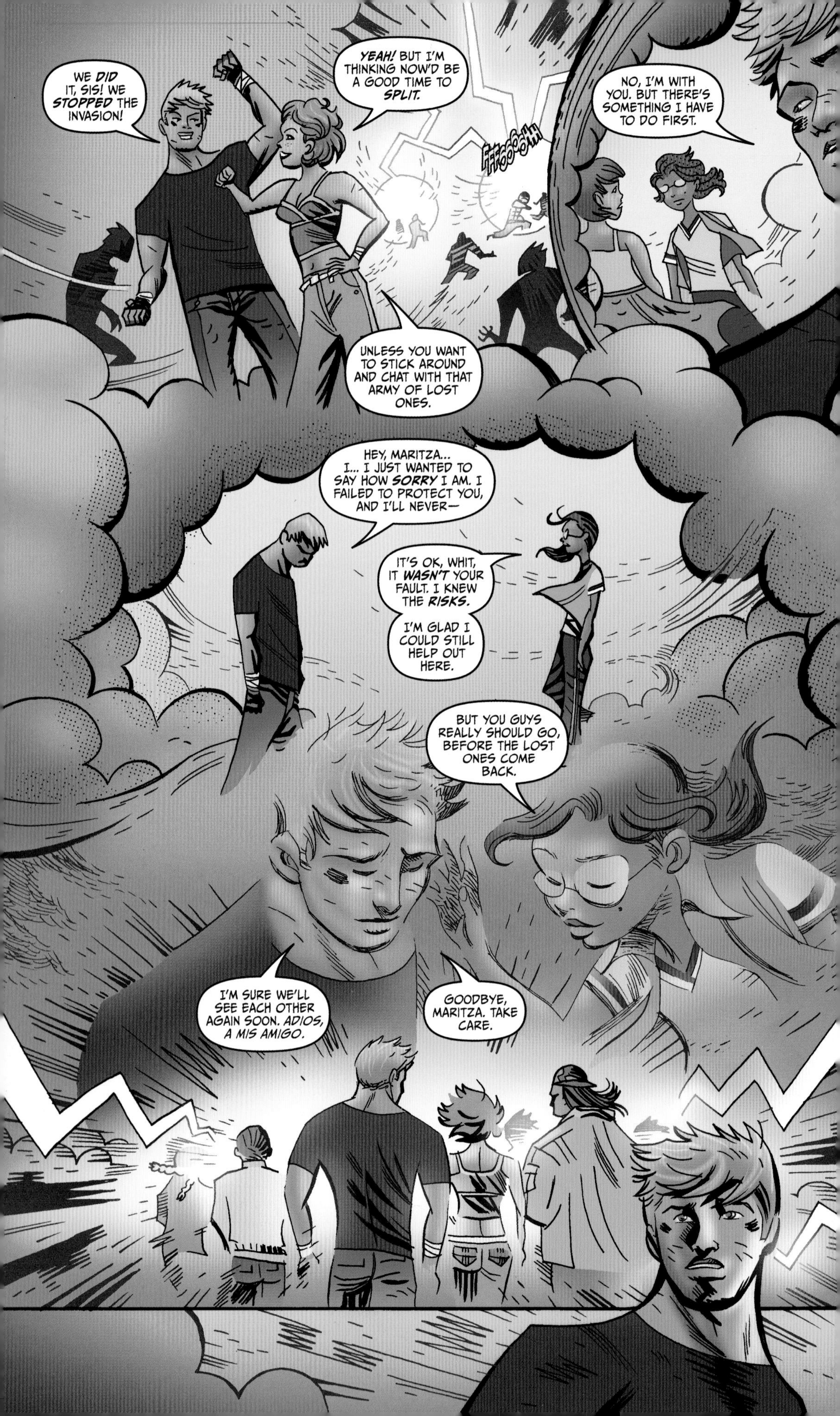
WE DID IT, SIS! WE STOPPED THE INVASION!
YEAH! BUT I'M THINKING NOW'D BE A GOOD TIME TO SPLIT.
FFFSSSSHH
NO, I'M WITH YOU. BUT THERE'S SOMETHING I HAVE TO DO FIRST.
UNLESS YOU WANT TO STICK AROUND AND CHAT WITH THAT ARMY OF LOST ONES.
HEY, MARITZA... I... I JUST WANTED TO SAY HOW SORRY I AM. I FAILED TO PROTECT YOU, AND I'LL NEVER—
IT'S OK, WHIT, IT WASN'T YOUR FAULT. I KNEW THE RISKS.
I'M GLAD I COULD STILL HELP OUT HERE.
BUT YOU GUYS REALLY SHOULD GO, BEFORE THE LOST ONES COME BACK.
I'M SURE WE'LL SEE EACH OTHER AGAIN SOON. ADIOS, A MIS AMIGO.
GOODBYE, MARITZA. TAKE CARE.

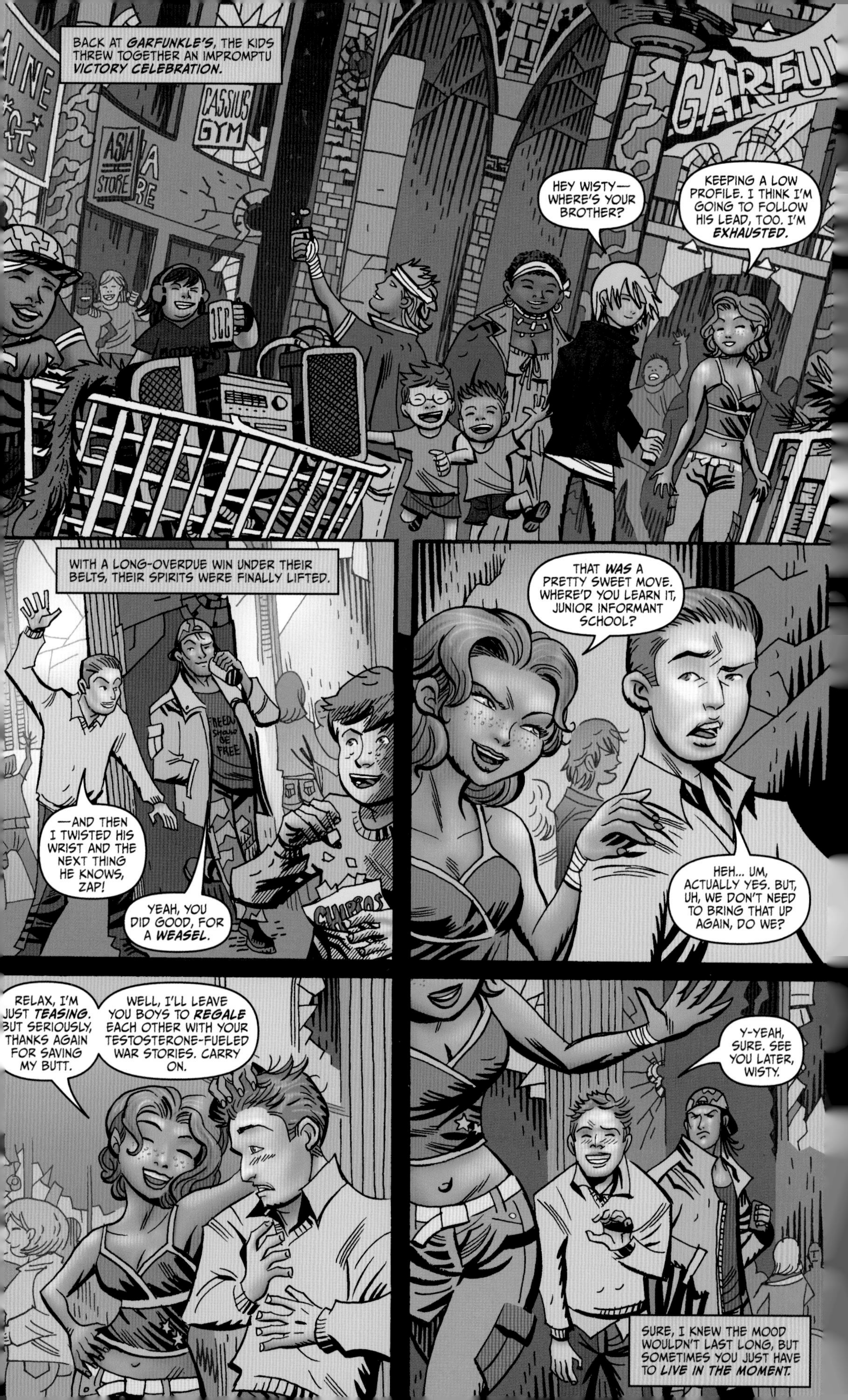
BACK AT GARFUNKLE'S, THE KIDS THREW TOGETHER AN IMPROMPTU VICTORY CELEBRATION.
CASSIUS GYM
ASIA STORE
GARFU
HEY WISTY— WHERE'S YOUR BROTHER?
KEEPING A LOW PROFILE. I THINK I'M GOING TO FOLLOW HIS LEAD, TOO. I'M EXHAUSTED.
WITH A LONG-OVERDUE WIN UNDER THEIR BELTS, THEIR SPIRITS WERE FINALLY LIFTED.
—AND THEN I TWISTED HIS WRIST AND THE NEXT THING HE KNOWS, ZAP!
YEAH, YOU DID GOOD, FOR A WEASEL.
THAT WAS A PRETTY SWEET MOVE. WHERE'D YOU LEARN IT, JUNIOR INFORMANT SCHOOL?
HEH... UM, ACTUALLY YES. BUT, UH, WE DON'T NEED TO BRING THAT UP AGAIN, DO WE?
RELAX, I'M JUST TEASING. BUT SERIOUSLY, THANKS AGAIN FOR SAVING MY BUTT.
WELL, I'LL LEAVE YOU BOYS TO REGALE EACH OTHER WITH YOUR TESTOSTERONE-FUELED WAR STORIES. CARRY ON.
Y-YEAH, SURE. SEE YOU LATER, WISTY.
SURE, I KNEW THE MOOD WOULDN'T LAST LONG, BUT SOMETIMES YOU JUST HAVE TO LIVE IN THE MOMENT.

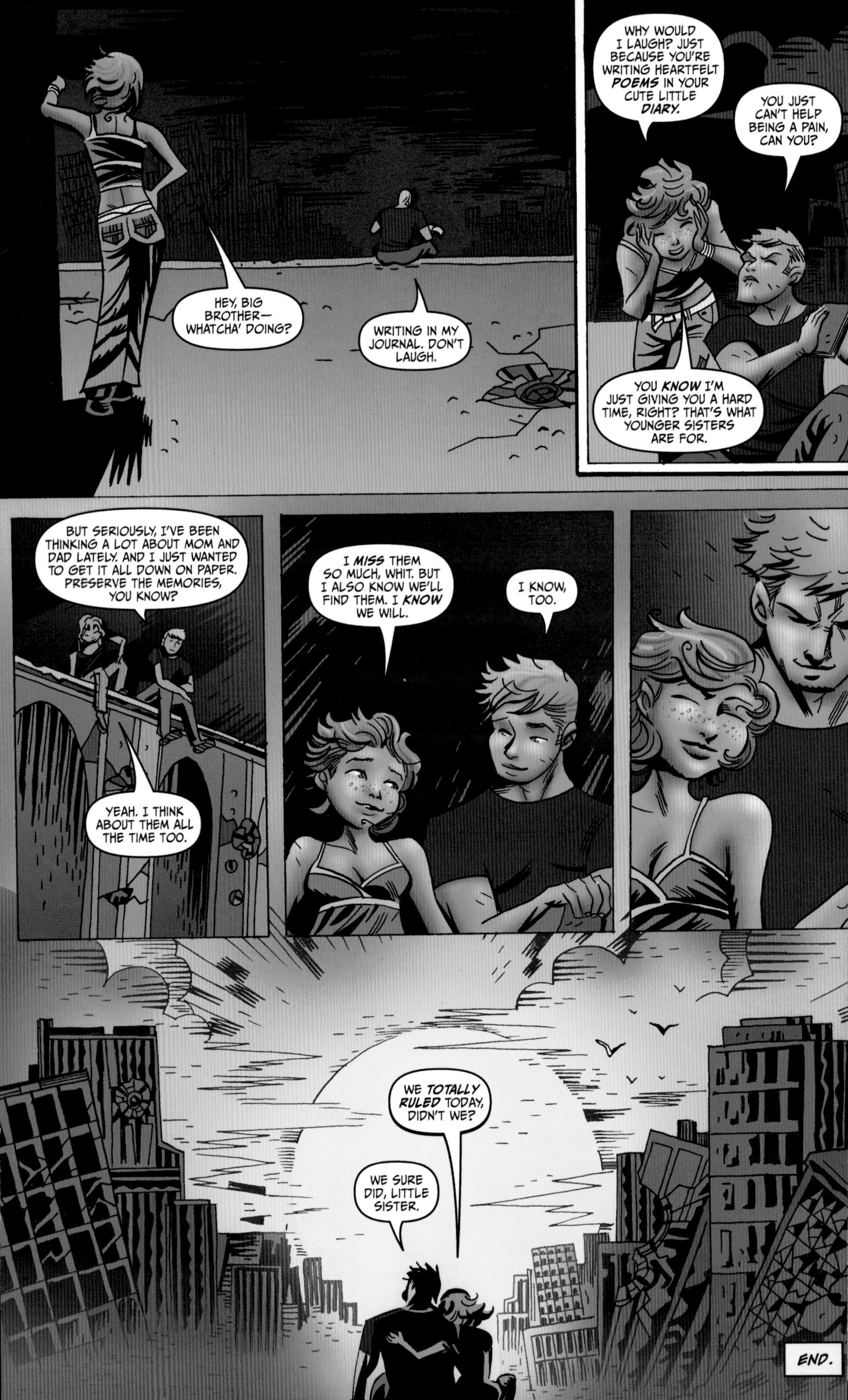
HEY, BIG BROTHER— WHATCHA' DOING?
WRITING IN MY JOURNAL. DON'T LAUGH.
WHY WOULD I LAUGH? JUST BECAUSE YOU'RE WRITING HEARTFELT POEMS IN YOUR CUTE LITTLE DIARY.
YOU JUST CAN'T HELP BEING A PAIN, CAN YOU?
YOU KNOW I'M JUST GIVING YOU A HARD TIME, RIGHT? THAT'S WHAT YOUNGER SISTERS ARE FOR.
BUT SERIOUSLY, I'VE BEEN THINKING A LOT ABOUT MOM AND DAD LATELY. AND I JUST WANTED TO GET IT ALL DOWN ON PAPER. PRESERVE THE MEMORIES, YOU KNOW?
YEAH. I THINK ABOUT THEM ALL THE TIME TOO.
I MISS THEM SO MUCH, WHIT. BUT I ALSO KNOW WE'LL FIND THEM. I KNOW WE WILL.
I KNOW, TOO.
WE TOTALLY RULED TODAY, DIDN'T WE?
WE SURE DID, LITTLE SISTER.
END.

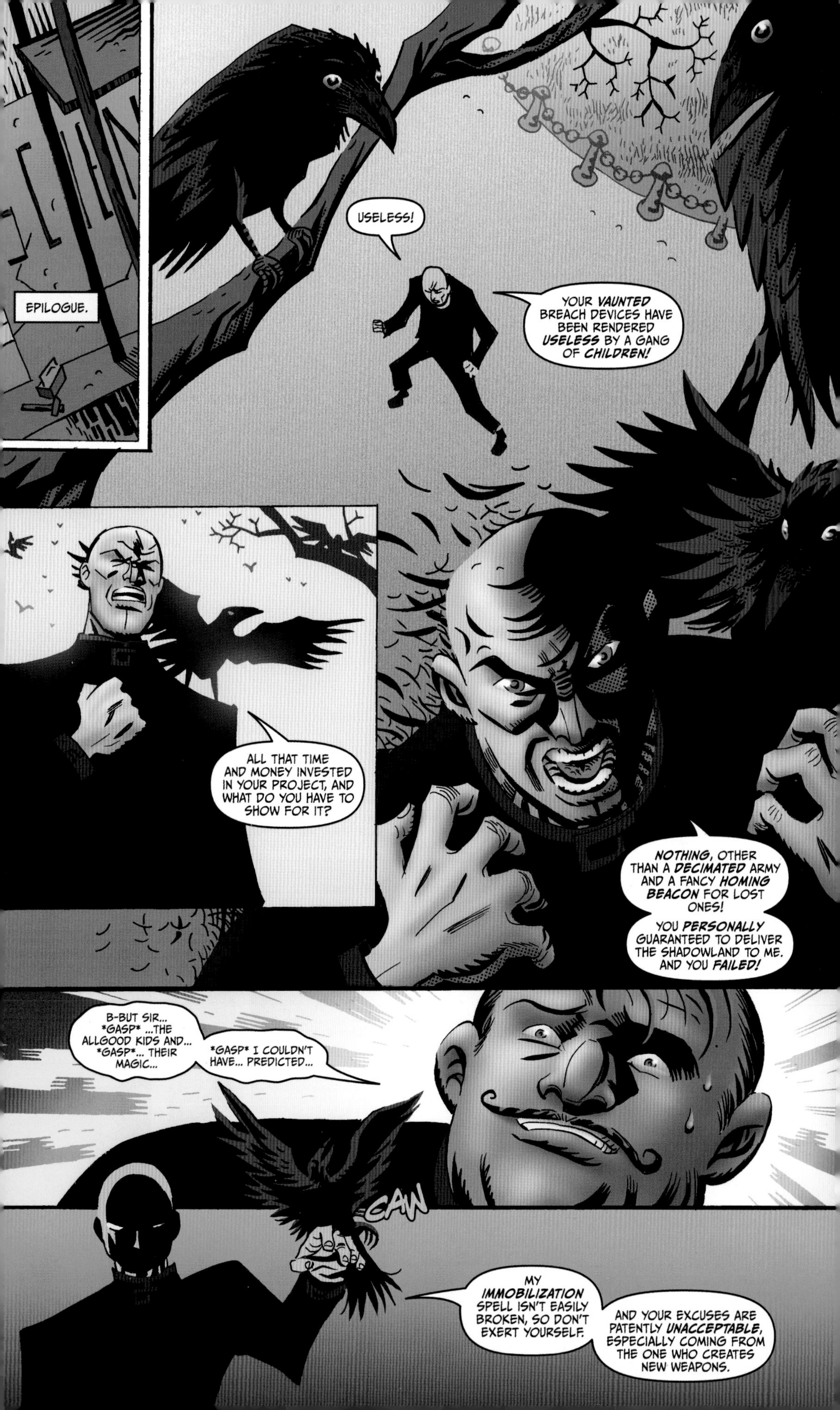
EPILOGUE.
USELESS!
YOUR VAUNTED BREACH DEVICES HAVE BEEN RENDERED USELESS BY A GANG OF CHILDREN!
ALL THAT TIME AND MONEY INVESTED IN YOUR PROJECT, AND WHAT DO YOU HAVE TO SHOW FOR IT?
NOTHING, OTHER THAN A DECIMATED ARMY AND A FANCY HOMING BEACON FOR LOST ONES!
YOU PERSONALLY GUARANTEED TO DELIVER THE SHADOWLAND TO ME. AND YOU FAILED!
B-BUT SIR... *GASP* ...THE ALLGOOD KIDS AND... *GASP*... THEIR MAGIC...
GASP I COULDN'T HAVE... PREDICTED...
CAW
MY IMMOBILIZATION SPELL ISN'T EASILY BROKEN, SO DON'T EXERT YOURSELF.
AND YOUR EXCUSES ARE PATENTLY UNACCEPTABLE, ESPECIALLY COMING FROM THE ONE WHO CREATES NEW WEAPONS.

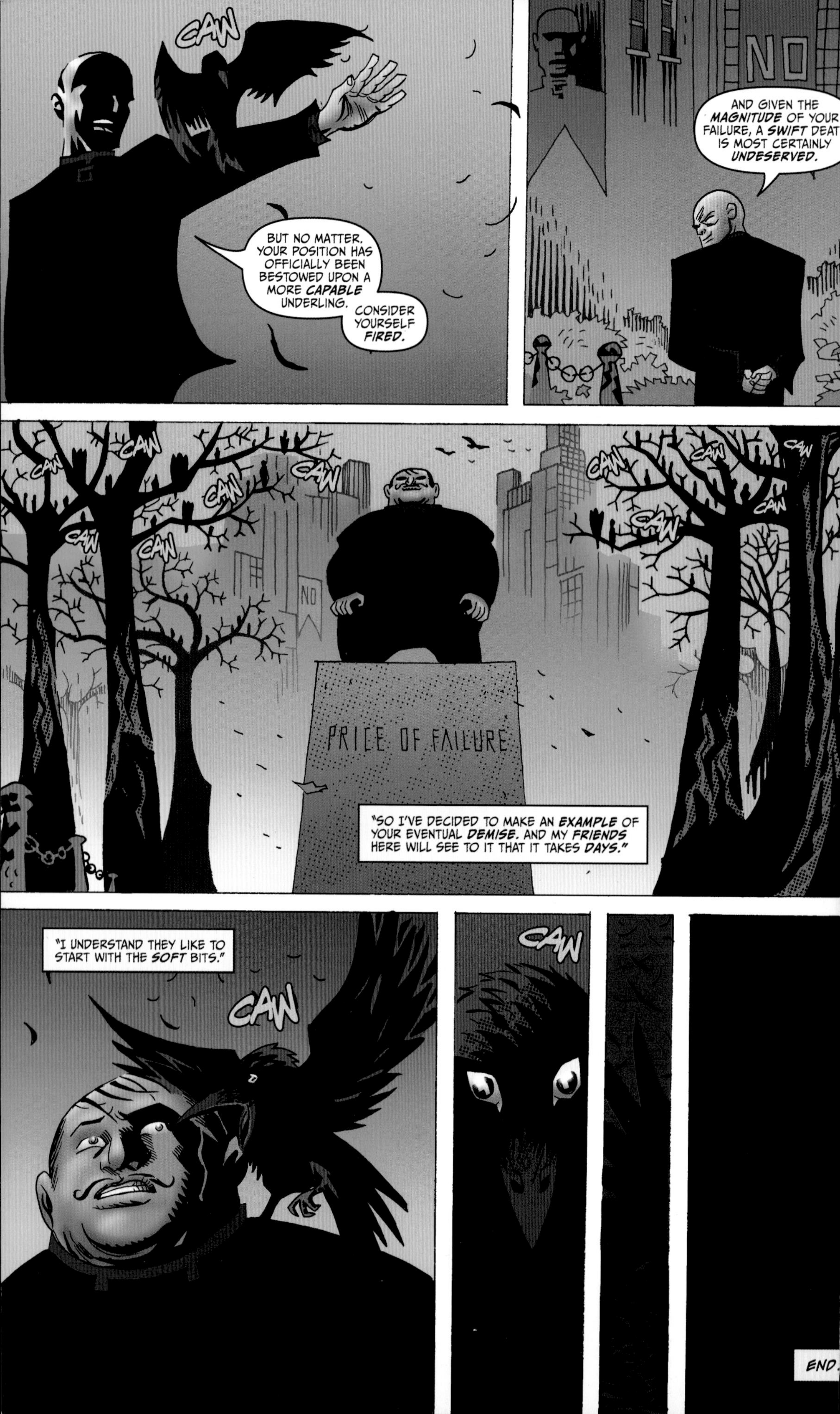
CAW
BUT NO MATTER. YOUR POSITION HAS OFFICIALLY BEEN BESTOWED UPON A MORE CAPABLE UNDERLING.
CONSIDER YOURSELF FIRED.
AND GIVEN THE MAGNITUDE OF YOUR FAILURE, A SWIFT DEAT IS MOST CERTAINLY UNDESERVED.
NO
CAW
CAW
CAW
CAW
CAW
CAW
CAW
CAW
CAW
CAW
NO
PRICE OF FAILURE
"SO I'VE DECIDED TO MAKE AN EXAMPLE OF YOUR EVENTUAL DEMISE. AND MY FRIENDS HERE WILL SEE TO IT THAT IT TAKES DAYS."
"I UNDERSTAND THEY LIKE TO START WITH THE SOFT BITS."
CAW
CAW
END.

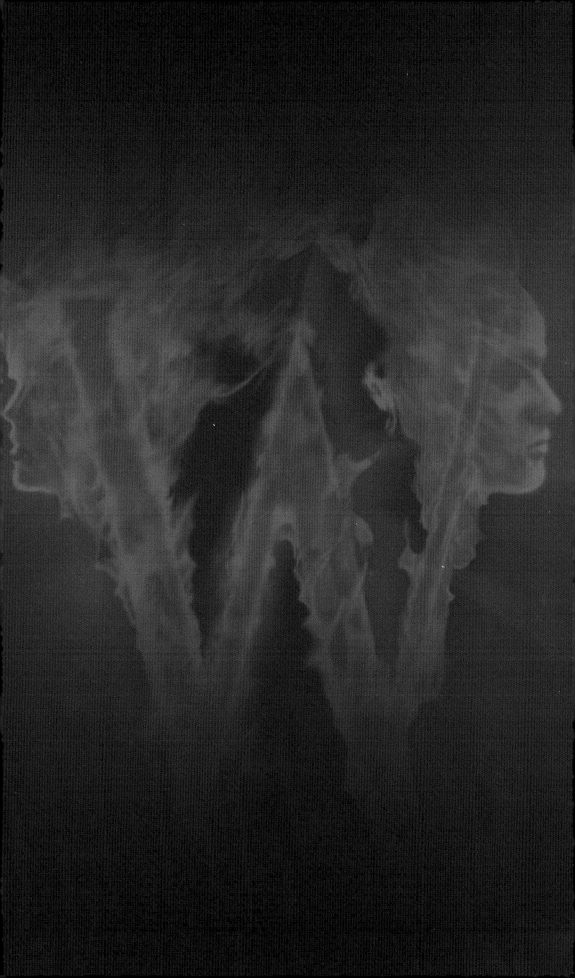

ART GALLERY

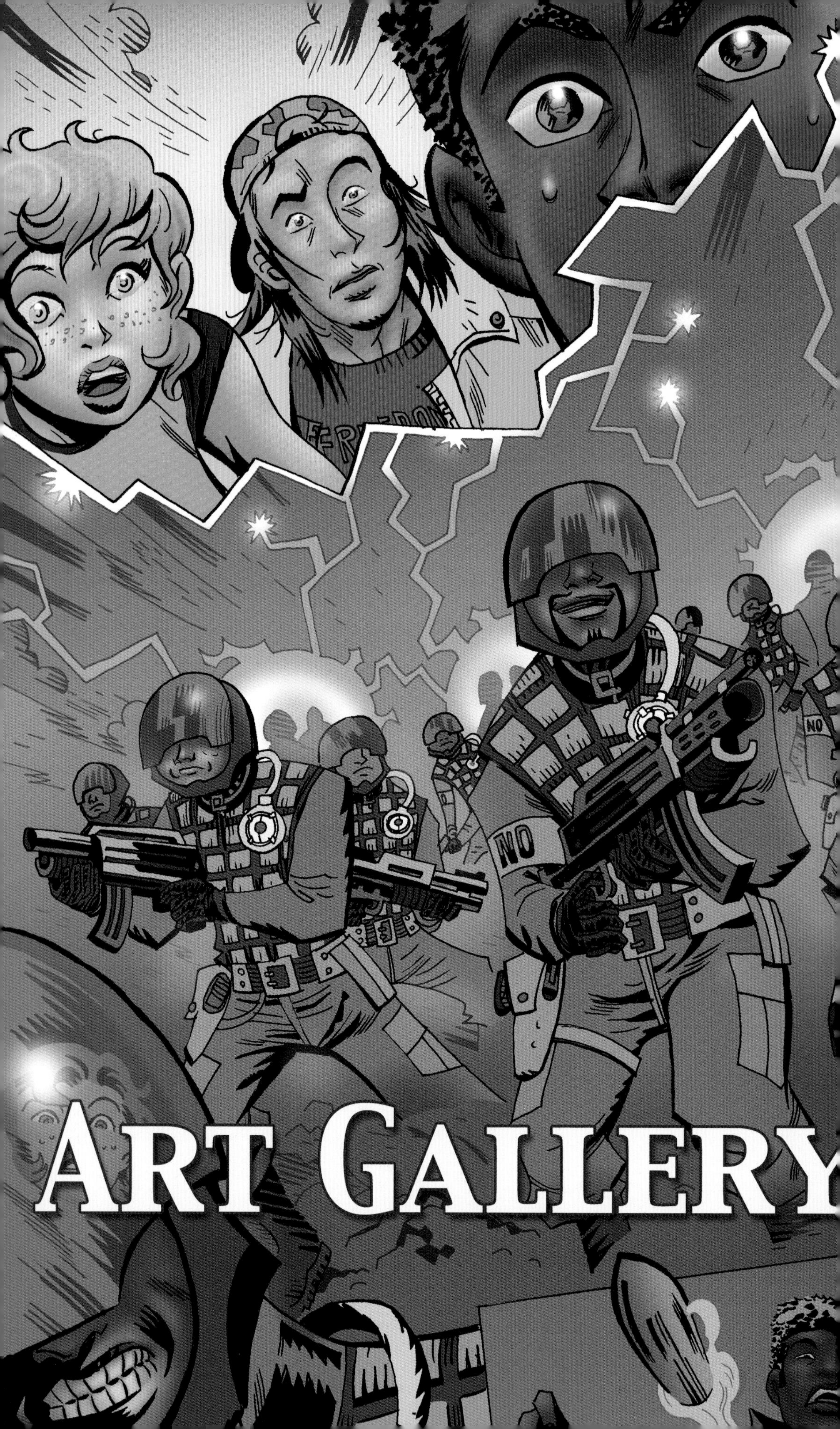
NO
NO

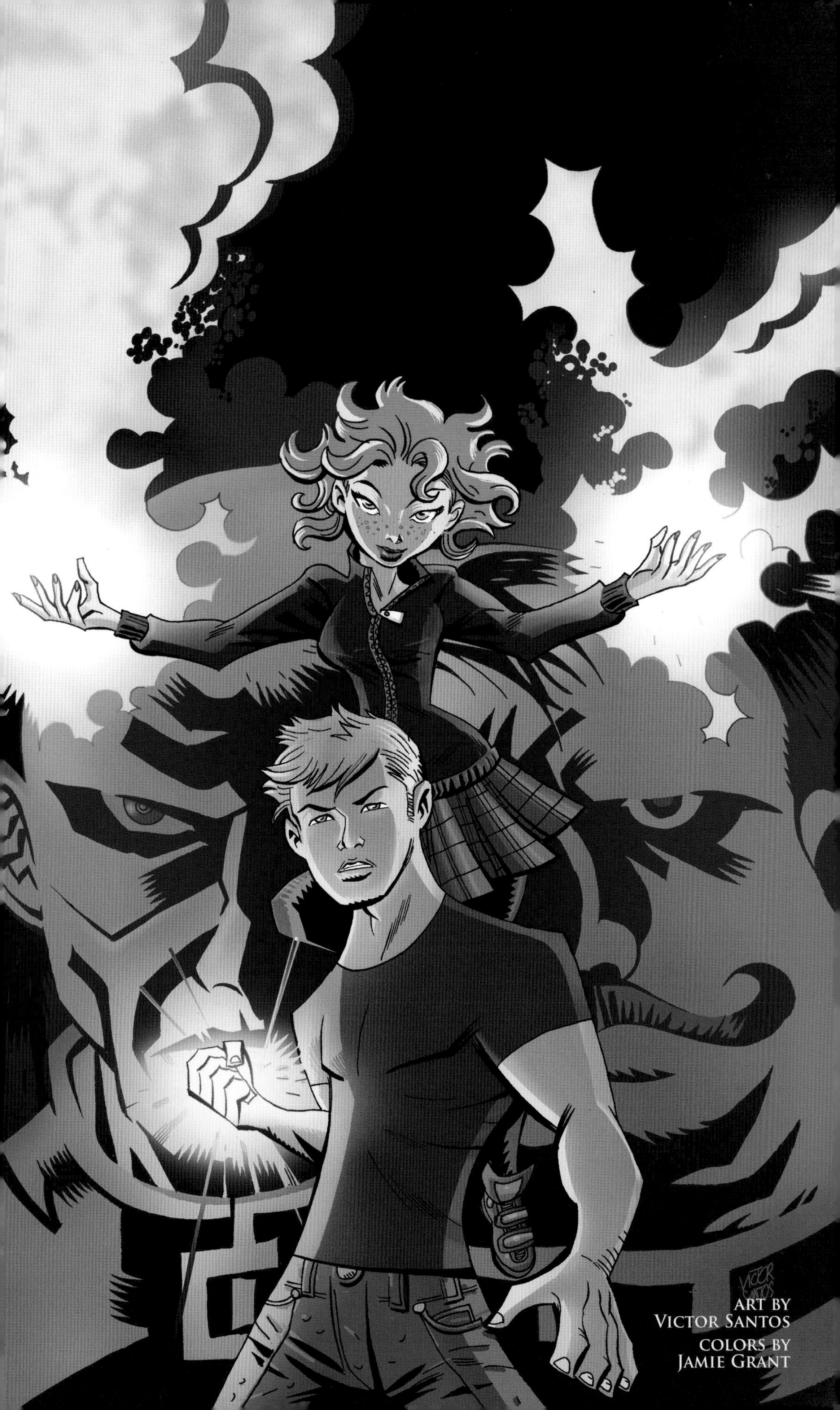
VICTOR SANTOS
ART BY
VICTOR SANTOS
COLORS BY
JAMIE GRANT

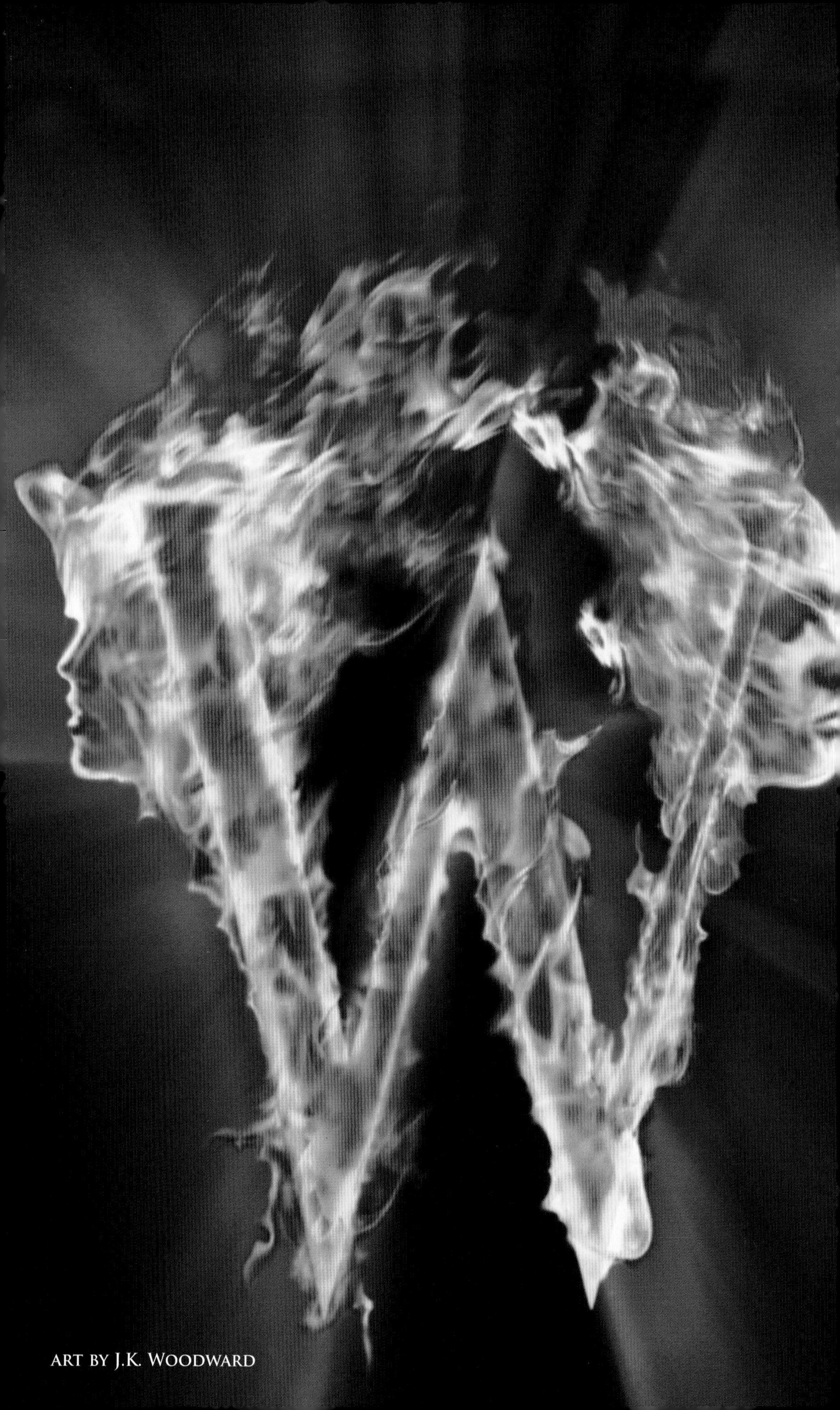

ART BY J.K. WOODWARD

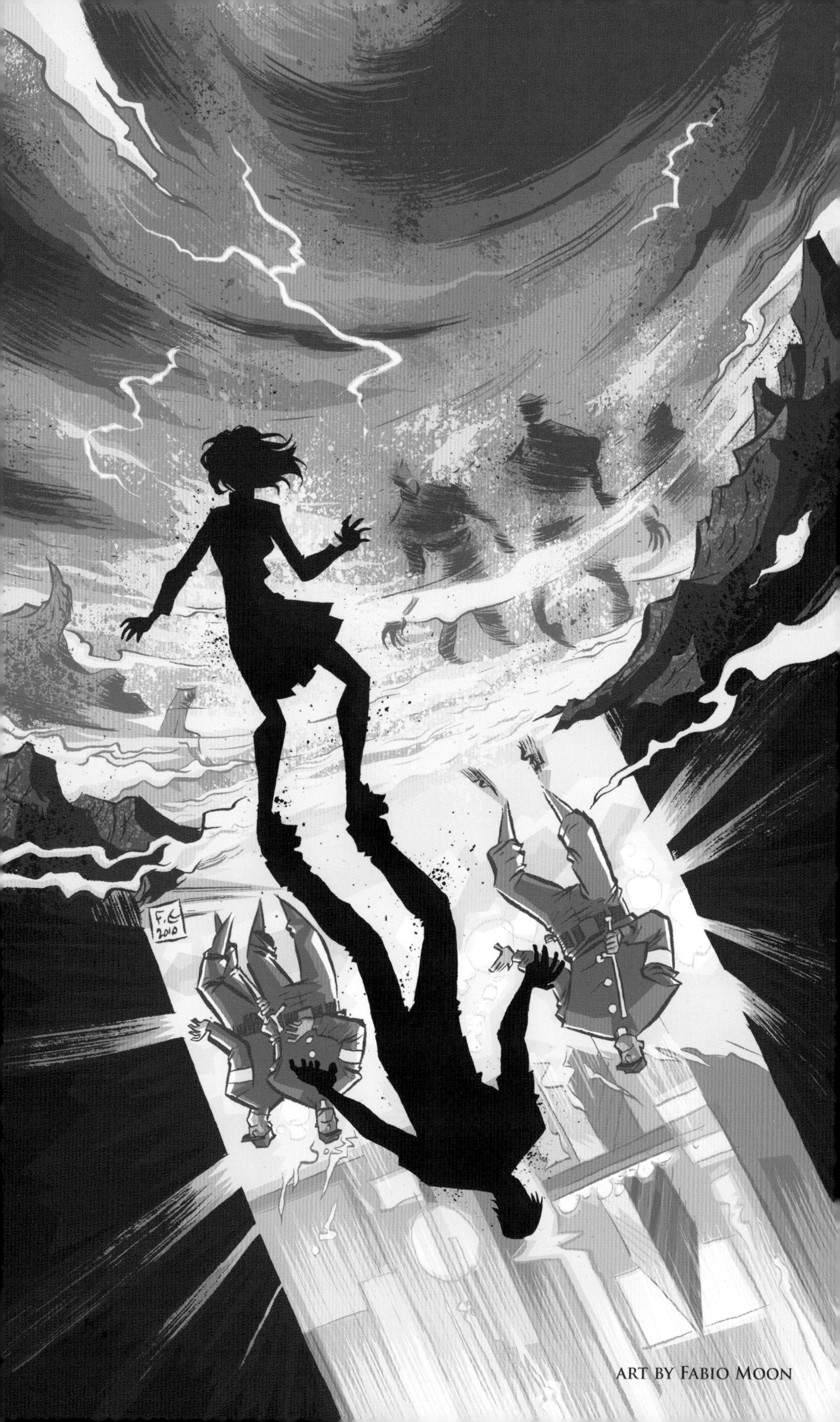

ART BY FABIO MOON

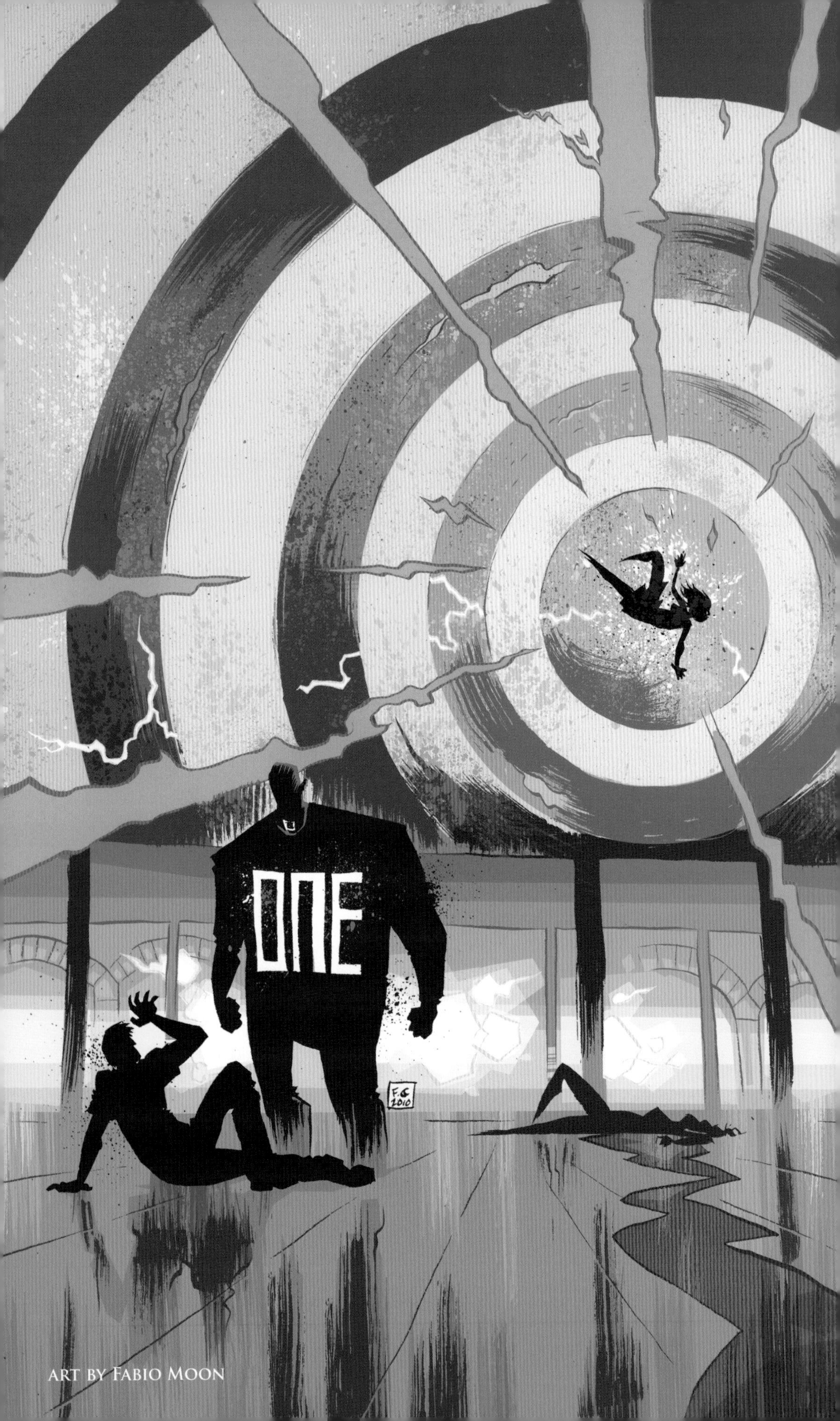
ONE
F.G
2010

ART BY FABIO MOON

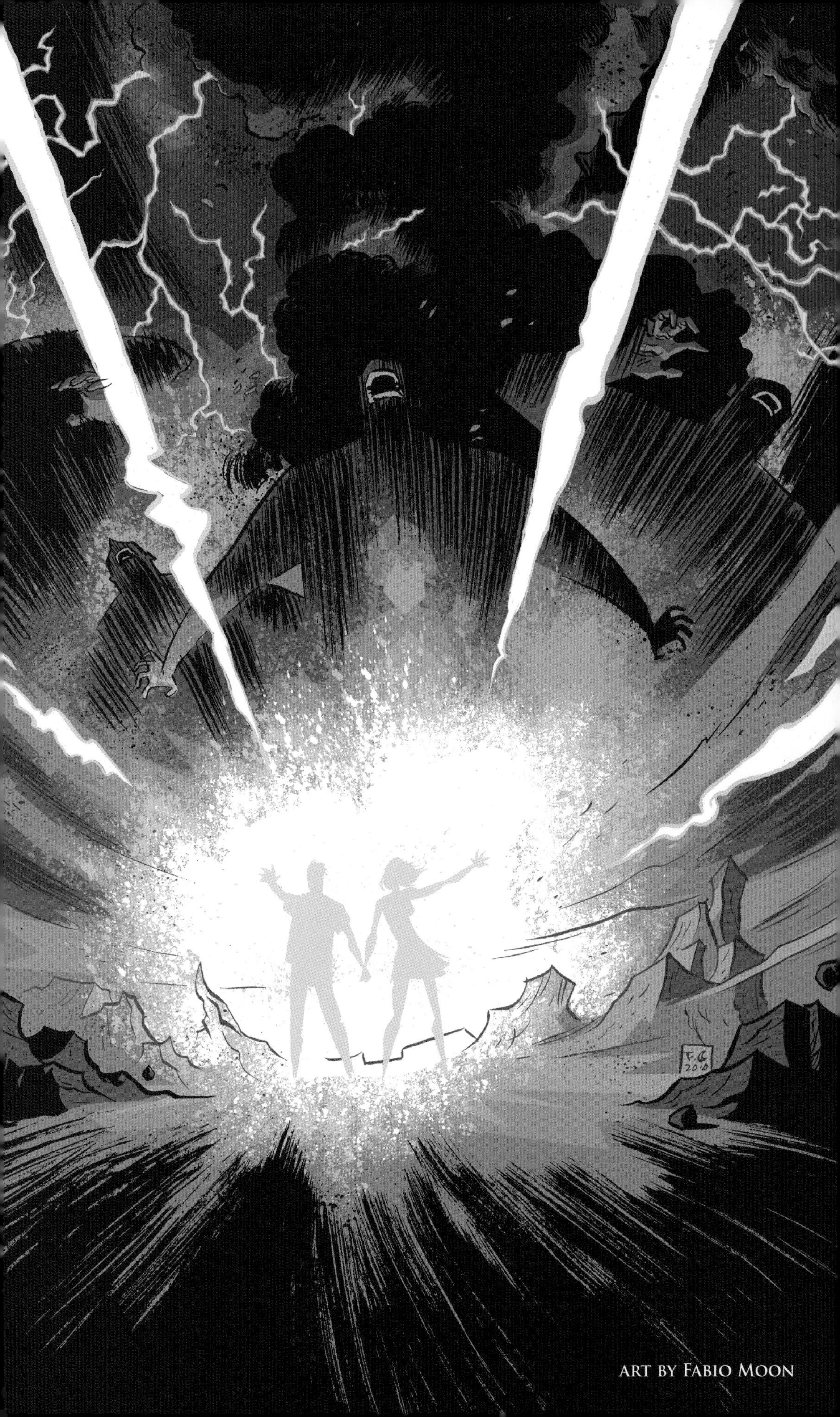

Art by Fabio Moon

Character Sketches
by Victor Santos

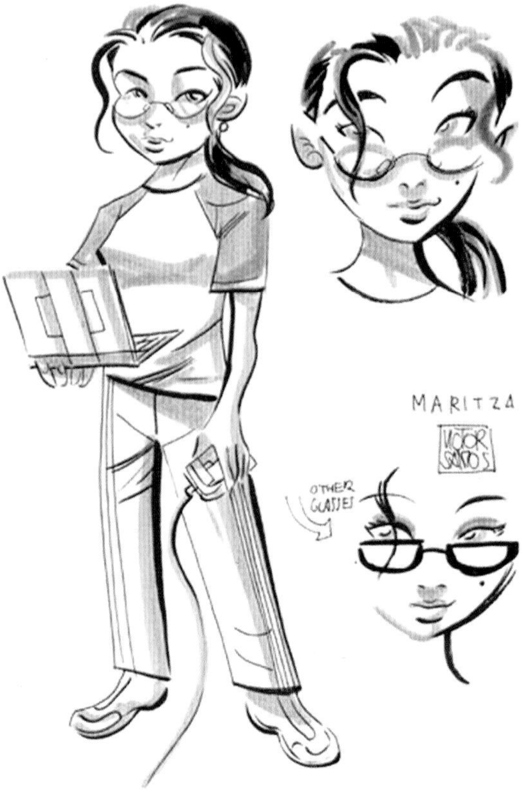
MARITZA
VICTOR SANTOS
OTHER GLASSES

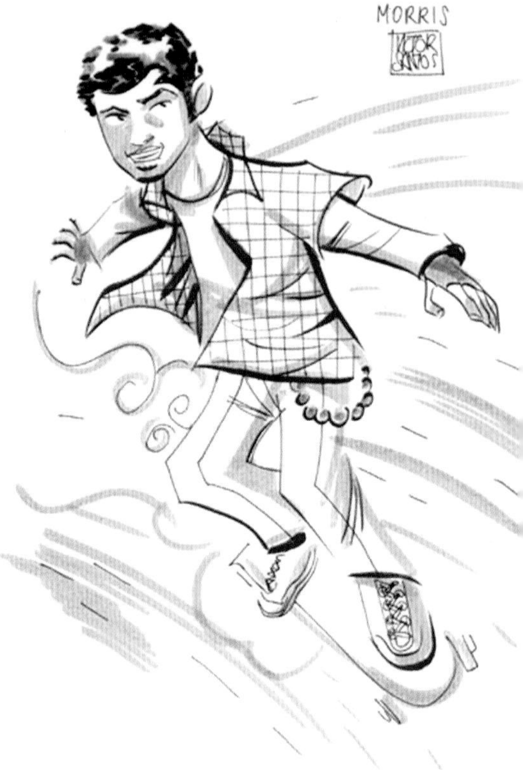
MORRIS
VICTOR SANTOS

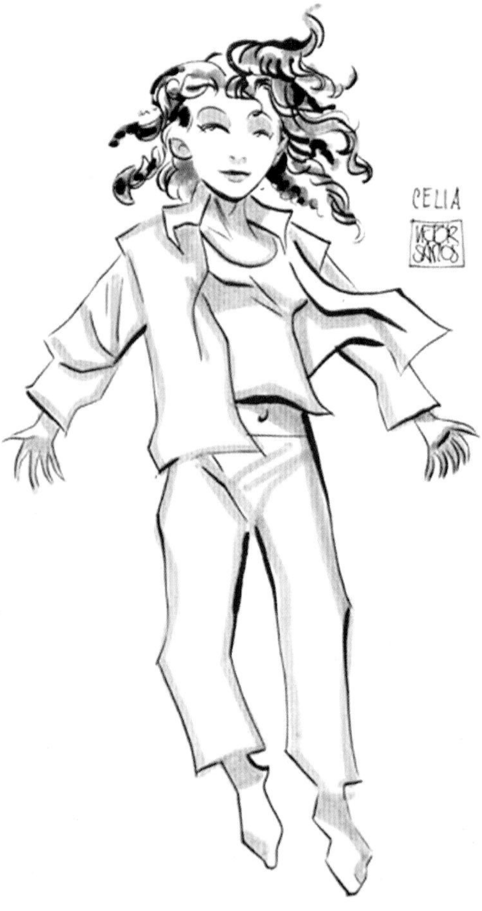
CELIA
VICTOR SANTOS

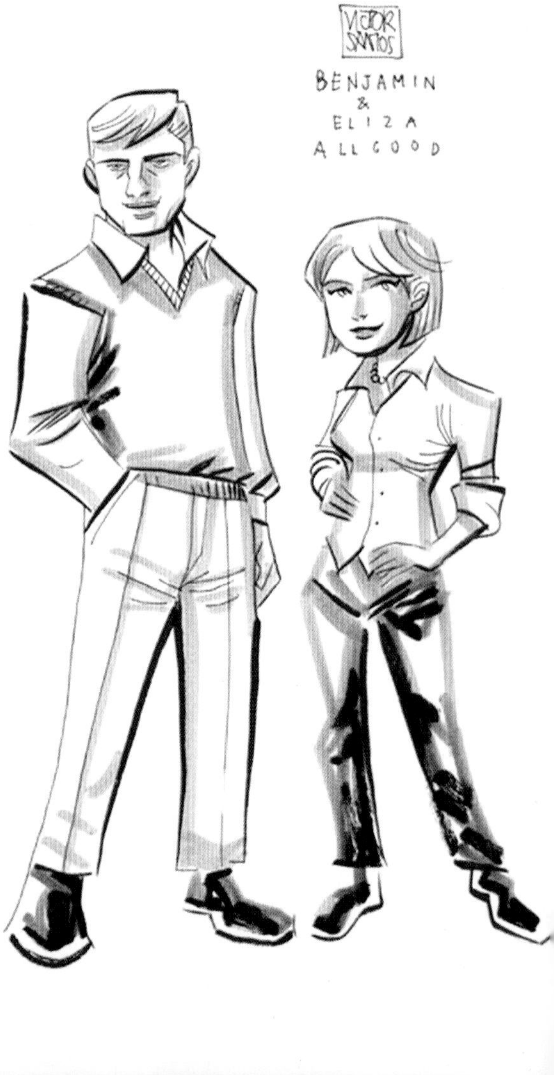
VICTOR SANTOS
BENJAMIN & ELIZA ALLGOOD

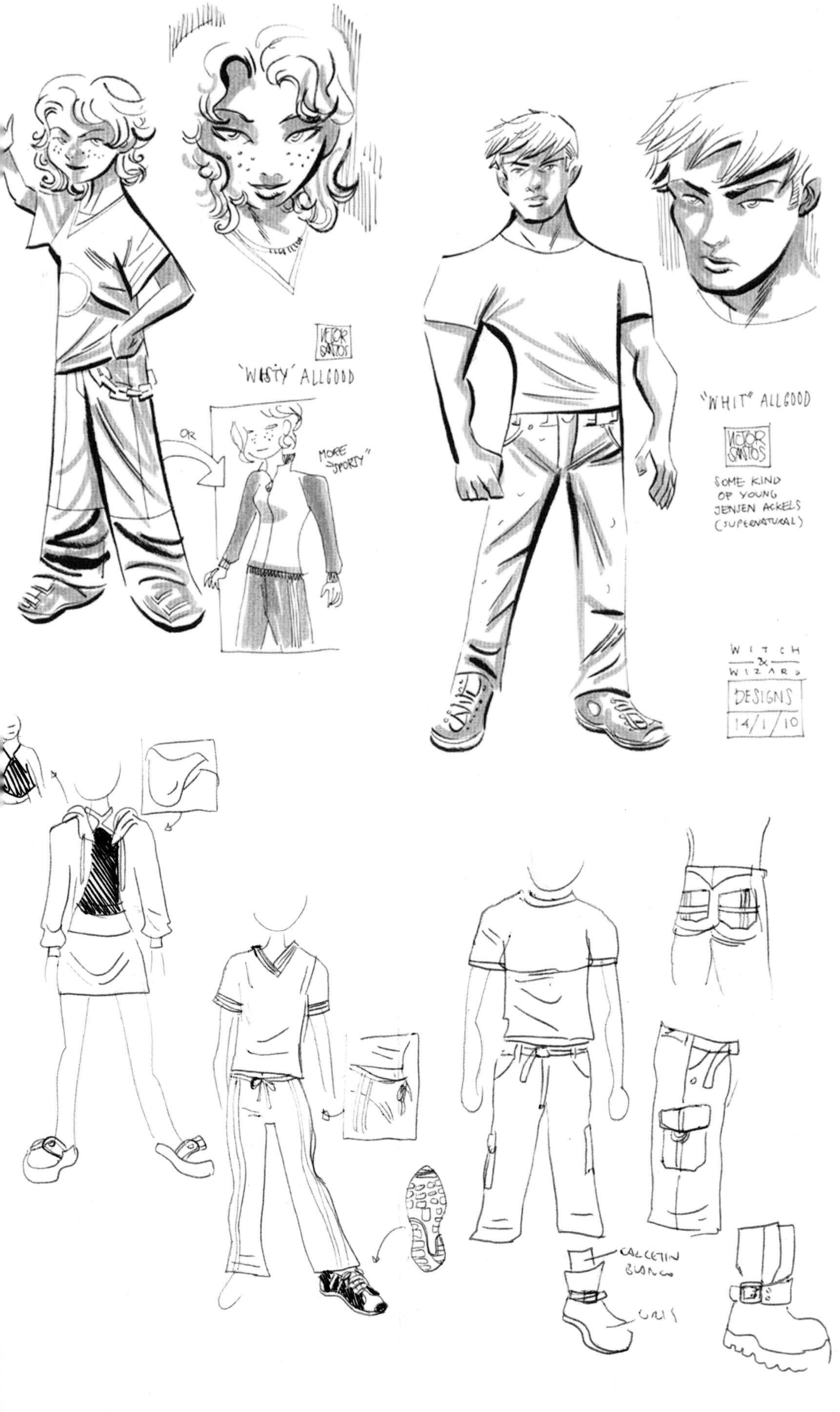
VICTOR SANTOS
'WISTY' ALLGOOD
OR
MORE "SPORTY"
"WHIT" ALLGOOD
VICTOR SANTOS
SOME KIND OF YOUNG JENSEN ACKELS (SUPERNATURAL)
WITCH & WIZARD
DESIGNS
14/1/10
CALCETIN BLANCO

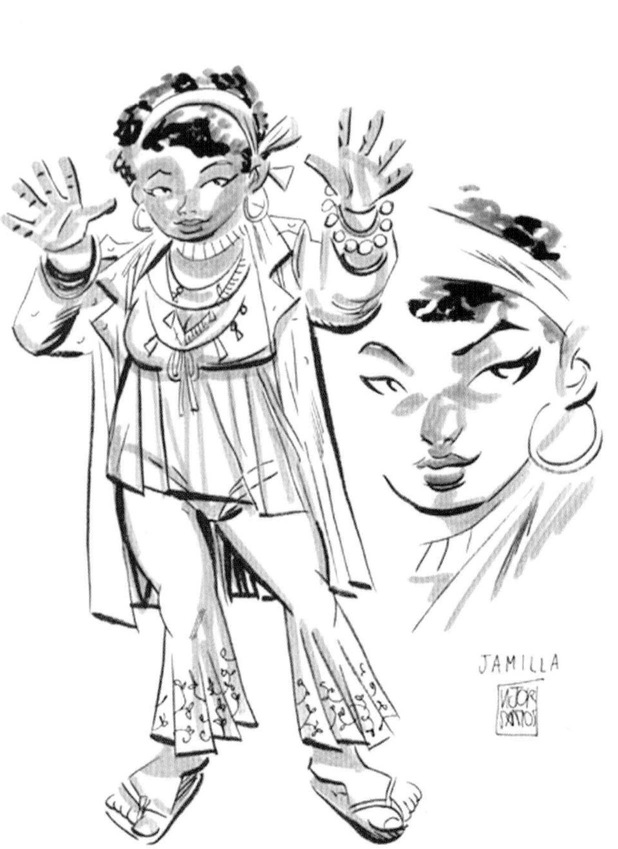
JAMILLA
VICTOR SANTOS

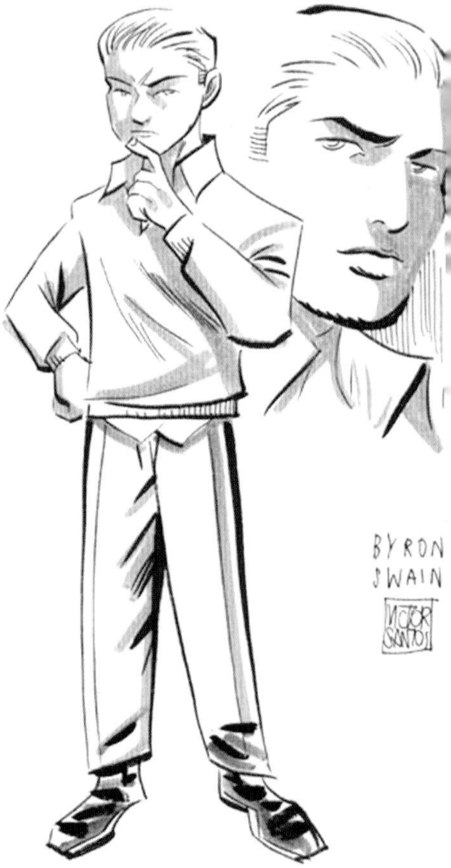
BYRON SWAIN
VICTOR SANTOS

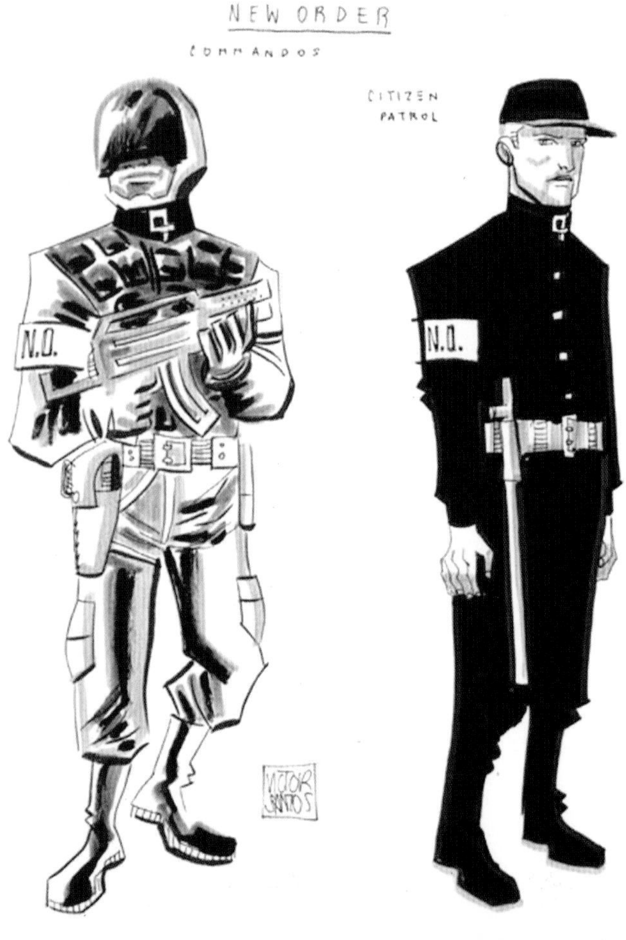
NEW ORDER
COMMANDOS
CITIZEN PATROL
N.O.
N.O.
VICTOR SANTOS

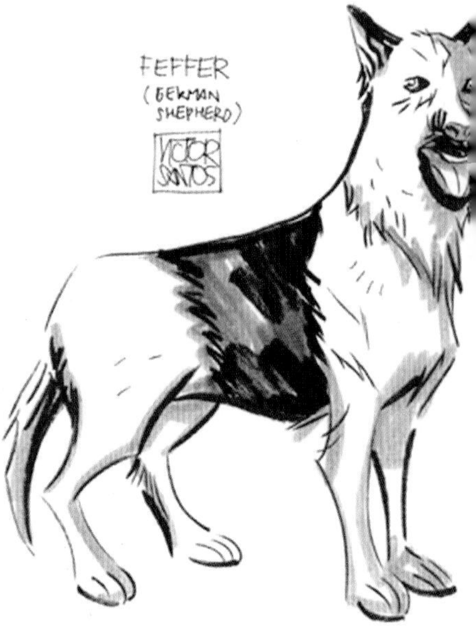
FEFFER
(GERMAN SHEPHERD)
VICTOR SANTOS

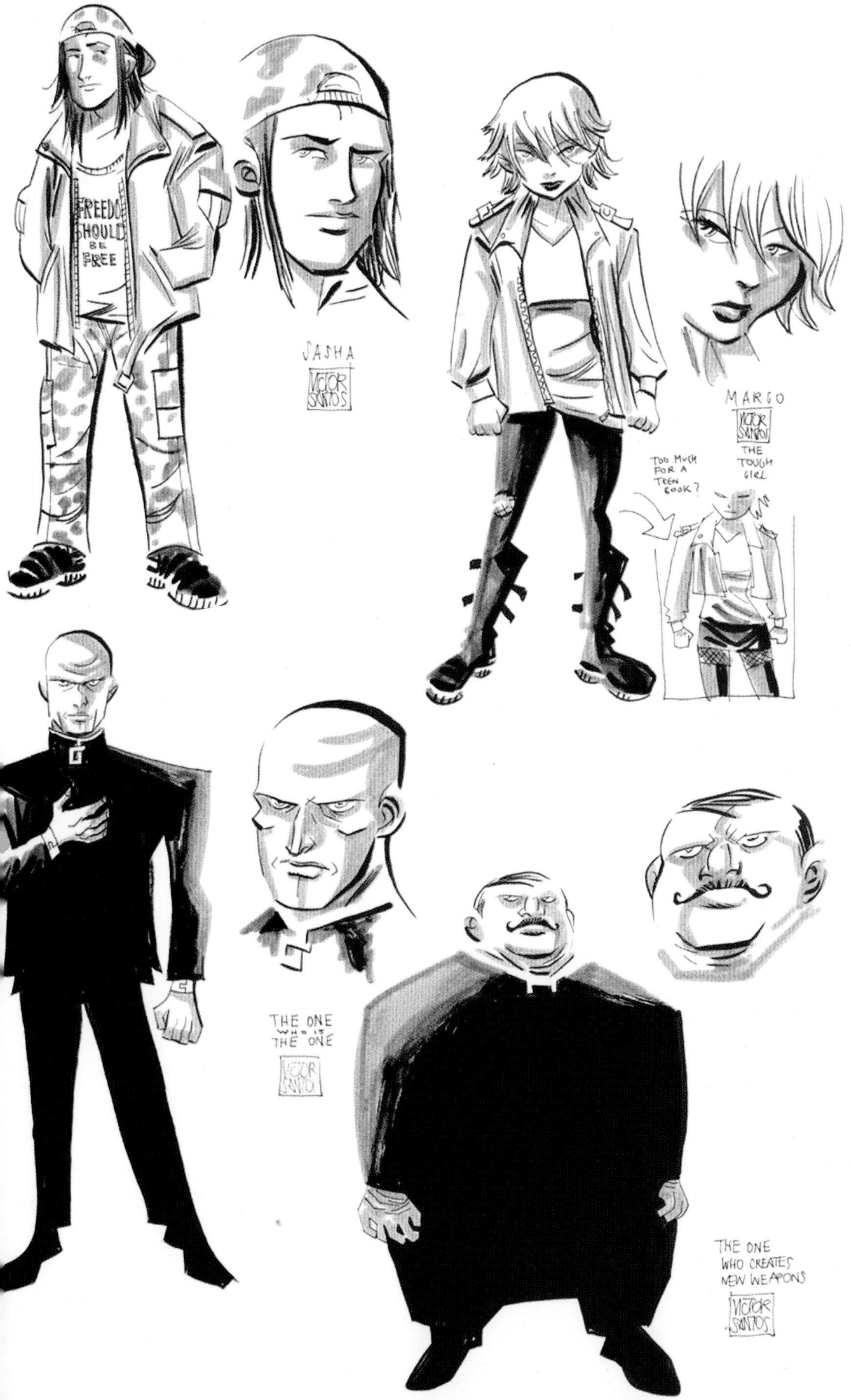
FREEDO
SHOULD
BE
FREE
SASHA
VICTOR SANTOS
MARGO
VICTOR SANTOS
THE TOUGH GIRL
TOO MUCH FOR A TEEN BOOK?
THE ONE WHO IS THE ONE
VICTOR SANTOS
THE ONE WHO CREATES NEW WEAPONS
VICTOR SANTOS

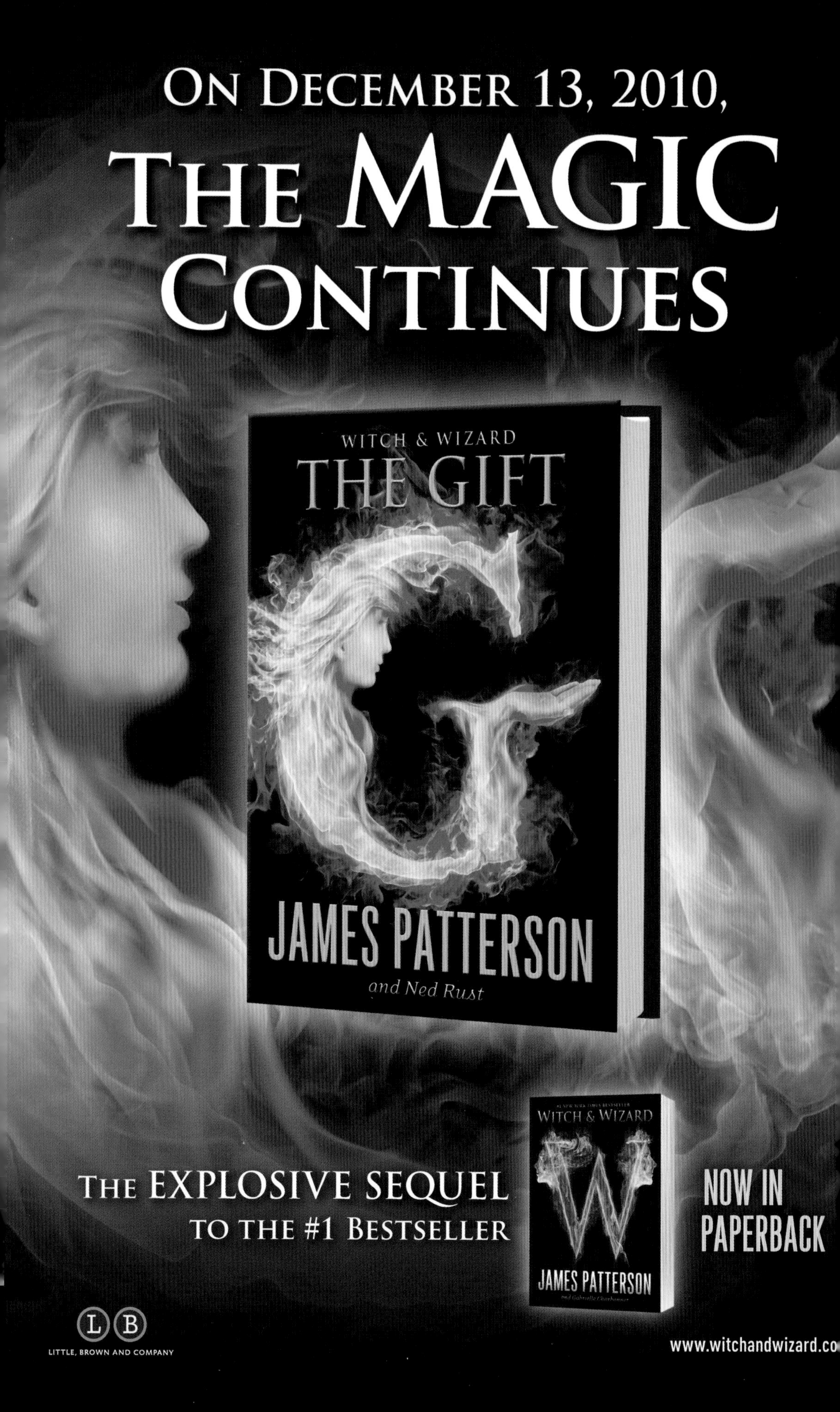
ON DECEMBER 13, 2010,
THE MAGIC CONTINUES
WITCH & WIZARD
THE GIFT
JAMES PATTERSON
and Ned Rust
WITCH & WIZARD
JAMES PATTERSON
THE EXPLOSIVE SEQUEL
TO THE #1 BESTSELLER
NOW IN PAPERBACK
LB
LITTLE, BROWN AND COMPANY
www.witchandwizard.co